Slavery and the Penal System

Slavery and the Penal System

J. THORSTEN SELLIN

ELSEVIER

New York / Oxford / Amsterdam

ELSEVIER SCIENTIFIC PUBLISHING COMPANY, INC.
52 Vanderbilt Avenue, New York, N.Y. 10017

ELSEVIER SCIENTIFIC PUBLISHING COMPANY
335 Jan Van Galenstraat, P.O. Box 211
Amsterdam, The Netherlands

Library of Congress Cataloging in Publication Data

Sellin, Johan Thorsten, 1896–
  Slavery and the penal system.

  Bibliography: p.
  Includes index.
  1. Punishment—History. 2. Slavery—History.
3. Corrections—History. I. Title.
HV8501.S43   364.6'09   76-19067
ISBN 0-444-99027-5

Manufactured in the United States of America

Designed by Loretta Li

Contents

Preface

In 1938, two notable historical works were completed. One of them, by Georg Rusche and Otto Kirchheimer, examined "punishment in its specific manifestations, the causes of its changes and development [and] the grounds for the choice or rejection of specific methods in specific historical periods."[1] The authors were looking for the social forces that shape penal systems, and they concluded that among these forces, economic and fiscal considerations dominated.

> That specific forms of punishment correspond to a given stage of economic development is a truism. It is self-evident that enslavement as a form of punishment is impossible without a slave economy, that prison labor is impossible without manufacture or industry, that monetary fines for all classes of society are impossible without a money economy. On the other hand, the disappearance of a given system of production makes its corresponding punishments inapplicable. Only a specific development of the productive forces permits the introduction or rejection of corresponding penalties. But before these potential methods can be introduced, society must be in a position to incorporate them as integrated parts of the whole social and economic system. Thus, if a slave economy finds the supply of slaves meager and the demand pressing, it cannot neglect penal slavery. In feudalism, on the other hand, not only could this form of punishment no longer be used but no other method was discovered for the proper use of the labor power of the convict. A return to the old methods, capital and corporal punishment, was therefore necessary, since the introduction of monetary fines for all classes was impossible on economic grounds. The house of correction reached a peak under mercantilism and gave great impetus to the development of the new method of production. The economic importance of the houses of correction then disappeared with the rise of the factory system. . . . The transition to modern industrial society, which demands the freedom of labor as a necessary condition for the productive employment of labor power, reduced the economic role of convict labor to a minimum.[2]

In short, the demands of the labor market shaped the penal system and determined its transformation over the years, more or less unaffected by theories of punishment in vogue.

The second work was an essay published by Professor Gustav Radbruch.[3] Several German historians of law had previously cursorily noted that the capital and corporal punishments that marked the criminal laws of early ages were originally domestic punishments meted out to erring slaves by their masters. Radbruch elaborated on the idea, showing that as the structure of Germanic society changed over the centuries, punishments originally reserved for those in bondage were later inflicted for crimes committed by low-class freemen, and ultimately on offenders regardless of their social status.

> To this day, the criminal law bears the traits of its origin in slave punishments. . . . To be punished means to be treated like a slave. That was symbolically underscored in olden times when to flogging was joined the shearing of the head, because the shorn head was the mark of the slave. . . . Slavish treatment meant . . . not just a social but also a moral degradation. "Baseness" is thus simultaneously and inseparably a social, moral and even an aesthetic value judgment. The lowly born is also a "mean fellow." . . . In both French and English the unfree peasant and the scoundrel are called villains. . . . In the illustrations in the *Sachsenspiegel* the faces of the common people are pictured as ugly and coarse. The diminution of honor, which ineradicably inheres in punishment to this day, derives from slave punishments.[4]

Both of these works have spurred me to write this book, which specifically examines the validity of Radbruch's thesis by tracing the influence of the social institution of chattel slavery on the evolution of penal practices in Europe and the United States from ancient time to the present. It is a dismal story, revealing the darkest and most brutal aspects of penal history and the social forces which resisted or nullified the labor of reformers seeking to humanize the treatment of adult major offenders. Considering the focus of the book, it seemed proper to begin it with a study of slavery and punishment in two great ancient societies, Greece and Rome, and to end it with a look at the subject in the two greatest slaveholding nations of the nineteenth century, Russia and the United States.

Two of the chapters have already been published, Chapter II in French translation in Volume Two of a *Festschrift* honoring Justice Marc Ancel (*Études de science pénale et de politique criminelle,* Paris, 1975), and Chapter III in one honoring Sir Leon Radzinowicz (*Crime, Criminology and Public Policy,* London, 1974). I am grateful for the permission to include them here. I also appreciate the care shown by Ms. Selma Pastor in typing the manuscript, and the fruitful discussions I have had with Professor Marvin E. Wolfgang concerning its contents.

J. Thorsten Sellin

Gilmanton, N.H.
March, 1976

Slavery and the Penal System

I: IN ANCIENT GREECE

Slavery was regarded as a natural and legitimate social institution in all ancient civilizations. Supplying manpower that could be exploited by the slave owners—private persons or religious, state, or municipal bodies—it served primarily an economic function. Information about slavery in antiquity is generally scant. Little is known about the practice in ancient Greece, except as it functioned in Athens during the fifth and fourth centuries B.C.

Athens was the most important of the city-states. Its political history has been immortalized by Herodotus and Thucydides, and its philosophers, poets, orators, and dramatists have cast some light on its social problems. Because of the character of this state, in which the working classes— commoners, alien resident craftsmen, freemen, and slaves—had little or no voice in government, contemporary historians and social commentators were naturally more concerned with the activities of the ruling classes— noble, propertied, military—than with the life of the common people, and especially of the slaves. This holds true also for Sparta, Athen's great rival, whose helots, though technically serfs, were in reality slaves.

The Slave Population

No one knows how many slaves there were in ancient Greece at any one time. Estimates by modern historians are based on partial and often fantastic figures in the writings of the ancients. It must be remembered that classical Greece was not one nation but a congeries of hundreds of independent or semi-independent city-states, i.e., communities of people living under one rule in a defined area that included the fortified seat of the religious cult and the government as well as the surrounding hinterland of farms and villages. Classical Athens was synonymous with Attica, an area of about 1,000 square miles, or half the size of the state of Delaware. Probably no more than half of its population lived in the town of Athens and its seaport, Peiraeus. In the early part of the fourth century, Sparta had an area of 3,300 square miles in the Peloponnesus, equal to the combined areas of Delaware and Rhode Island. It is doubtful that any of the other city-states occupied as much as 400 square miles, and some were no larger than present-day

1

Andorra or Liechtenstein. It is thus not surprising, that population data cited by authors pertain to only a few of the largest and most important city-states.

A. H. M. Jones has made an ingenious analysis of the population of Athens, noting that until the last half of the fourth century even the most rudimentary statistics are lacking. For that time he calculated that there were about 20,000 slaves in a total population of circa 144,000.[1] Other estimates for the same period are cited by Victor Ehrenberg. One of them, attributed to A. W. Gomme, gives a total population of 258,000, including 104,000 slaves. Another estimates the population at between 140,000 and 190,000, including between 30,000 and 60,000 slaves.[2] William Westermann concluded that the slaves of Attica, during the early part of the Peloponnesian War, which began in 431 B.C., numbered from 60,000 to 80,000, or about a third or possibly a fourth of the population, but he added that "it must be granted that this statement is no more than a reasonable suggestion."[3] In other words, the size and the composition of the population of Athens are not known very accurately even though much is known about Attican slavery.

For Sparta, data are even more meager. Gustave Glotz assumes that it had a population of about 400,000, including 275,000 helots, but he fails to specify the date.[4] Ehrenberg cites an estimate for the fourth century, which gave corresponding figures of 270,000 and 200,000.[5] They apparently apply to a period antedating the loss of Messenia, which considerably reduced the territory of Sparta. In any case, the figures are speculative.

Sources of Supply

Slaves were acquired in a variety of ways. Wars brought captives, the spoils of the victors, who, if not ransomed, could be sold to the traders who followed the armies or in the open market or, if kept, bought their lives with their freedom. Most slaves, however, were purchased in special slave markets. These were largely provisioned by sea-faring merchants or by pirates who raided the Mediterranean shores as far as Libya for human merchandise. The areas bordering on the Black Sea and Asia Minor were favored sources of supply.

There were other ways too of acquiring slaves. Children born to female slaves became the property of the mother's owner. Infants, abandoned by those too poor to support them, might either be raised or sold by the finder. Farmers in debt to a landlord could be enslaved with their families if they defaulted on their debts. Slaves could be inherited like other property. Finally, enslavement might, in certain cases, be a punishment for crime.

2

Except for the indigenous Spartan helots, most slaves were imported non-Greek foreigners. Plato (429–347 B.C.) in his *Republic* voiced the sentiment that no Hellene should own another Hellene, but there were exceptions. Thucydides (471–391 B.C.) gives many examples of internecine wars between city-states that resulted in the conquest of a fortified town, the killing of all able-bodied defenders by the victors, and the sale of the women and children into slavery, but it is not clear whether this merchandise was destined for foreign markets or retained at home. By and large, Plato's sentiment was shared by his fellow Greeks, who considered themselves superior to the "barbarians"—i.e., all whose mother tongue was not Greek—and who found in their superiority ample justification for enslaving their inferiors. Plato's *Statesman* noted that most people "in this part of the world" assumed that Greeks "are a class apart, and they group all other nations together as a class."[6]

Aristotle on Slavery

This snobbish belief engendered many myths about the characteristics of foreigners. Aristotle (c. 384–22 B.C.), in line with then current ideas about geographical and climatic influences on the constitution and nature of man, thought that peoples of cold countries, especially in Europe, were of poor intelligence and skills although spirited, and that they, though comparatively free, were incapable of governing others. Asians, on the other hand, were both skilled and intelligent, but their lack of spirit made them fit for subjection and slavery. The Greeks, who lived in an intermediate geographical environment, possessed all admirable qualities.[7]

Among Greek thinkers, Aristotle supplied the finest analysis of slavery in a society where the family was the basic social institution and kinship was of fundamental importance in the organization and life of the state. His view of slavery as a natural component of the social structure is attested to by the fact that he regarded a household without slaves as incomplete. A complete household would have a stock of property consisting of instruments both inanimate and animate. The slave was "an animate article of property," and like any other such article "an instrument intended for the purpose of action" and "separable from its possessor," i.e., could be sold or otherwise disposed of. "The use which is made of the slave diverges but little from the use made of tame animals; both he and they supply their owner with bodily help in meeting his daily requirements."[8]

The basic condition of slavery in a community like the city-state was the presence of two elements, one "able by virtue of its intelligence to exercise forethought" and, therefore "naturally a ruling and master element," and another "able by virtue of its bodily power to do what the other element plans; a ruled element, which is naturally in a state of slavery." For one who was a slave "by nature," his condition was "both beneficial and just." He was mentally fitted for this condition "if he is capable of becoming (and this is the reason why he also actually becomes) the property of another and if he participates in reason to the extent of apprehending it in another though destitute of it himself," being "entirely without the faculty of deliberation." He was also different from the freeman physically, having a body with "strength for the menial duties of life," while the freeman possessed a physique "upright in carriage and useful for the various purposes of civil life—a life which tends, as it develops, to be divided into military service and the occupations of peace." The irony of nature was not lost on Aristotle, for "the contrary of nature's intention often happens; there are some slaves who have the bodies of freemen—as there are others who have a freeman's soul. But if nature's intentions were realized . . . it is obvious that we should all agree that the inferior class ought to be the slaves of the superior."[9]

Who were these people who were by nature slaves? Barbarians, of course. Being incapable of governing others, they had no "naturally ruling element" in their communities and thus were slaves by nature. "That," said Aristotle, "is why our poets have said, Meet it is that barbarous people should be governed by the Greeks—the assumption being that barbarian and slave are by nature one and the same. . . ."[10]

Aristotle was familiar with arguments against slavery advanced by legal scholars and philosophers. He acknowledged that they had some justification, considering that beside natural slavery there existed another kind, based on convention. The law that regarded an enemy captured in war as booty belonging to the victor was, in fact, a convention claimed by many jurists to be contrary to law. "They regard it as a debatable notion that any one who is subjugated by superior power should become the slave and subject of the person who is his superior in power." If a war were unjust, for instance, it would be unjust to make captives slaves. If a person did not deserve to be a slave—presumably because he was not one by nature—he was not *really* a slave. Otherwise, "men reputed to be of the highest rank would be turned into slaves . . . if it happened to them . . . to be captured and sold. . . . This is the reason why Greeks do not like to call such persons slaves, but prefer to confine the term to barbarians. But by this use of terms they are . . . driven . . . to admit that there are some [i.e., barbarians] who are everywhere and inherently slaves and others [i.e., Greeks] who are

4

everywhere and inherently free." The same reasoning, he observed held true for nobility. Greeks thought of themselves as absolutely noble, whether at home or abroad, but not so barbarians, who could not be noble outside their own countries.[11]

The coexistence of natural and conventional slavery created problems. When freemen and slaves owed their respective positions to nature, there was "a community of interest and a relation of friendship between master and slave," but when slavery rested "merely on legal sanctions and superior power," and both slaves and masters were either freemen by nature or both deserving of slavery, conflicts arose and troubled the state.[12]

Aristotle's assumption that barbarians were natural slaves, devoid of reason and otherwise inferior, was attacked by the Sophists, who saw slavery as an institution invented by society. In his work *On Truth,* Antiphon remarked that "those descended from noble ancestors we reverence and honor; but those from no noble house we neither reverence nor honor. In this we treat each other barbarously, since by nature we are all alike fully adapted to be either barbarians or Hellenes."[13] Alcidamas taught that "God created us all free; Nature makes no slaves," an idea shared by the playwright Philemon, and expressed by an actor in one of his comedies, who said, "Though one is a slave, he is a man no less than you, master; he is made of the same flesh. No one is a slave by nature; it is fate that enslaves the body."[14] Such equalitarian notions may have had some influence on the treatment of slaves, but they did not abolish the institution, which was so integral a part of the social class system that only a revolution working fundamental changes in the political organization and social structure of the state could have done so.

Social Classes

In early Athens, the inferior orders of peasants, laborers, and slaves ruled over by a land-owning aristocracy constituted the vast majority of the population. Farming was the chief industry. The poverty of the peasantry and the urban lower class was aggravated by the oppressive rule imposed on them. Civil strife was frequent. Plutarch (c. 48 B.C.–c. 125 A.D.), in his biography of Solon, wrote that

> the inequality between the poor and the rich occasioned the greatest discord, and the state was in so dangerous a situation that there seemed to be no way to quell the seditions. . . . So greatly were the poor [farmers] in debt to the rich [land-

5

lords] that they were obliged either to pay them a sixth part of the produce of the land . . . or else engage their persons to their creditors, who might seize them on failure of payment. Accordingly, some made slaves of them, and others sold them to foreigners. Nay, some parents were forced to sell their own children (for no law forbade it) and to quit the city to avoid the severe treatment of those usurers.[15]

Solon (640–558 B.C.) was called upon to put an end to the disorders. The laws he promulgated changed the social structure of Athens. He abolished slavery for debt, recalled those who had fled, and ransomed those sold abroad. He distributed the monopoly of power and privilege that the nobility had enjoyed among four classes according to income. According to Plutarch, the highest class contained the men whose estates produced at least five hundred measures of corn, oil, and vinegar annually; the next highest was composed of those with property yielding at least three hundred measures; they were the *hippeis,* or knights, who could afford horse and armor when called to war. The third class, the *zeugitai,* had land producing at least two hundred measures; armored at their own expense they were infantry men, *hoplites,* in war time. The lowest class, the *thetes,* could hold no office; they were allowed to vote in the Assembly, the permanent "town-meeting" of Athens, and could appeal a verdict of a lower court to the assembly sitting as a court of appeal.

The total membership of the four classes—the voters of Solon's state—was small, probably less than twenty per cent of the population. Estimates for much later periods placed it at between forty and fifty thousand at the beginning of the Peloponnesian War, when the population of Athens was at its peak, and at only nine thousand after the Macedonian conquest in 322 B.C., when the peace settlement of the following year provided for disfranchisement of more than twenty-thousand citizens who were not wealthy.

The rest of the free adult population who had no vote but full civil rights were the women and the resident aliens, or *metics.* The *metics* came from other Greek city-states or from foreign lands. They were immigrants who made Athens their permanent home. Although liable to military duty and paying taxes, they were not allowed to own houses or land, the prerogative of citizens. They were craftsmen, artists, merchants, bankers, or industrial entrepreneurs, occupations held in low esteem by the citizens.

Pride in Athenian birth and ancestry was a common trait of the citizens. Rarely was a *metic* admitted to the status of citizen, and then only for some conspicuous service to the state, and cases of freedmen granted citizenship were rarer still. Ancient writers tell of a slave who, having become a freedman and ultimately a very rich and influential banker, finally reached that goal. At

6

least on one occasion, when the state was in great danger, all slaves of military age were drafted and promised their freedom after the war, thus swelling the ranks of the *metics.*

Finally, there were the slaves, who had no rights, being "articles of property," and the freedmen, manumitted slaves still temporarily bound to their masters until they had fulfilled certain obligations to him. Once that was accomplished, they were enrolled among the *metics,* to mark their alien origin.

In time the timocratic state fashioned by Solon was transformed into a citizen's democracy, largely by Pericles (c.495–429 B.C.). After the victory of Athens and her allies over Persia, the *thetes* who had valiantly manned the galleys by the thousands, demanded greater political recognition and a voice in the government. The resultant reforms made all public offices available by lot to all citizens above thirty, and all judicial matters were submitted to juries of hundreds of citizens also drawn by lot. The same procedure was used to fill the posts of the many administrative boards of a now wealthy and important empire. Gradually, the acquisition of citizenship was made easier, a policy which induced Demosthenes (386–322 B.C.), in his oration *On the Duty of the State,* to castigate the Assembly because, contrary to earlier custom, it was allowing "the vilest of mankind, menials and the sons of menials to be your citizens."[16] In an ironical commentary on the times, the Old Oligarch conceded tongue in cheek that it was only proper that the poorer classes and the common people be given more recognition than men of birth and wealth, since they, as steersmen, boatswains, lieutenants, look-out men at the prow, and shipwrights, were responsible for making the state powerful, but what galled the conservative antidemocrat most was that slaves and *metics* were so tolerantly treated that slaves did not step aside to let one pass in the street and that both dressed so well that they looked like citizens and occasionally were even allowed to live munificently because it served the purpose of the state.[17] He reflected an attitude toward manual labor found in the writings of Plato and Aristotle.

Both these philosophers lived during the century that ended with the Macedonian conquest of Athens in 322 B.C., the year of Aristotle's death: he had survived his old teacher by a quarter of a century. Both were upper-class gentlemen of a conservative bent. Their views of the duties of citizenship and the role of the working classes were probably shared by most of the members of the master class.*

---

*When Socrates spoke to Callicles about the worth of "engineers," he added, "All the same you despise him and his art and use the term 'mechanic' as a term of contempt, and you would not

7

In the imaginary state of Magnesia, for which Plato prepared his *Laws,* a citizen was to devote his life to civic activities. Neither he nor his servants were to be artisans, retailers, or wholesalers "or perform any service whatever for private individuals, who are not his equal in status, with the exception of those services that a free man will naturally render to his father and mother and remote ancestors and to all free persons older than himself."[18] Only *metics* or temporary visitors were to be merchants; the transgression of this rule by a citizen would entail punishment.

The education of children should ensure conformity to these views. It should not, according to Aristotle, make children "mechanically minded," and he explained that "the term 'mechanical' *(banausos)* should properly be applied to any occupation, art, or instruction which is calculated to make the body, or soul, or mind of a freeman unfit for the pursuit and practice of goodness." To do something to satisfy a personal need or help a friend would be proper, but to do it repeatedly at someone's request would be menial and servile. Leisure, i.e., freedom from labor, should exist in a well-ordered state, and in an ideal state citizens should not be mechanics or shopkeepers, "which is ignoble and inimical to goodness." Nor should they labor on farms, for "leisure is a necessity both for growth in goodness and for the pursuit of political activities."[19] He admitted that it was not easy to see how such a society might be realized.

Nor was it realized in Athens. The wealthy citizens did enjoy leisure and could devote themselves to civic tasks. They had large landholdings and could operate their farms and factories by slave labor or lease their slaves for work on government projects. The small farmer, who might own a slave or two, worked with his family in his fields and vineyards. The poorest class, the *thetes,* had small land parcels which partially sustained them, but half of that population was landless and had to work in town in their small workshops or become hired hands, but to become anyone's servant was repugnant to Athenians, who could not quite rid themselves of the idea that all paid labor contained an "element of slavishness." As the wealth of Athens grew and the political agencies of the democracy demanded more and more public service of its citizens in the Assembly, on the juries, and in the various administrative departments of the state, and compensated them financially for all such services, an approximation to the ideal state pictured by Aristotle was reached.

---

hear of marrying your daughter to his son or taking his daughter to wife yourself" (Plato, *Gorgias,* trans. and with an Introduction by Walter Hamilton [Baltimore: Penguin Books, 1971.], p. 512).

Spartan Helotry

Slavery took such a different form in Sparta that Plato regarded the "helot-system . . . probably just about the most difficult and contentious institution in the entire Greek world."[20] The helots far outnumbered the citizens, who according to estimates constituted only about five percent of the population at the outbreak of the Peloponnesian War.[21] About three-fourths of the population were helots, and one-fifth noncitizen merchants and artisans.

Spartan citizens were rigorously trained for war and the exercise of civic virtues, not for manual labor. The helots, public slaves owned by the state, were assigned to the citizens for the cultivation of their farms. In one sense they resembled serfs, being bound to plots of land and having to deliver part of their produce to their masters. Even though some of them achieved a measure of economic independence, other circumstances made their lot harder and more precarious than that of the Athenian chattel slaves. Historically they were of native stock subjugated by invading conquerors, and their oppression by their masters led to many bloody uprisings. They were feared by the citizenry, whose policy of repression was, according to Thucydides, based on "the necessity of taking precautions against them."[22] The laws gave them little protection. Indeed, a kind of ritualistic official proclamation of a state of war between citizens and helots is said to have been made annually, making the killing of a helot an act of war instead of murder. In his biography of Lycurgus, Plutarch described the occasional manhunts organized by the superintendents of education, who selected the cleverest of the Spartan youths to ambush and kill helots by night or invade the fields in broad daylight and kill the ablest and strongest of the laborers.[23] Thucydides claimed that once during the Peloponnesian War fear of an uprising led the Spartans to assemble two thousand of the most courageous helots and secretly murder them.

Slave Labor

Athenian slaves performed a variety of tasks. Of those privately owned many, whether male or female, were domestic servants. Others were field hands or were engaged in their masters' workshops or small industries as laborers or skilled workers. If a master had no personal use for a slave, he could hire him out or permit him to practice a trade or even a profession; his earnings belonged to his master. It is claimed that Nicias, the ill-fated general of the Sicilian expedition, owned a thousand slaves whom he leased to mining operators.

Many slaves were owned by the state. Some of these public slaves held highly responsible positions, considering their legal status. The various government agencies needed employees. Streets had to be cleaned and repaired, roads constructed, public stores inventoried and guarded. Magistrates needed clerks, registrars, and accountants, the jail had to have guards and an executioner. Weights and measures had to be inspected, and policemen were needed to maintain order. All these tasks devolved on public slaves. Being permanent employees, they became the professional experts in public service, because turnover among their employers— magistrates and executives—was great.[24] These slaves were well treated. According to Glotz, "they could have their own house; their furniture was their own, they kept their savings. They were free to take a wife and to bring up their children."[25]

Private slaves enjoyed no such privileges. Their treatment was capricious. Alfred Zimmern describes it, as applied during the fifth century, in ideal terms that suggest that masters were always kind and considerate.[26] Plato painted a different picture. He acknowledged that some people knew of slaves who had done more for their masters than sons or brothers would have done and had often been "the salvation of their masters' persons and property and entire house," but others claimed that "a slave's soul is rotten through and through and not to be trusted. Some people . . . treat them like animals and whip and goad them so that they make the souls of their slaves three times—no, a thousand times—more slavish than they were. Others follow precisely the opposite policy."[27] He believed that although kindness and moral instruction were the best way of treating a slave, any misconduct on his part should be punished. "One should always address a slave in the language of command. One should not sport or jest with slaves, whether male or female; for though this is often done, it is a senseless practice and its result is to spoil the slave, making his life of servitude more difficult to bear and the authority of the master harder to maintain."[28]

There was one group of slaves whose lives were no bed of roses, namely, those working in the silver mines at Laureion in the southern tip of Attica. These mines, though state property, were run by slave-owning or slave-hiring operators under government leases. The mines had been of little importance before the fifth century, but the discovery of rich lodes in 483 B.C.

led to rapid and extensive exploitation and a great expansion of slave labor, with a concomitant rise in the revenues of the state, until overexploitation almost dried up the source after a few decades.

The extraction of the ore was done in deep galleries. "These galleries are winding . . . and were kept very narrow . . . generally 2–3 feet high and 2–3 feet broad; ventilation was provided by occasional airshafts. . . . The miners worked with small clay lamps, for which niches were made in the rock; these remained alight for ten hours and almost certainly marked the length of the daily shift. . . . [The miners] worked in chains and almost naked and were branded with their master's stamp."[29] During their most profitable period, it is said that some ten-thousand slaves were employed in them.

Mining is still a hazardous occupation today. Under the conditions described it must have been very dangerous indeed, and responsible for a heavy loss of life. No free man cared to expose himself to these dangers; slaves were expendable. Since they worked in chains and in continuous shifts they must have been lodged above ground during rest periods, under strict surveillance to prevent their escape. No mention has been found, however, of slave prisons similar to the Roman *ergastulum*.

Crime in Athens

There exist no statistics on criminality in ancient Greece. The old historians relate many incidents of treasonable acts or other glaring misconduct by persons prominent in the political or social life of the states, but the ordinary run-of-the-mill criminality did not engage their attention. That it existed is self-evident even though its dimensions are unknown. Commentaries on its causes are not lacking, however. The aristocratic Old Oligarch, for instance, blamed the common people for the crimes committed. "Within the ranks of the people will be found the greatest amount of ignorance, disorderliness, rascality—poverty acting as a strong incentive to base conduct, not to speak of lack of education and ignorance, traceable to the lack of means which afflicts the average of mankind." In the better class—"the cream of society," which he claimed was everywhere in the world opposed to democracy—one found, on the other hand, "the smallest amount of intemperance and injustice, together with the highest scrupulousness in the pursuit of excellence."[30]

Philosophers also pondered the causes of crime. Plato believed that tendencies to violence and crime were found in communities where the juxtaposition of wealth and poverty produced feelings of jealousy and envy. In his discussion of voluntary homicide, he made "as complete a list as possible" of its causes.

The chief cause is lust, which tyrannizes a soul that has gone wild with desire. This lust is usually for money, the object of most men's strongest and most frequent longing. Because of the innate depravity of men and their misdirected education, money has the power to produce in them a million cravings that are impossible to satisfy—all centering on the endless acquisition of wealth. The cause of this incorrect education is the pernicious praise given to wealth by the public opinion of Greeks and non-Greeks alike. . . . Second, an ambitious cast of mind: this breeds feelings of jealousy. . . . In the third place, many a murder has been prompted by the cowardly fears of a guilty man. When a man is committing some crime, or has already committed it, he wants no one to know about it, and if he cannot eliminate a possible informer in any other way, he murders him.[31]

Aristotle thought that some crimes were due to the lack of necessities, and that if equality in landed property could be achieved men would not steal simply to escape cold or satisfy hunger. "But want is not the only cause of crimes. Men also commit them simply for the pleasure it gives them, and just to get rid of an unsatisfied desire . . . they may [even] start some desire just in order to enjoy [by crime] the sort of pleasure which is unaccompanied by pain."* Owning property and employment would prevent crimes caused by the lack of necessities, but a temperate disposition and the aid of philosophy would be needed by the pleasure-seekers to restrain them. As for the greatest crimes—and here he seems to contemplate crimes of state—they are committed "not for the sake of necessities, but for the sake of superfluities. Men do not become tyrants in order to avoid exposure to cold."

Based on these cited fragments of notions about the roots of criminality we may assume that the ordinary offenses like theft and personal violence, in ancient Athens as elsewhere up to the present day, were most prevalent among the poor, whether free or slave, who formed the largest substratum of the population.

The Penal System

We have noted that philosophers intimated that economic and educational reforms might eliminate some of the most important forms of criminality, but the most practical means was believed to be laws that would punish offend-

---

*Op. cit., 1267a. Plato had already formulated this hedonistic principle, saying that "we want to have pleasure; we neither choose nor want pain; we prefer the natural state, if we are thereby

ers. The principal purpose of criminal legislation was formulated by the philosophers in terms that have survived to the present day. Protagoras (481–411 B.C.) taught that "he who desires to inflict rational punishment does not retaliate for a past wrong which cannot be undone; he has regard to the future and is desirous that the man who is punished, and he who sees him punished may be deterred from doing wrong again. He punishes for the sake of prevention, thereby clearly implying that virtue is capable of being taught."[32] Socrates (c.470–399 B.C.) held that "the object of all punishment which is rightly inflicted should be either to improve and benefit its subject or else to make him an example to others, who will be deterred by the sight of his sufferings and reform their own conduct."[33] In his oration against Aristogeiton Demosthenes said: "For there are two objects for which all laws are framed—to deter any man from doing what is wrong and, by punishing the transgressor, to make the rest better men."[34]

The criminal law, then, should not be retaliatory. It should aim to prevent crime by reforming the offender by his punishment and to make that punishment, at the same time, an effective warning to others. The possibility of achieving these aims did not go unchallenged. Theognis, a Megaran poet of the sixth century B.C., questioned the reformatory value of punishment, saying that "no man has ever discovered a way to make a fool wise or a bad man good. . . . You will never make the bad man good by teaching."[35] The deterrent power of punishment was also questioned, as shown in the first recorded debate on the appropriateness of using the death penalty to punish rebels.

The Mityleneans had revolted against Athens in 427 B.C., and Cleon, a leading member of the assembly, had demanded that a punitive expedition be dispatched with orders to execute all the rebels as a warning to potential rebels. In opposition to this proposal, Diodotus delivered a speech in which he questioned the deterrent power of punishment in general:

> All states and individuals are alike prone to err and there is no law that will prevent them; or why should men have exhausted the list of punishments in search of enactments to protect them from evildoers? It is probable that in early times the penalties for the greatest offenses were less severe, and that, as these were disregarded, the penalty of death has been by degrees in most cases arrived at, which is itself disregarded in like manner. Either then some means of terror more terrible than this must be discovered, or it must be owned that this restraint is useless; and that as long as poverty gives men the courage of necessity, or plenty fills them with the ambition which belongs to insolence and pride, and the other conditions of life remain each under the thraldom of some fatal and master passion,

---

relieved of pain, but not if it involves the loss of pleasure. We want less pain and more pleasure . . ." (*op. cit.*, 733).

so long will the impulse never be wanting to drive men into danger. Hope also and cupidity, the one leading and the other following, the one conceiving the attempt, the other suggesting the facility of succeeding, cause the widest ruin, and, although invisible agents, are far stronger than the dangers that are seen. Fortune, too, powerfully helps the delusion, and by the unexpected aid that she sometimes lends, tempts men to venture with inferior means. . . . In fine, it is impossible to prevent . . . human nature doing what it has once set its mind upon, by force of law or by any other deterrent force whatever. We must not, therefore, commit ourselves to a false policy through a belief in the efficiency of the punishment of death, or exclude rebels from the hope of repentance and an early atonement of their error.[36]

The punishments used in Athens to achieve the desired aims of the law reflected the social class structure of the state. For most offenses citizens were fined, and so were *metics* who had resources. In some instances citizens were banished, especially for offenses against the cult and occasionally for having reached such heights of political eminence that they had incurred the envy of powerful opponents who could sway the assembly. In that event, the victim was ostracized and exiled for ten years. Treason was punished by death, the execution taking place in the jail; the executioner was a public slave whose function was considered so odious that he had to live outside the city walls. For some offenses certain demeaning punishments fell upon a citizen designed to shame him by public exposure. But no citizen was sentenced to be flogged. The rare exceptions cited by Plato do not materially affect the rule.

Flogging was the preeminent punishment for slaves and half-free freedmen, nor did *metics* escape it. Demosthenes said that the chief distinction between the freeman and the slave was that the latter was punished in his body and the former in his property.[37] Private slaves had no property. Whether public slaves, who might have some savings, could be fined is not known. Private slaves accused of serious crimes could be confiscated by the state and put to death. Most offenses by slaves, however, were settled between their owners and the victims, who were often other slave owners. The victim could be compensated for damages or the culprit simply transferred to him. If the victim was the owner of the offender, he could discipline the slave by any means he chose, even kill him, which was not a public crime. If a citizen killed someone else's slave, he could pay the cost of replacement or, under certain circumstances, double the slave's value.

The administration of justice also favored citizens. If the testimony of a slave was admissible or required in a criminal trial, torture was used to extract it. *Metics* and other aliens could be similarly treated.[38] "The slave was not believed unless he confirmed it under pains of torture. Slaves were

14

things. As things, they could not logically be assumed to know the innate force of truth and the sanctity of the oath."[39] Public slaves and private slaves taken by the state from their masters were tortured by the public executioner, but in the case of an offense that was settled between owner and victim, the torture used to learn the "truth" took place in the household.

Citizens summoned as defendants or witnesses could not be tortured to secure confessions or to compel them to testify. Dictators or tyrants who now and then seized control of a city-state who violated this rule did so in disregard of law and custom. Demosthenes does tell of Antiphon, who led the oligarchic revolution in Athens toward the end of the Peloponnesian War and was later tried for treason, tortured, and executed in 411 B.C. for his role in that event, but that "torture" was probably an aggravated death penalty.*†

The most common instrument of torture employed in the punishment of slaves was probably the whip. Aristophanes (c.448–c.380 B.C.) may have used poetic license when, in *The Frogs,* he has one of his characters offer his purported slave for torture and, on being asked what form it should take, replies: "Anything you say: lash him to a ladder, suspend him, scourge, flog, rack, pour acid up his nose, pile rocks on him."[40] This may, however, not have been far fetched. Human ingenuity in such matters in later ages has been shown to be unlimited. If a slave died under torture or was permanently disabled, only a piece of property was lost or damaged and could be written off one's inventory or compensated for by payment.

Historians of criminal justice have agreed that imprisonment as the preventive detention of persons accused of a crime or awaiting the execution of a sentence has always existed in some form or other, but they have generally claimed that imprisonment as a punishment for common-law crimes is a relatively modern invention. This view is erroneous and based on a legal fiction which will, it is hoped, be amply demonstrated in this book. Imprisonment as detention was used in Athens as elsewhere. Persons accused of crimes to be adjudicated by the courts were guarded in the city jail, and so were those awaiting the execution of their sentences—witness the case of Socrates. Detention was also used to coerce a convicted offender into paying a fine, and it could be prolonged indefinitely if such payment could not be exacted. In the latter case, some scholars[41] claim that the imprisonment was actually an alternative punishment. It was undoubtedly felt to be such by the

---

*Demosthenes, *Orations, op. cit.*, p. 66.

†That traitors might receive very harsh treatment is intimated by Polus, who in a conversation with Socrates hypothetically referred to a man "arrested for the crime of plotting a dictatorship and racked and castrated and blinded with hot irons, and finally, after suffering many other varieties of exquisite torture and seeing his wife and children suffer the same, is crucified or burnt at the stake . . ." (Plato, *Gorgias,* 473).

insolvent culprit, but that it was a legally established and independent form of punishment for the nonpayment of a fine is debatable.

If we believe Socrates, who listed imprisonment as one of the punishments in use, the others being flogging, fine, banishment, and death, the practice did exist. And, if it is true that the detailed provisions in Plato's *Laws* are generally based on those of Athenian law, one would have to accept that punitive imprisonment occurred. Plato's provisions, however, are so bound up with his ideal plan for his Magnesia that one may doubt that he always portrayed contemporary reality.

For instance, he provided for three prisons in his state, "a public one near the market place for the general run of offenders, where large numbers may be kept in safe custody; one called the 'reform center' near the place where the Nocturnal Council assembles, and another in the heart of the countryside, in a solitary spot where the terrain is at its wildest; and the title of this prison is somehow to convey the notion of punishment."[42] Except for the jail, where any one accused of a crime could be held for trial or execution and any one except slaves could be detained for the nonpayment of a penalty, the other institutions were to serve a population of about five thousand citizens and their families.

Who was to be punished by imprisonment? First, a person guilty of a religious offense. If he committed that crime out of foolishness and was a decent fellow, he was to be sent to the reform center for at least five years, where only members of the Nocturnal Council would visit him to admonish him and ensure his spiritual salvation. When he was released and seemed to "enjoy mental health," he "should go and live with sensible people, but if appearances turn out to be deceptive and he is reconvicted on a similar charge" he was to be executed. More atrocious atheists were to be confined, upon conviction, in the third kind of prison, denied visits by free men, served their food by slaves, and after death thrown naked over the border of the state, not buried.[43] This last provision may have been metaphorical, for which neighboring state would allow its soil to be defiled in such manner?

A citizen who engaged in retail trading was to be imprisoned for one year for sullying his paternal hearth. A second conviction for the same offense meant two years in prison, and for each subsequent offense of like nature the term would be doubled indefinitely.[44] A citizen convicted of assaulting any man twenty years older than himself was to be imprisoned for a year or more. A nonresident foreigner would, for such crime, be sentenced to two years, and a resident *metic* to three years or more.[45]

It is evident that Plato had advanced ideas on punishment, but we are left in the dark on where the imprisonment was to be executed, except when offenders against the cult were involved. His prison system appears to be a theoretical construct for there is no evidence that anything like it ever existed in the Athens of his day or that his prison sentences had any counterparts in Athenian law.*

One form of punishment involving the deprivation of freedom is not mentioned by Plato, namely penal slavery, although it existed in all Greek states, where some made "civic degradation, or *atimía,* an ingenious preliminary to slavery."[46] Athens did sentence to slavery *metics* who fraudulently enrolled on the list of citizens or failed to pay the *metic* tax, foreigners who married an Athenian, and freedmen who did not meet their obligations to their old masters.[47] What became of them is not known. Did they become public slaves, sold or exported, employed in government projects, or perhaps leased to the operators of the marble quarries on Mount Pentelicus or the silver mines at Laureion? Answers are lacking.

Penal slaves were employed in the mines of Egypt by the Hellenistic Ptolemies, as is evident from the report of Diodorus Siculus, an historian and world traveler from Syracuse who lived in the first century B.C. In his history he described the condition of these slaves in the following words.

At the extremity of Egypt and in the contiguous territory of both Arabia and Ethiopia there lies a region which contains many gold mines . . . and here the overseers of the labor in the mines recover the gold with the aid of a multitude of workers. . . . For the kings of Egypt gather together and condemn to the mining of the gold such as have been found guilty of some crime and captives of war as well as those who have been accused unjustly and thrown into prison because of their [i.e., the kings'] anger, and not only such persons but occasionally all their relatives as well, by this means not only inflicting punishment upon those found guilty, but also securing at the same time great revenues from their labors. And those who have been condemned in this way—and they are a great multitude and are all bound in chains—work at their task unceasingly both by day and throughout the entire night, enjoying no respite and being carefully cut off from any means of escape, since guards of foreign soldiers who speak a language different from theirs stand watch over them, so that not a man, either by conversation or by some contact of a friendly nature, is able to corrupt any of his keepers. . . . And since no opportunity is afforded any of them to care for his body and they have no garments to cover their shame, no man can look upon the unfortunate wretches without feeling pity for them because of the exceeding hardship they suffer. For no leniency

*Morrow, *op. cit.,* p. 67, cites a law of fourth-century Mylasa, in Asia Minor, making the violation of a certain banking ordinance punishable by a fine it committed by a freeman, but by fifty lashes and six months' imprisonment if the offender was a slave. A second-century inscription from Pergamum prescribed that if a slave polluted a well without his master's knowledge, he was to lose his possessions, given one hundred lashes, imprisoned for ten days, and then brought out and flogged again, not less than fifty lashes. In this case, imprisonment was probably merely detention to permit the slave to recover from his first beating.

or respect of any kind is given to any man who is sick, or maimed, or aged, or in the case of a woman for her weakness, but all without exception are compelled by blows to persevere in their labors, until through ill-treatment they die in the midst of their tortures.[48]

Penal slavery was probably not introduced by the Hellenistic rulers, who had occupied Egypt since the death of Alexander the Great in 323 B.C., when his empire was divided by his generals. Forced labor had existed in Egypt since time immemorial. It had built the tombs, pyramids, and monuments, impressed by rulers who owned all the natural resources and whose subjects were in reality their bondsmen.[49] It is not impossible that such forced labor was used as a punishment for crime at quite an early date. In fact, Sabbacus, an Ethiopian king of Egypt in the eighth century B.C., abolished the death penalty during his reign and substituted penal labor in chains on public works.[50]

Ancient historians refer to the stone quarries of Syracuse, a Greek colony in Sicily, as a place where penal slaves were employed. Plutarch described them briefly as "a place where malefactors, felons and slaves were put to punishment."[51] They were spacious enough to serve as a prisoner-of-war camp after the successful defeat of the Athenian invaders during the Peloponnesian War. Thucydides reported that several thousand of them were kept in the quarries under frightful conditions, but whether they were also kept at labor is not told.

As we have seen, ancient Greece can be said to have had two penal systems, one for citizens and one for noncitizens—slaves, freedmen, *metics*, and foreigners. Offending slaves were at a particular disadvantage, for as "articles of property" they were subject to the domestic discipline of their owners and could even be killed with impunity. When brought to public trial as either witnesses or accused, they as well as other noncitizens could be subjected to judicial torture, which no citizen had to endure. If convicted they could be punished by flogging, which citizens were spared. And, in some instances, *metics* but not citizens could be condemned to penal slavery. There is no evidence that the two systems ever merged and made slave punishments applicable to all law violators. Conclusive evidence of that evolutionary process is found in the history of Rome.

II: SLAVERY AND PUNISHMENT IN ANCIENT ROME

The history of ancient Rome makes clear the impact of slavery on a society and its institutions. Of the many threads in the web of that history only one concerns us here, namely, the influence of slavery on the transformation of the penal system. As that system developed, slavery put its imprint on it both indirectly and directly; indirectly, because the institution degraded the free laborer and, during the late Empire, contributed to reducing him to a state of servitude almost indistinguishable from slavery, and directly, because the peculiar status of the slave subjected an offending slave to judicial procedures and punishments originally not applicable to free men, but finally regarded as proper for all but the small privileged aristocracy of birth or wealth.

To the Romans, slavery was a normal social institution sanctioned by universal usage. Their great wars of conquest, which in a few centuries had made Rome into a world power, and by the beginning of the Christian era master of the Mediterranean world and central and western Europe, brought vast numbers of enslaved war captives into the Republic, providing manpower for the expanding economy, especially for agriculture, Rome's chief industry. The slave population is said to have reached its height during the first century B.C. It has been conservatively estimated that in the Italian peninsula at that time nearly forty per cent of its population was enslaved and about thirty per cent of the population of the city of Rome.[1]

Most slaves were unskilled or semiskilled workers, but some, especially those brought in from the East, were used in domestic service, often in highly trusted posts in the great households. Most were privately owned, but the largest slave-owner was the state, who employed them on a variety of public works. Municipalities owned slaves, and large numbers were used on the imperial domains, mostly land and mineral resources.[2]

Slavery seems to engender a feeling in the master class of actual or potential slaveholders that the inherent character of the slave explains and justifies his lowly status. Aristotle's views on that were shared by the Romans. His status of slave tainted his occupation. Manual labor, in particular, was regarded as proper for slaves and not fit for free men. In his essay on moral duties, written when slavery was at its height in Rome, Cicero, a slave-owner and a humane man, thought it wise to treat slaves like hired free workers. One is tempted to assume that this meant that he wanted to see the status of the slave improved, but later in the same essay he condemned "the base and menial work of unskilled laborers, for the very wages the laborer receives is a badge of slavery. . . . The work of the mechanic is also degrading; there is nothing noble about a workshop."[3] The stigma of slave labor attached to the free laborer's occupation was to contribute significantly to his abasement during the late Empire.

In considering the treatment of the slave, it is important to remember that he was a chattel, an object, albeit a live one, and that in civil law he was a nonperson whose treatment by his owner was of no concern to the state, at least during the Republic.[4] Law and custom protected the rights of the master; the slave had none. Consequently, his treatment depended on how well he performed his assigned tasks, on his skills and intelligence, on the temperament of his owner or overseer, and even on the cost of his replacement, which varied, depending on the market.

In spite of some examples to the contrary, domestic slaves were probably treated fairly well. The grossest mistreatment occurred in the state-owned mines leased to contractors and worked by slaves. Speaking of the Spanish silver mines which at times employed as many as forty-thousand slaves, Diodorus of Sicily, who visited them during the last half of the first century B.C., wrote that

the slaves who are engaged in the working of them produce for their masters revenues in sums defying belief, but they themselves wear out their bodies both by day and by night in the diggings under the earth, dying in large numbers because of the exceptional hardships they endure. For no respite or pause is granted them in their labors, but compelled beneath blows of the overseers to endure the severity of their plight . . . indeed, death in their eyes is to be more desired than life because of the magnitude of the hardships they must bear.[5]

The time would come when these hardships would be regarded as the proper punishment of convicted plebeian criminals.

On the large plantations and cattle ranches, which at times employed hundreds of slaves, conditions were also deplorable. Run by slaves or freedmen overseers for mostly absentee landlords, they were worked by a motley crew of largely unskilled slaves whose days were spent in physical labor from dawn to dusk under the whiplash of slave guards, and often in chains to prevent escapes. From time to time their miseries triggered uprisings, some of which grew into major wars, like the revolt in 72–71 B.C. of the slaves—mostly Germans, Gauls, and Thracians—of the gladiatorial school

20

at Capua led by the Thracian Spartacus. When finally suppressed by the legions under Crassus, the rebels had mustered over seventy-thousand fighting men.[6]

The Offending Slave

Although in law the slave was only a piece of animate property for whose behavior his owner was responsible, he was also a human being with passions and desires, fears and resentments. When he offended against his master he was subject to domestic discipline, for as *dominus* his master had the power of life and death over him. If the slave was suspected of wrongdoing, his master could have him tortured to secure a confession, and have his fellow slaves tortured to secure evidence. Once his guilt was established, or if he was caught in the act, his punishment was at his master's discretion.

Whipping was the most common punishment, but the culprit might be chained, and if he was a recaptured fugitive he could be branded on the forehead with the letter F. He could be mutilated, confined in stocks which clamped his ankles and even his neck and wrists, or made to carry the *furca,* a V-shaped yoke, around the neck to the points of which his outstretched arms were tied. For very serious offenses, his master might execute him by having him beaten to death or burned alive. A slave in Petronius' *Satyricon* speaks of "gentle fire, the cruelest death to which an angry master can sentence his slave."[7] Crucifixion was the preferred method of execution for slaves within the domestic establishment. At Trimalchios' famous banquet, his secretary reported that among recent events on that wealthy freedman's estates was the crucifixion of the slave Mithridates "for blaspheming the guardian spirit of our master Gaius."[8] After the suppression of the revolt of Spartacus, Crassus had six thousand captured slaves crucified along the Appian Way and, after the burning of Rome, Nero had many Christians, falsely accused of arson, crucified or burned alive, i.e., punished like slaves.[9] Most of them probably were slaves, freedmen, or aliens. At best, the offender might be traded or sold.

Still another punishment might await him, especially on the larger domains, namely imprisonment in the estate's private *ergastulum* (from the Greek *ergasterion*—workshop), where he would be kept in fetters at hard labor, such as milling corn. Little is known about these *ergastula.* The agronomist Columella suggested that they be so constructed that only the upper part of the building, with windows beyond reach, would be above ground level.* The abuses prevalent in these establishments gave rise to national scandals at times. When young Tiberius was *quaestor,* he was sent by Augustus in 20 B.C. to inspect them because they were said to house many army deserters and kidnaped freemen. Hadrian sought to suppress them, but without success, because in the late Empire when a slave was sentenced by a magistrate to public labor, whether temporarily or for life, he would, with his owner's consent, be returned to serve his term in chains in his owner's private prison.[10]

The disciplinary power of the *dominus* over his slave was but slightly curbed during the Empire. In 61 A.D., for instance, masters were forbidden "to punish their slaves by making them fight beasts . . . unless the cause had been approved as sufficient by a magistrate."[11] Domitian forbade masters to castrate their slaves for sale as eunuchs, and tried, ineffectually, to discourage the practice by fixing a low maximum price for the product. Hadrian added teeth to the law by threatening the slave's owner with the confiscation of his property, and the consenting slave and the surgeon with capital punishment. He also forbade the master to kill his slave without a judgment by a magistrate, or to sell her or him without proper cause to a procurer or a provisioner of the gladiatorial games. Antoninus Pius made a master who killed his slave liable to a charge of homicide, and ordered a slave who had sought asylum at the emperor's statue to escape a cruel master to be sold to a more clement person.[12] However, since Constantine later had to reiterate that a master was guilty of homicide if he killed his slave willfully or by "wantonly cruel" punishment, it is evident that all these restrictions little interfered with time-honored practices of domestic discipline, especially when the master was a person of power and prestige.

Social Classes

As Roman society evolved from a primitive small city-state to a multiple-nation world-state, social and economic forces were operating to produce changes in political structure, the focus of political power, the concept of citizenship, and the stratification of social classes, which in turn ultimately produced a penal system that applied ancient slave punishments to the vast majority of the population.

---

*L. J. M. Columella, *On Agriculture* (3 vols.; Cambridge: Harvard University Press, 1941–55), I, 63. He also advised masters to "call over the names of the slaves in the prison, who are in chains, every day and make sure that they are carefully fettered and also whether the place of confinement is well secured and properly fortified" (I, 22).

The freeborn Roman took great pride in his status as citizen. It was a privilege he jealously guarded. By virtue of it he could, through popular assemblies, participate in the legislative process and, to some degree, in the administration of justice. Therefore, when he by conquest incorporated new territories into the state, he was reluctant to grant citizenship, except sparingly. Even in Italy proper, only second-rate citizenship was granted to people of the conquered towns. This exclusiveness was to change as Rome grew more prosperous after the great wars of conquest. A liberal policy of manumitting slaves added new and foreign elements to the body of citizens. Between 81 and 49 B.C., for instance, some five hundred thousand were freed.[13] This helps to explain Tacitus' claim that, in Nero's time, the freedmen of Rome supplied "the majority of the voters, servants of public offices, attendants to magistrates and priests, and soldiers even in the city cohorts . . . if the freedmen were to be segregated, the freeborn would be shown to be very thin on the ground."[14] Gradually, citizenship was granted to people in certain territories and to demobilized veterans of barbarian stock, and finally by Caracalla, in 212 A.D., to nearly all freeborn males within the Empire. What had once been the proud possession of a select group had become degraded. The freeborn barbarian of the provinces and the Roman descendant of slaves were not the typical citizens of the Empire. It is not illogical to assume that these developments had an effect on the evolving penal law. They paralleled important changes in the class structure of Roman society.

Democracy was a hollow word in Rome. True, during the Republic citizens, in public convocations, passed legislation and elected magistrates, but the two important assemblies—the Centuriate and the Tribal—were so constituted that in the former the wealthiest class could outvote the others, and in the latter the ancient client relationship between the common citizen and his wealthier patron practically guaranteed that the interests of the upper classes would be protected and served. The Senate was for centuries controlled by a handful of patrician families who also supplied most of the elected magistrates. Its power remained unchallenged until a group of nouveau-riches did so successfully during the later years of the Republic.

The wars of expansion laid the conquered lands under tribute, subjected their inhabitants to taxation and imposts, and stimulated trade and the exploitation of their natural resources. Since senators, forbidden to engage in foreign trade, were largely satisfied to cultivate their acres and invest their profits, another wealthy class came into being, the *equites,* or knights. They collected tribute and taxes and custom duties under contract with the state, operated mines leased from the state, and engaged in trade, banking, and construction work, etc., amassing great wealth in the process, especially as tax collectors. As a class, they too formed a hereditary nobility, a notch below the senatorial class, and finally, they were to fill vacancies in the Senate and, during the late Republic and early Empire, acquire seats in the jury courts.

A third class, the *decurions,* emerged after the fall of the Republic. With the establishment of Roman colonies and towns, the government of these municipalities was fashioned on that of Rome. The town senate, or *curia,* was its governing body. Its members were property owners in the town and the surrounding territory under their jurisdiction. They constituted the rural nobility, lowest on the aristocratic scale, but an important segment of the upper classes whose members were collectively referred to as *honestiores* in the penal laws of the later Empire.

Below them were the common citizens, ranging from the propertyless laborer or proletarian, that class of the population thought useful mostly for procreation, to the artisan, the shopkeeper, the small industrialist. They were the plebeians, the humble, the *humiliores,* below whom came the slaves.

These class distinctions had a significant influence on the development of the penal system during the Empire, when the process of converting the old slave punishments into official legal punishments was completed. That process was accelerated by the catastrophic political and economic developments which ultimately dismembered the Empire in the fifth century. We must limit comments to the period beginning with the accession of Diocletian (284–305 A.D.) to the imperial throne, the first occupant to assume absolute power after half a century of gross misrule by a series of emperors, made and unmade by the army, whose wars with rivals and foreign foes had ruined the economy of the state.

Diocletian's ability as a field commander who restored order and secured the frontiers of the Empire was matched by his administrative skill. He enlarged and restructured the army, reformed the administration of the realm, and centralized its control. The result was the creation of a vast bureaucracy and a need for greater revenues to meet the mounting costs of government. His ingenious tax system, based on the productivity of land and labor, brought the entire class of *decurions* to ruin. These town councilmen were obliged to assess the value of property in their districts, establish the amount of the land tax, and then collect it from the taxpayers. They were held liable for eventual deficits. The onus of these responsibilities soon became unbearable and they sought every means of escape: enlistment in the army, joining holy orders, ceding their land to some larger landowner, turning sharecroppers *(coloni),* or joining some craft guild, perhaps exchanging one plight for another.

The *coloni* also sank under the fiscal burdens and many deserted the land. This loss of manpower in agriculture became so serious that in 332 A.D. Constantine decreed

> that the *coloni* who might flee or might plan to flee from their overlords must be returned to them and be shackled in irons—"so that they might fulfill, under the merited condemnation to servitude, the obligations which befitted them as free men." . . . Although they continued to be differentiated formally from the rustic slaves *(servi rustici),* the *coloni* later came to be referred to as "slaves of the land itself to which they were born." This change in terminology expresses realistically the degree of descent toward enslavement which the *coloni* had undergone.[15]

They were tied to the land and sold with it when it changed owner. Their status was hereditary.*

Urban workers met a similar fate. The craft guilds were placed under state control and their members bound to their craft, which was made hereditary. This leveling process, which made manual workers "slaves of the craft," so to speak, was exemplified in the many state factories throughout the Empire. "In the state industries," writes Jones, "it is difficult to find other than technical differences between the *fabricenses,* or arms manufacturers, who were legally soldiers, and the workers in the mints, weaving mills and dyeworks, who were legally slaves. Both were bound with their children to their trades; *fabricenses* were branded to facilitate their detection if they escaped."[16]

The above-described debasement of the working class stood in glaring contrast to the hereditary privileges and status enjoyed by the politically and economically powerful aristocracy and landed gentry and those whose financial and business success had gained them titles of nobility. The ancient Roman upper-class views of the indignity of manual labor were reinforced when the working classes were actually reduced to a slavelike status. Thus it seemed appropriate to subject humble citizens who committed crimes to punishments originally reserved for slaves.

The Penal System

We have noted that the repression of illicit conduct within the domestic establishment rested on ancient prerogatives of the head of the family. Much of what today is prosecuted by the state as crime therefore fell outside the

---

*Converting the technically free *coloni* into "slaves of the land" was easy, because so many of them had originally been manumitted slaves, whose previous owners, derived more profit from

province of the penal law. In primitive Rome, treason and parricide were offenses against the state punishable by death.[17] The traitor, hands bound and face covered, was beaten and hanged on the "accursed tree" or in the *furca*.† The Twelve Tables, which in 451 B.C. codified ancient law, prescribed burning arsonists alive, hurling perjurers from the Tarpeian Rock, and drowning parricides sewn up in a sack. A slave caught stealing was beaten and thrown from the Rock; a freeman thief was given to his victim for enslavement. One who accidentally caused a fire paid damages unless he was too poor, in which case he was flogged, as was the thief of crops under the age of puberty. A few other offenses were also punished by death but, as we shall see, death sentences were rarely executed when the offender was a citizen, because in their struggle with the patricians for a share of political power, the plebeians, in 509 B.C., had forced the adoption of a law which prohibited the magistrates from flogging Roman citizens or executing them for crimes before receiving the approval of the Centuriate Assembly to which the offender had the right to appeal.

This procedure was to have a dramatic effect on penal justice. Roman citizens were not detained before trial as a rule, and since the convocation of the Assembly took some time, the defendant could flee into exile, which usually happened. The magistrate then outlawed him by "interdiction of fire and water," and if he returned to Rome without authorization, he faced execution. Exile and interdiction did not become punishments per se until 63 and 58 B.C., respectively.[18] During the Empire they would be transformed into relegation and deportation.

Slaves and noncitizens did not have the right to appeal to the assembly. They were subject to the arbitrary justice of the magistrate, who could pass sentence of death, crucify slaves, flog, fine, confiscate property, etc.[19] Considering the character of the population of Rome toward the end of the Republic, there was no dearth of candidates for the cross, the stake, and the lash.

As the Roman state expanded and the body of citizens increased in the city of Rome, the Centuriate Assembly, which was always convoked in the city, became too unwieldy for the administration of justice. Other means had

---

sharecroppers who maintained themselves and their families by their labor than from costly slaves maintained at their expense; (*see* Marc Bloch, "Comment et pourquoi finit l'esclavage antique," *Annales*, 2:30–44, 161–70, 1947, p. 24, reproduced in M. I. Finley [ed.], *Slavery in Classical Antiquity* [Cambridge, Heffer, 1968]).

†When Nero heard that the Senate had declared him a public enemy and that "he would be punished 'in the ancient style' when arrested, he asked what 'ancient style' meant and learned that the exeuctioners stripped their victim naked, thrust his head into a wooden fork and then flogged him to death with sticks" (Suetonius, *Nero*, 49, in *The Twelve Caesars* [Baltimore: Penguin Books, 1957]).

to be found. The result was the creation of permanent courts, composed of thirty or more jurors and chaired by a praetor. At first the jurors were all drawn from the senatorial class, but later the knights also won the right to serve. Each court dealt with only one crime, the definition of which usually embraced a variety of acts, sometimes tenuously related. The laws creating the courts fixed mandatory punishments which could not be appealed. The oldest was passed in 149 B.C. to deal with extortion by provincial governors. Most of them date from the first century B.C., except for an Augustan law of 9 A.D. They dealt with cases of lese majesty (including treason), adultery, murder, crimes of violence, parricide, forgery, bribery, extortion, kidnapping, embezzlement, and illegal practices in the food trade, and only charges brought by a citizen were acted on. Slaves, freedmen, and aliens could not bring accusations; their masters or patrons had to assume that role on their behalf.

Equality of Roman citizens before the law was Republican doctrine. Death, fines, and removal from office remained as punishments, but exile and/or outlawry continued to serve as administrative substitutes for death, except in rare instances when some law proscribed them.

Drastic changes were to occur in this system during the Empire. The roles of the Centuriate Assembly and the jury courts in the administration of justice were appropriated by the Senate, which took criminal jurisdiction over cases affecting its members or their families, until Diocletian deprived it of this prerogative, and by autocratic emperors, who transferred the functions of the jury courts to courts served by appointed magistrates not bound to apply only the punishments which the jury courts had had to use. Imperial edicts, mandates, and rescripts, and the opinions of learned jurists in the service of the throne, expanded the scope of the penal law. New punishments were adopted and old ones preserved, including all the arbitrary ones traditionally available to magistrates. The ancient principle of the equality of citizens before the law was discarded. Citizens would soon be sentenced to punishments once reserved to slaves, and the upper classes that had controlled and manipulated government even during the Republic would acquire a privileged status that was reflected both in the trial procedure and in the punishments.

For instance, in order to discover evidence for the prosecution of a defendant, torture was used during the Republic, but only on slaves.[20] Indeed, this was regarded as the only means of extracting the truth from them. The practice continued during the Empire, but Tiberius began to subject freemen to it in lese-majesty and treason cases. From then on it must have occurred in other cases of serious crime too, because in the third century it was expressly forbidden to torture town councillors *(decurions)* and their children. This means that the higher classes of nobility, senators, and knights, were also exempt, and that, at the discretion of the magistrate, judicial torture could be used on the accused or a witness belonging to the lower classes—plebeians, aliens, freedmen, and slaves.[21]

An upper class citizen, *honestior,* was spared many of the punishments of the low-class offender, *humilior.*[22] If he was convicted of a capital crime—i.e., one which no longer was punishable only by death, as during most of the Republican period, but which now meant a crime that on conviction deprived a citizen of his status as a freeman, his citizenship, his family, and sometimes his life—he was almost always deported for life to an island and saw his property confiscated. If he was actually sentenced to die, he was simply beheaded with a sword, a prerogative claimed by nobles up to modern times. For noncapital crimes he might be relegated, i.e., exiled for life or a term of years, without loss of citizenship or his freeman's status. He could not be sentenced to die in the arena fighting wild beasts or as a gladiator, to expire in torments on the gallows, the cross or at the stake, nor to ignominious penal labor fit for slaves unless he had previously been degraded to the status of a *humilior* for whom such punishments were proper.

Hard labor as punishment for crimes committed by freemen was not used during the Republic. Its prototype was the *ergastulum* already described and reserved for criminal slaves. It was during the Empire that hard labor was to develop into a favored punishment of lower-class criminals. Its most severe form was a sentence to the imperial mines *(ad metalla),* i.e., metal mines, chalk and sulphur pits, quarries, and salt mines. The sentence was for life and reduced the prisoner to the status of a public slave of the imperial fisc, until Antoninus Pius declared him to be "slave of the punishment," a condition known in modern times as penal servitude.[23] The prisoners had to wear heavy chains; their life expectancy was short. A variant of this punishment was the sentence, also for life, to "mining" *(ad opus metalli).* Such prisoners wore lighter chains and presumably worked at tasks other than the extraction of the ore. Slaves who had belonged to private masters and who were not condemned to other brutal punishments were sent to the mines because they could not be sentenced to "public work" *(opus publicum),* which consequently became reserved for low-class freemen. These sentences were for life or limited terms. The prisoners wore chains and were occupied in building or repairing roads, cleaning sewers, caring for the public baths, working in state bakeries, etc. If sentenced for life, the offender lost his citizenship.*

---

*That hard labor could be used as punishment was, of course, known to Republican Rome. It was in use in Syracuse when Sicily became a Roman province in the third century B.C., and Diodorus

The Roman passion for games gave rise to new punishments during the Empire. Spectacles in the amphitheater of fights with wild beasts and duels or pitched battles of gladiators, with slaves the actors or contestants, were popular during the late Republic. Criminal slaves were sometimes sold by their masters to the gladiatorial schools and thus could suffer a punishment not yet prescribed for freemen by law. That lack was remedied during the Empire, which at its height saw not only slaves but *humiliores* sentenced to die in the arena, mangled by beasts, or killed by gladiators.[24] Other gruesome methods of execution also threatened them—burning alive after smearing the offender with "the pitch that turns the victim's body into a living flaming torch" [25] or crucifixion, which had been regarded as a slave punishment until Constantine in deference to the Savior, substituted hanging.

Lower-class offenders were also subject to corporal punishments for certain misdemeanors. Freemen were beaten with rods, slaves were whipped. Mutilating punishments were in use in the late Empire because Justinian, in a Novella, abolished the amputation of hands and feet and the dislocation of joints as punishment, substituting amputation of one hand if the thief was armed and caught in the act.[26]

This completes our cursory examination of the evolution of the penal system of ancient Rome and the influence exerted by the institution of slavery. The end product of that evolution—the penal system of the late Empire—bore the stamp of slavery. Punishments once applicable only to slaves became proper for certain classes of citizens. Slavery itself remained a form of punishment. Upper-class offenders were spared the brutal capital and corporal punishments which the poor had to suffer. This was the penal system Rome left as a legacy to the Middle Ages.

---

of Sicily had described its use in Ptolemaic Egypt before Augustus' conquest of that country. Nevertheless, it was not a prescribed punishment in the laws that created the jury courts, although it is conceivable that magistrates, exercising arbitrary justice, may occasionally have used it for criminal slaves or aliens, but evidence is lacking. Mommsen (*Römisches Strafrecht* [Graz, 1959], p. 949; reprint of 1889 ed.) believed that it began to be used under Tiberius. However, when Strabo visited Sinope on the Black Sea, a colony founded by Caesar, he noted that convicts were working in the mines, and since Strabo died in the seventh year of Tiberius' reign at the age of seventy-plus, it seems unlikely that he undertook any arduous trips that late in life.

Punitive labor in mines and on public works, a punishment that gained popularity during the Empire, was probably the result of a manpower shortage. Slaves had traditionally furnished the needed manpower, but when the end of the wars of conquest cut short the supply of captives, convict labor offered a reasonable partial solution.

III: IN THE MIDDLE AGES

When Sir Frederick Pollock casually mentioned that among the Anglo-Saxons "slaves were liable to capital and other corporal punishments, and generally without redemption," he added that "the details have no material bearing on the general history of the law and may be left to students of semi-barbarous manners."[1] Some students of early Germanic law did not dismiss these "details" so cavalierly. Indeed, they maintained that slavery had a crucial influence on the history of penal law. This was noted in 1882 by Ludwig von Bar,[2] among others; but the outstanding advocate of the idea was Gustav Radbruch, who elaborated it in a remarkable essay originally published in 1938.[3] Contrary to the views of some earlier historians who believed that punishments introduced into the public penal law of the Germanic peoples during the Middle Ages were offshoots of ancient rituals of human sacrifice or of outlawry, Radbruch held that they originally were private domestic punishments of slaves and over the centuries made applicable to all offenders. He saw this transformation as a product of changes in the structure of Germanic society and rooted in that primitive community which Tacitus, most eminent of Roman historians, described in 98 A.D. in his *Germania,* a slim monograph still the chief source of information about the political, economic, and social life of the many independent tribes—he named half a hundred of them—of central and northern Europe in his day.

Slavery was firmly established among the Germans.[4] It must have been widespread, for manual labor was considered beneath the dignity of free men, who preferred hunting, feasting, gambling, and especially fighting. Most slaves were the spoils of war. They lived in huts assigned to them by their masters on plots of land which they cultivated. They raised cereal crops and livestock, part of which had to be delivered to their masters. This may make them appear like sharecroppers, but they were in fact chattels without rights and could be traded like the oxen and horses of their owners. Their lowly status set them apart from the society of free men, tainted them even when freed, and subjected them to a justice peculiar to chattel slavery.

According to Tacitus, the chief punishment in the unwritten law of a tribe was death. It was imposed for crimes committed during warfare. The offenses were adjudicated by the tribal assembly of freemen authorized to bear arms, and convened on specific days or in an emergency to deliberate and decide matters of public policy and to function as a court of justice. They were acts threatening the safety of the tribe and odious to the gods, whose standards were carried into battle and whose invisible presence on the field inspired the warriors. The importance of the cult may be gleaned from the fact that only priests were authorized to execute the death sentences imposed by the assembly, as well as the punishments of fetters or flogging for minor offenses during warfare and the unspecified punishment for disturbing the peace of the assembly.

Death sentences were promptly and publicly executed, and the two methods used were geared to the nature of the crime. "Traitors and deserters are hanged on trees; cowards, shirkers and sodomites* are pressed down under a wicker hurdle in the slimy mud of a bog.† This distinction in the punishments is based on the idea that offenders against the state should be made a public example of, whereas deeds of shame should be buried out of men's sight."‡ Soldiers who threw away their shields were punished by being barred from the assembly and sacred rites, so great a disgrace that they often committed suicide.

In this manner the assembly, acting as a kind of collective court-martial, dealt with serious offenses against the tribal community. Historians who have claimed that offenses such as harmful sorcery or murder were public crimes in ancient times are not supported by Tacitus. Nor did the assembly, if its criminal jurisdiction has been completely described, declare any man an outlaw, expel him from the community and expect him to be killed by his pursuers or any one encountering him. This practice arose later, when public vengeance began to supplant the private vengeance which a primitive community regarded as the proper means of exacting retribution for private wrongs.

In Tacitus' time, homicides, woundings, robberies, thefts, and the like were the private concern of the kinship groups that made up a tribe. We are not specifically told how such events were dealt with when they occurred *within* a given kinship group, but if a member of such group killed or injured a member of another, a kind of private war broke out, which might last for some time, since heirs were obligated to take up the feud of a father or

---

*The meaning of *corpore infames*, which learned translators have assumed to denote homosexuals, has been disputed (*see* Dieter Feucht, *Grube und Pfahl* [Tübingen, 1967], pp. 90–92, 125–27).

†Evidence of this practice in the time of Tactitus has been unearthed, especially in northwest Germany and Denmark (*see* P. V. Glob, *The Bog People* [Ithaca, N.Y., 1969]).

(Tacitus, chap. 12. I have used Mattingly's translation, as revised by Handford and published in *The Agricola and Germania* (Penguin Books, 1970). The notes are mine.)

kinsman. Ultimately a feast of reconciliation would be held after an inter-group agreement was reached, by which a stated number of livestock were transferred by the offender and his kin to the victim or his kin as compensation for the wrong done. If a private settlement could not be reached, the injured party could bring the matter before the assembly. If the plaintiff's cause was decided in his favor, the assembly would order his adversary to indemnify him and his kindred in an amount proportionate to the injury and consisting of horses and cattle, and similarly pay the tribe an amount proportionate to the indemnity.* Tacitus does not tell us what action the assembly was wont to take if its order was not obeyed, nor does he mention what role the social rank of the victim might have played in fixing the amount of these fines. Radbruch noted that "the prerogative of feud and indemnity, which is central to the arrangements antedating the criminal law, was a prerogative of those only who could demand satisfaction and could pay."[5] Since enslavement could result from inability to pay a gambling debt, an insolvent defendant might become the slave of the victim or of his family and be delivered to their mercy.

The disciplinary power of the head of a household was unlimited and of no concern to the tribal state. If his wife misbehaved sexually, he could cut off her hair, strip her naked, and flog her through the village in the presence of kinsmen. We are told that a woman so treated would find it difficult to get another husband. As for slaves, their masters could deal with them at will. They could be flogged, fettered, put to hard labor, or even killed. These were the domestic punishments specifically mentioned by Tacitus, but since no external official restraints were placed on the slave-owner, other painful methods were probably also used, then as later, in the disciplining of offending slaves.

The report by Tacitus on the public administration of criminal justice among the primitive Germans and on their custom of settling private feuds is not complete, and in the absence of documentary evidence, modern historians have tried to fill the gaps by retrojecting later beliefs and customs, because four centuries were to pass before information about Germanic legal customs became available again. These were the years of the great westward migrations of the tribes into Italy, Gaul, and Spain in the fourth and fifth centuries graphically described by Gibbon in his *Decline and Fall of the Roman Empire*. Rome accepted them as confederates and granted them large shares of land, livestock, and slaves at the expense of the native

*Minor wrongful acts were adjudicated by magistrates elected by the assembly. With the aid of a panel of one hundred assessors, they administered justice in districts and villages.

populations. As the Roman empire crumbled in the West, the barbarian kings established sovereignty over their territories of settlement or conquest—the Ostrogoths in northern Italy, the Visigoths in southwest Gaul and the Iberian peninsula, the Burgundians in eastern Gaul and western Switzerland, and the Franks in northern Gaul. We do not know exactly when they began to put their legal customs in writing. The Goths had been given an alphabet by Bishop Ulfila a century earlier than the first known fragments of law—in Latin—issued by the Visigothic king Euric about the year 480 A.D.[6] They marked the end of the first dark age of German legal history and foreshadowed the many written "barbarian codes" or folklaws of later centuries.[7]

The barbarian codes were mostly concerned with penal justice. They evidence a growing effort by the state to limit the practice of private vengeance and feuding. Indeed, the Visigoths prohibited it, as did the Bavarians much later—neither with conspicuous success. Chief reliance was instead placed on fixed or agreed indemnities (composition) imposed or approved by order of a court and paid by an offender to his victim or his victim's kin, in default of which he could be delivered to his adversary for retaliation or enslavement. Indemnities were of two kinds: specific amounts, called *wergeld,* for killing, wounding, or assaulting another person; and others which basically correspond to the value of property stolen, damaged, or destroyed. They were usually expressed in units of Constantine's gold solidus, even though payments were more often made in kind than in coin. In all but a few exceptional cases, an offender also had to pay a fine to the state treasury, often far in excess of the indemnity, and it tended to increase proportionately as the administration of justice was found to be a most lucrative source of revenue. Prosecutions were initiated by the aggrieved party, and centuries were to pass before public prosecution made its first halting appearance. All but capital cases were adjudicated in the courts of counts or village justices; these were usually dealt with in the king's high court.

The barbarian codes mirrored societies where class differences rendered even freemen unequal before the law. The Burgundian code,[8] for instance, subdivided them into noble, middle, and lower classes. Below these were the half-free freedmen and serfs, whose legal status was often barely distinguishable from that of the lowest class—the slaves. The basic value—the *wergeld*—placed on their lives in part reflects the position of these classes on the social scale. For a noble, this sum was 300 solidi, for a middle-class man 200, and for one of the lower class, 150. If a master killed his own slave no punishment awaited him, but if he killed another's slave, the indemnity he had to pay depended on the slave's occupation, i.e., his market value. An ordinary slave—unskilled worker, ploughman, swineherd—was worth 30 solidi; a carpenter, 40; a blacksmith, 50; and a trained house servant or messenger, 60; but a silversmith or steward cost 100 solidi, a royal steward as much as a lower-class, and a goldsmith as much as a middle-class freeman. If someone knocked out the tooth of a slave, he had to pay his owner 2 solidi; if the victim was a freedman he owed the victim 3 solidi, and the tooth of a lower-class man would cost him 5 solidi.

A freeman charged with a crime could clear himself by oath and the oaths of his sons or parents and twelve relatives; but if this procedure, fraught with the risk of perjury, was invalidated,* the judge would order him to engage in a trial by combat,[9] i.e., a duel with his accuser, permitting a judgment—*Urtheil,* ordeal—of God to decide the issue. Although this may strike us as a novel way of settling a dispute, it must have seemed quite natural to a people who were known in Tacitus' time to have used the outcome of a duel by champions as an omen of the result of an impending battle.

The Burgundians threatened any freeman who murdered another freeman or royal servant of barbarian origin, or who was privy to such murder by his slave, with death. Assaulting a Christian priest was a capital offense if committed by a Jew. A freeman could be executed for plundering houses or treasure chests and for stealing oxen, horses, mares, or cows. If he committed adultery, both he and his partner could be killed. A freeman's daughter who voluntarily united with a slave could be executed, or might instead be made the king's slave. The ancient punishment of live burial in a bog awaited a wife who deserted her husband. Otherwise the method of execution was not spelled out in the Burgundian code. The judge would "hand over" the offender to be publicly killed by the accuser and his kin.

Most offenses by freemen against persons or property were settled by payment of indemnities, often without official intervention. In some cases, these indemnities were punitive and amounted to treble or even ninefold the damage suffered. If the defendant could not raise the amount in money or in kind, he was doomed to enslavement by his accuser. This must have been the common fate of poor defendants considering that a *wergeld* of 150 solidi to satisfy the kin of a slain lower-class freeman, for instance, was equivalent to 75 oxen, 150 sheep, or 30 draft horses. Enslavement by the parents of an

---

*In the earliest Anglo-Saxon laws, we find kinsmen being replaced as oath-helpers by men "of the same class" as the accused. Even this was considered likely to tip the scale of justice in favor of the accused. Before the end of the seventh century, the principle had been well established that at least one man of high social rank should be among the oath-helpers (*see* F. E. Stenton, *Anglo-Saxon England* [3d ed.; Oxford, 1971], pp. 316–17).

abducted girl would definitely await an indigent abductor, and if a horse thief was executed, his wife and children over fourteen years of age became the slaves of the horse's owner.

A mutilating punishment was stipulated in Burgundian law. A freeman might suffer the amputation of a hand if he aided a fugitive to escape or removed or destroyed boundary markers. In the latter case, at least, he could avert the punishment by paying an indemnity, and this was probably also possible in the first instance. If a Jew struck a Christian he had to pay 10 solidi to save his hand.

In Tacitus' time slave-owners were held as responsible for the misdeeds of their living chattels as if they themselves had committed them. Later the notion developed that the slave had a will of his own and should share responsibility for his crime and suffer public punishment.[10] The choice of appropriate punishments, however, posed a problem for the barbarian legislator. Some punishments suitable for freemen could not be imposed on a slave. Outlawing him would give him freedom, however precarious, and since he had no possessions he could not pay fines and indemnities. If he was a suspect he could not exercise a freeman's prerogative of calling on oath-helpers to swear to his innocence. Substitutes for these expedients had to be devised, and they were at hand. The legislator simply made the practices employed by slave-owners within the domestic establishment—flogging, castration, cutting off the hand, blinding, death,* and physical force to elicit confessions—into public punishments and judicial procedures. These devices were hallowed by tradition, and since slaves were held to be inferior to other human beings, these were considered appropriate punishments. They seemed equally proper for serfs and freedmen and, in time, even for those humble, impoverished freemen, unable to purchase immunity from physical punishments. Eventually they were to place an indelible stamp on the penal law of the Middle Ages and made applicable to most everybody, free or unfree, until the end of the eighteenth century. Some of them have survived until today in the penal laws of some countries and in the disciplinary practices or regulations of "correctional" institutions.

Under Burgundian law flogging was the paramount punishment for slaves

---

*(Von Bar, *op. cit.* [English ed.], p. 74 No. 4). As previously noted, in the time of Tacitus death was not an official punishment for offenses against the life or property of private persons. It was imposed only for certain crimes which during warfare threatened the security of the state or the success of a war enterprise—treason and desertion. Tacitus did mention that minor military offenses were punished by flogging, and Heinrich Brunner (*Deutsche Rechtsgeschichte* [2 vols.; Leipzig, 1887, 1892], II, 607) believed that freemen were thus punished. Since even the earliest folk laws did not permit the flogging of freemen, it is not unlikely that the offenders thus treated were not freemen soldiers but unfree servants, alien camp followers, and the like.

and serfs. No freeman was subjected to this treatment, one which through-out history has been regarded as the most degrading of punishments. The number of blows allowed ranged from 75 to 300, depending on the offense. Theft of livestock, grain standing in sheaves, or a beehive earned the maximum penalties. In most instances, the owner of the culprit also had to indemnify the victim of the crime according to a fixed tariff, varying from a third of a solidus for a stolen goat to 10 solidi for a fine horse. An ox was worth 2 solidi, and a cow, pig, or sheep one solidus. A slave who voluntarily knocked out the tooth of a freeman was not only flogged but also might lose a hand.

Murder, theft, and robbery were capital offenses for freemen and slaves alike, but slaves could also be condemned to death for manslaughter, assaults on freewomen, sexual relations with free girls, aiding a fugitive to escape, and removing or destroying boundary markers, while freemen only had to pay indemnities.

When a slave or serf was accused of crime, the court could order him tortured to help establish his guilt or innocence. Strangers were not exempt, because they were generally believed to be fugitive slaves or serfs. If a stranger entered a community, any one learning of it was in duty bound to bring him before a judge, who might order him tortured to find out who owned him.

Freemen were not subjected to judicial torture. The use of oath-helpers and ordeals was more in keeping with their status. Generally speaking this held true for all Germanic folk laws, with one exception: Visigothic law not only permitted the flogging of freemen for most offenses, but also allowed the torture even of nobles and dignitaries charged with capital crimes and of lower-class freemen accused of crimes carrying indemnities of 300 or more solidi. The Visigothic code was a mixture of Germanic and Roman elements in which the latter strongly dominated; its penal provisions showed this influence most clearly.[11] A few exceptions have also been noted in other codes. An Alamanic law of the late sixth century permitted the torture of suspected witches, slave or free, and the Council of Reisbach in Bavaria circa 800 A.D. prescribed torture of suspected sorcerers. But, as the use of ordeals everywhere increased during the feudal period, judicial torture seems to have disappeared, until it was to fill the void caused by the firm stand against ordeals by the Lateran Council in 1215 A.D.[12]

Judging from its provision of capital punishments and its adoption of judicial torture in proceedings against the unfree, the Burgundian code was to some degree contaminated by Roman law. Its more famous contemporary, the law of the Salian Franks,[13] was more representative of early medieval

Germanic law. It was compiled under King Clovis about 500 A.D. Before his death, in 511, he had subjugated Burgundy and most of Gaul. The Merovingian Dynasty, of which he was the most eminent head, was succeeded in the late seventh century by the Carolingians, whose greatest ruler, Charlemagne (768–814), extended Frankish dominion over most of Italy and central and western Europe from the Pyrenees to the Baltic, and was crowned head of the Roman Empire in 800 A.D. Soon after his death the Empire disintegrated, and by the end of the ninth century the Frankish era had ended.

The data needed for an examination of Radbruch's hypothesis belong mainly to that era. They are quite meager considering that the history of four centuries is involved—a period equal to the time from the landing of Columbus in the West Indies in 1492 to the beginning of the present century—but they dry up completely during the next three hundred years—the second dark age or "silent centuries" of Germanic legal history[14]—before they resume again in the early thirteenth century.

During the Frankish era the stigma of slavery consigned the slave and his near social kin—the freedman and the serf—to discriminatory treatment in the administration of justice. Salic law did not permit the torture of freemen, but it authorized the torture of a slave accused of theft sufficiently large to cost a freeman thief an indemnity and fine of 15 solidi. The suspect was stretched on a bench and given up to 120 blows with switches as thick as the little finger. If he did not confess, his accuser could demand that the torture be continued; and if he continued to insist on his innocence, his accuser had to buy him from his owner, which placed him at the mercy of his new proprietor. If he confessed to a theft which a freeman thief could settle by a payment of 35 solidi, he was castrated, the only mutilating punishment known to Salic law.[15] However, his original owner could save him from the lash by a payment of 3 solidi, and from castration by a payment of 6 solidi.[16]

In early Frankish times, mutilating punishments, such as blinding or the amputation of a hand, the nose, or an ear, were legally defined slave punishments. Occasionally, a freeman's death sentence might be commuted to mutilation, but after the sixth century freemen could be directly sentenced to such punishment "for offenses disclosing a slavish and base mind." [17] It was always redeemable in accord with a minutely detailed table of values. A Lombard law of the same century threatened counterfeiters with the loss of a hand.

The use of mutilating punishments increased during the Carolingian period, partly for crimes like theft, which previously had been capitally punished, and partly for crimes like perjury, which had been redeemable. A law of Charlemagne threatened a conspirator with the loss of his nose and the recidivist thief with the loss of an eye as well. Similar provisions were found in contemporary Lombard law. Slaves found guilty of sex crimes were occasionally castrated. Blinding, considered the most serious mutilation, was sometimes substituted for capital punishment.[18] Bavarian folk law punished a slave who set fire to church property at night with the loss of a hand and an eye. Cutting off an ear became a common punishment for thieves during the Middle Ages and far into modern times. In addition to being painful, it served as permanent identification.

Punishments "to hide and hair" were slave punishments during the Frankish era and exclusively so in all early laws except the Visigothic. Under the Carolingians, thieving freemen could be flogged, theft being regarded as a most shameful crime evidencing a slavish mentality; but as a rule, freemen were fined and slaves beaten.[19] The Merovingians whipped low-class persons but fined the well-to-do for violating Sunday prohibitions and a west-Frankish law of the ninth century punished slaves and serfs with flogging for falsifying measures; freemen were fined. If a freeman was flogged his head was shorn. Short hair was the mark of a slave; freemen wore theirs long.

Branding does not seem to have been a frequent punishment in the Frankish kingdom. A Lombard law of the eighth century ordered thieves branded, and after the ninth century counterfeiters were branded in France.

The early folk laws were sparing in carrying out the death penalty, partly because the Church opposed it, but mostly because the ancient custom of resolving interfamily conflicts by a financial settlement prevailed even after the state gradually assumed authority to regulate and enforce such proceedings. The purpose of death sentences meted out to freemen was a threat to compel the payment of fines and indemnities rather than death itself. Thieves caught in the act could be killed on the spot with impunity, but failing this, Salic law provided a court death sentence. The punishment, however, was redeemable by payment of *wergeld,* the amount depending on the offender's social status. The reluctance to put freemen to death is clearly shown in the Bavarian law, which actually forbade their execution except for treason, an offense broadly defined to include lese-majesty.

The execution of corporal or capital sentences was at first the duty or prerogative of the accuser and his kin. Salic law, for instance, provided that if a slave was found to have had sexual relations with his free mistress, he was to be handed over to her kin to be "broken," a method of inflicting death that became popular in the French and German laws of the late Middle Ages and remained in common use until the late eighteenth century. A Lombard law of the eighth century specified that a slave found guilty of theft and not redeemed should be killed by his master or, if the latter refused, by the victim of the crime. If he, too, refused, the thief was to be executed by the court, in which case his owner had to pay an indemnity nine times the value of the stolen property.[20] This threat undoubtedly served as an incentive for the slave's owner to carry out the court's sentence. As time passed and the state assumed more direct control over penal justice, officers of the court executed the penalties publicly. Professional hangmen did not appear until the thirteenth century.

Judging from the data, then, the punishment actually suffered by an offender during the Frankish era depended less on his crime than on his caste or social status. The unfree person—slave, freedman, and serf—was subject to judicial torture, from which freemen were exempt. He was liable to corporal punishment as prescribed by law. Flogging and mutilation were at first reserved for him, and his only avenue of escape from these punishments or from torture lay in his master's or patron's willingness to purchase his exemption if the law allowed it. In later centuries, when these slave punishments first came to be used on freemen, it was not manly crimes of violence openly committed that were thus sanctioned, but shameful clandestine theft indicative of the base and slavish nature of the offender.

A freeman unable to clear himself of a criminal charge by oath or ordeal could usually buy his exemption from punishment; but if he was unable to pay the often ruinous indemnities and fines, he was subject to mutilation or death, or to enslavement by the victim or his heirs, which lost him the rights of freemen. These rights could also be lost if he was declared an outlaw by the court because he had escaped justice or had refused to face his accuser in court. If he persisted in his contumacy, his house was razed and his goods forfeited to the state, "his wife became widow, his children orphans, his kin strangers." [21] None could with impunity give him shelter or aid. Like the wolf of the forest, he was any man's legitimate prey.

The "silent centuries" that followed the collapse of the Carolingian Empire saw the culmination of the political and economic debasement of the common people by a military aristocracy of big landowners. By "the tenth and eleventh centuries most of the peasants tended to be serfs who were bound to the soil and whose lives were virtually at the mercy of their lord . . . a very few held their land just as the lord held his—from the king or another great lord. Others were in varying degrees of servitude." [22]

No longer did the emperor's traveling judges supervise the administration of justice by the counts and dukes who were rulers of their domains. The old folk laws and royal capitularies were forgotten and old tribal customs revived. Among the landed gentry feuding, never completely eliminated, flourished again and was no longer limited to the blood feud. Constant disorders and the oppression of the peasantry by the magnates added to the number of fugitive slaves and serfs, who joined the outlaws making the highways unsafe.*

Repression of crime became more and more savage. The powerful and the wealthy settled their conflicts in their own way by payments;[23] but the poor were doomed to increasingly cruel corporal and capital punishments, partly in the belief that this would counterbalance the glaring inefficiency of law enforcement. It was easy to evade justice by flight. The effect was noted by Maitland in describing the visit of the justices of Eyre to Gloucester in 1221 A.D. They

> listened to an appalling tale of crime, which comprised some 330 acts of homicide. The result was that one man was mutilated and about 14 men were hanged, while about 100 orders for outlawry were given. . . . In 1256, the justices in Northumberland heard of 77 murders; 4 murderers were hanged, 72 were outlawed. They heard of 78 other felonies, for which 14 people were hanged and 54 outlawed. In 1279 their successors in the same country received reports of 68 cases of murder, which resulted in the hanging of two murderers and the outlawing of 65, while for 110 burglaries and so forth, twenty malefactors went to the gallows and 75 were left "lawless" but at large.[24]

Similar conditions prevailed on the Continent.

Exemplary punishment of the few who were caught was believed to be a salutary deterrent to crime, but it was a self-defeating policy.

> Public executions of capital, mutilating, corporal and dishonoring punishments, often aggravated by horrible methods of inflicting them, dulled the aim of deterrence and harmed general deterrence by brutalizing the conscience of people. Equally disastrous was the effect of this penal law from the point of view of individual prevention. The outlawed, the banished, the mutilated, the branded, the shamed, the bereft of honor or stripped of power it expelled from the community of decent people and thus drove them out on the highway. Therefore the penal law itself recruited the habitual and professional criminals, who flourished in those days.[26]

---

*The general demoralization of the age was seen by Fulcher of Chartres as the reason that Pope Urban II called for the first crusade in 1095 A.D. "He saw that the faith of Christianity was being destroyed to excess by everybody, by the clergy as well as the laity. He saw that peace was altogether discarded by the princes of the world, who were engaged in incessant warlike contention and quarreling among themselves. He saw the wealth of the land being pillaged continuously. He saw many of the vanquished, wrongfully taken prisoner and very cruelly thrown into foulest dungeons, either ransomed for a high price or tortured by the simple torments of hunger, thirst, and cold, blotted out by a death hidden from the world. He saw holy places violated, monasteries and villas burned. He saw that no one was spared of any human suffering and things divine and human alike were held in derision" (*Chronicle of the First Crusade,* trans. Marthy Evelyn McGinty [Philadelphia, 1914], p. 11).

By the end of the twelfth century, the slave punishments of earlier days had been enshrined in public penal law and made applicable to free and unfree alike.[28] Political and economic changes connected with maturing feudal institutions had fostered this process by reducing most of the peasantry to a state of praedial servitude, which largely eliminated the need for chattel slaves except in domestic service. The punishment inflicted on a criminal no longer depended on whether he was a slave or a freeman, but whether he was a noble or a commoner, a burgher or an outsider, a wealthy man or a poor man. The system of criminal justice was dominated and managed by aristocrats—kings and ecclesiastical or laic manorial lords, or wealthy burghers who were gaining control over town government.* These noble or upper-class people looked at manual workers and more or less unfree peasants generally living on the brink of poverty and lacking political power, even though they constituted the vast majority of the population, as an inferior breed providentially created to serve the economic needs of their betters. In such a society equality before the law was an illusion, as Maitland so well illustrates. Writing of the English law of the twelfth century, he observed that

> a *wité* [fine] of £ 5 was of frequent occurrence and to the ordinary tiller of the soil this must have meant ruin. Indeed there is good reason to believe that for a long time past the system of *bót* [indemnity] and *wité* had been delusive, if not hypocritical. It outwardly reconciled the stern facts of a rough justice with a Christian reluctance to shed blood; it demanded money instead of life, but so much money that few were likely to pay it. Those who could not pay were outlawed or sold as slaves. From the very first it was an aristocratic system; not only did it make a distinction between those "dearly born" and those who were cheaply born, but it widened the gulf by impoverishing the poor folk. One unlucky blow resulting in the death of a thegn [noble] may have been enough to reduce a whole family of ceorls [serfs] to economic dependence or even to legal slavery. When we reckon up the causes which made the bulk of the nation into tillers of the lands of lords, *bót* and *wité* should not be forgotten. . . . The debasement of the great bulk of the peasants under a law of villeinage . . . gave their lords a claim upon those chattels that might otherwise have paid for their misdeeds.[27]

In such a society, a noble sentenced to die was honorably beheaded, thus spared the infamy of hanging, the lot of the poor thief. And, because in such a society the chief determinant of the penal consequence of a crime to the

---

*Commenting on an Augsburg ordinance of 1276 A.D., von Bar (*op. cit.,* p. 108) observed that it was administered by a "hard-hearted citizen-body, proud of their wealth, caring everything for property and little or nothing for the life or misery of a poor man [and] willing to inflict the loss of a hand for merely entering an orchard or grass plot with intent to steal."

offender was his lack or possession of wealth, a man of means could buy his freedom from physical punishment, while the poor man went into slavery or the life of an outlaw, or to the wheel, the gallows, the mutilation block, or the whipping post to suffer a capital or corporal punishment prescribed by law but originally reserved for slaves, a "detail" which, as Radbruch demonstrated, does have a "material bearing on the general history of the law" and should not "be left to students of semi-barbarous manners."

IV: GALLEY SLAVERY

Among the Germanic nations, whose penal system has just been described, enslavement did exist as a punishment for a criminal act. It may well have been extensively used, since a poor offender unable to indemnify his victim could be enslaved by his lay or ecclesiastical creditor or the fisc. The labor or services he had to render to his owner can only be surmised. We do know that when Alfonso X of Castile (1252–84) revised and romanized the Visigothic laws in his *Siete Partidas,* he introduced slavery as a punishment for certain crimes, perhaps under the influence of the revival of Roman law in the preceding century. He decreed that the offender was to spend his life in chains digging "in the mines of the king or laboring in other works of his or serve those who do so."[1]

However, the capital and corporal punishments characteristic of the late Middle Ages and early modern times grew increasingly harsh until the eighteenth century. More and more offenses were punished or made punishable by death, new corporal punishments were invented and added to those hallowed by tradition, and new devices were introduced to stigmatize and degrade offenders—all in the hope of deterring potential criminals. The dominant aims of the law were intimidation, retaliation, and retribution. Reform was generally understood to mean the effect of punishment on those who witnessed it, not on those who suffered it.

The catalogue of punishment was horrendous. Public spectacles of criminals being hanged, beheaded, drawn and quartered, broken on the wheel; buried, burned, boiled, or disemboweled alive; stoned to death, torn by red-hot tongs, branded, blinded; mutilated by having their tongues torn out or clipped; ears, hands, feet, or fingers amputated; castrated; whipped, pilloried, or exposed in the stocks were not uncommon. The refined cruelty and torture that marked some of these practices is easily imagined.[2] That refinement received full play in the torture chamber, where confessions, regarded as necessary for conviction, were painfully extorted, a practice which had become nearly universal by the end of the fourteenth century.

Perhaps this savage penal system demonstrated a contempt for the value of human life. It certainly was a response to a criminality so extensive that public authorities were incapable of coping with it and applied punishments believed to possess the greatest deterrent force. The large majority of offenders came from the poor classes of peasants and laborers held in very low esteem by the small upper classes of nobles, large landowners, and patrician burghers who dominated the administration of justice.

The efforts to repress crime were rendered powerless, however, by the political and economic forces that created a social plague which bedeviled all the countries from feudal times into the eighteenth century—i.e., the mounting flood of beggars and vagrants who beleaguered the towns and infested the countryside. A few of them were actually invalids or others licensed to seek alms for themselves or some worthy cause, but most of them lived by their wits. They were the professionals who artfully and deceitfully played on the sympathy of benevolent people. From their ranks were recruited the bands of thieves, burglars, and robbers who made the highways unsafe, and the outlaws and bandits (i.e., those banished from their towns) whose hideouts were in the sheltering forest.[3]

The conditions that produced this social evil have been described by historians. Suffice it to say that as time passed and the punishments in vogue proved ineffective, public authorities were compelled to consider other means of punitive control. They were prompted to do so in part because the brutality of the punishments were arousing public sympathy, and religionists were beginning to question the justification for some of the penalties. In this connection, the influence of the Reformation was considerable. The Protestant reformers urged the abolition of the death penalty for theft and the discontinuance of infamizing whipping and banishment, because the Bible did not sanction them.[4] Others found corporal punishments objectionable because the branding or maiming of offenders stigmatized them and prevented their pursuit of an honest livelihood.* Finally, as economic changes placed a premium on labor, public authorities realized that the traditional punishments deprived the state or the town of available manpower. Instead of killing, maiming, whipping, or banishing criminals, they could be put to work for the profit of the government. Forced labor was the answer; its prototypes had already been created by the ancient Romans, whose sentences to mines (*damnatio in metallum*), mining labor (*opus*

---

*The *Rules for Judges* composed by the Swedish reformer Olavūs Petri in the early sixteenth century contains this statement: ". . . all punishment should aim for betterment, and, if possible, a punishment should be such as not to prevent him who is punished from reforming himself. As occurs in the case of those who have stolen. They stand on the scaffold, lose their ears and are banished from the community. If such persons go to other lands where no one knows them and wish to reform and conduct themselves well, they are never trusted. The punishment is a hindrance to him who is punished and he becomes desperate and worse than before. It might have been better for him to lose his life immediately."

metalli), or public labor *(opus publicum)* were now being revived. Therefore, it might be instructive to take another look at these prototypes before examining the changes they would undergo when adapted to the needs and conditions of later ages.

Under Roman law certain crimes were capital offenses punishable by death, immediate or delayed, or by life sentence to mines or mining labor. In either case, the convict, if a freeman, lost his citizenship and status and became a slave. This happened if he was sentenced to the mines, which was always for life, and he remained a slave even if he was dismissed. This was also the case if he received a life sentence to mining labor, but if sentenced to *opus publicum* he lost only his citizenship. Sentences to *opus publicum* could be for life but were usually to specific terms. The convict in the mines—whether iron, copper, silver, or salt, or stone quarries, lime, sulphur, or chalk pits—always wore heavy "irons," the one in mining labor lighter chains. Otherwise they were treated alike. The laborer in *opus publicum* was also in chains; this punishment was also referred to as "public chains," *vincula publica.*[5] What is clear is that the Romans differentiated between penal slavery, a capital punishment, and the *opus publicum,* even though they had one thing in common—forced labor.

The miners were slaves. Those sentenced to *opus publicum* did work formerly usually done by slaves. It has been defined as "forced labor on a public construction or a public work as a punishment for crime . . . committed by persons of the lower classes. . . . Working in an opus publicum comprised the construction or restoration of roads, cleaning of sewers, service in public baths, bakeries, weaving-mills (for women) and the like."[6] Obviously these convicts worked in enterprises managed by public authorities. The bakeries and weaving-mills were public works, and we may assume that the numerous state and imperial factories scattered over the domains of the late Empire also employed some convict labor. It is important to note that public labor was performed both outdoors or indoors.

When forced labor as punishment was first resurrected in the Middle Ages, penal slavery, a slightly less severe penalty than death, reappeared as a form of capital punishment. It was, at times, served in mines, but in the maritime nations it also took the form of slavery in galleys and bagnes, and, in the landlocked nations, of fortress labor or forced labor on fortifications. The Roman *opus publicum* not only came back as outdoor labor on streets, etc., but as indoor labor in houses of correction and prisons. The clear legal distinction seen by the Romans between penal slavery and the *opus publicum* disappeared. According to the Austrian code of 1768, "public labor

45

punishments" were administered in fortresses, houses of correction, galleys, or mines, or comprised street-cleaning, waiting on the sick in hospitals, and the like, but whatever the form of these public punishments, those subjected to them always had to wear fetters and "irons."[7] In time, these punishments came to replace corporal and most capital penalties, and since they foreshadow the development of the penal system of the nineteenth century they merit our attention.

Galley Slavery

In ancient times, seaborne commerce and warfare in the Mediterranean were dependent on vessels moved by winds and manpower. Those carrying freight were bulky square-rigged ships of small tonnage; the warships were galleys moved by rowers and carrying auxiliary lateen sails. The crews of the merchant ships were usually slaves. The status of the galley oarsmen depended on the nation they served. The Greeks drew them from the lowest class of freemen, the Romans mostly from the class of freedmen. Service in the Roman legions were the prerogative of citizens. In those rare instances when slaves, in times of great national danger, were impressed into the army, they were usually given their freedom beforehand and placed in special detachments regarded as inferior to the legions.[8] The navy was not as highly esteemed as the army. The life of rowers was unbearably hard, the pay low, and the period of service, twenty-six years, much longer than that of a soldier, at least during the Empire.[9] Freedmen were accepted as oarsmen and marines and could even advance to the rank of admiral. Aliens were also enrolled as rowers, especially those from Dalmatia, where the light pirate galleys served as veritable training schools for the art of rowing triremes. Even slaves were made rowers in times of national emergency, being requisitioned from owners who had to pay for their maintenance for a fixed period of time. After his capture of New Carthage in Spain in 209 B.C., Scipio set numerous slaves—war captives—to work at the oars of his galleys, promising them their freedom after the campaign.[10] However, although it has been claimed that during ancient times "the galley fleets depended upon slave power" [11] and that "as the Romans quickly built fleets . . . freedmen and slaves were employed as marines or rowers,"[12] the data to support such sweeping assertions are lacking.[13] Indeed, the history of naval warfare up to the late Middle Ages records little about the composition of crews and nothing about the use of their labor as a punishment for crime.

The French Galleys

No one seems to know when or where penal slavery at the oars originated. Fernando Cadalso[14] claims that in Spain it dated back to a decree of Emperor Charles V of 1530, but a Castilian ordinance of 1348, known as the Ordinance of Alcalá, threatened certain offenders with sentences of ten years to the galleys.[15] In France, Jacques Coeur, great international merchant and the "moneyman" of Charles VII, is credited with being the first to use forced labor in the galleys that escorted his trading vessels. In 1443, he was granted royal permission to seize by force "idle persons, vagabonds, and other scum" to fill his crews.[16] From then on galley captains were periodically authorized to requisition and collect convicts from courts, which had been ordered to cooperate. A regular system of delivering convicts to the galley ports was not instituted until the seventeenth century.[17]

The men destined for penal slavery at the oars were a motley crowd. In 1490 a royal letter addressed to all judicial authorities in France called on them to supply "all malefactors . . . who have merited the death penalty or corporal punishment, and also those whom they could conscientiously declare to be incorrigible and of evil life and conduct."[*] The effect of this order may be noted in the fact that four years later eighteen of the twenty-four vessels of the galley fleet were manned by convict oarsmen.[18] From time to time other edicts specified what kind of convicts should have the traditional punishments for their crimes converted into galley slavery. Men in good health, neither too young nor too old were generally preferred. At first the courst evidently imposed short terms, because in 1564 an edict forbade the fixing of terms of less than ten years.

The number and proportion of convict-rowers depended on several factors, such as the availability of other manpower, the size of the galley fleet, and the capacity of its vessels. Originally the crews were composed of volunteers and slaves. The latter were infidels—Moslem Turks or Moors[†]—

---

[*](Masson, *op. cit.,* p. 83.) They came to be referred to as galerians. The term "forçat," forced laborer, also came into use. A royal decree of 1677 declared that "criminals condemned to serve on our galleys as 'forçats' " and who "after their sentence mutilate their members or cause them to be mutilated shall be punished by death" (Saint-Edme, *op. cit.,* "Forçat").

[†]"Turk" referred to any subject of the Ottoman Empire, which by the middle of the sixteenth century included Asia Minor, Mesopotamia, Syria, Egypt, the entire North African coast, Greece, Bosnia, Serbia, Albania, and Hungary.

captured in raids on the Barbary Coast or in victorious engagements with the fleets of the Ottoman Empire or with the numerous pirate fleets that infested the Mediterranean. Others were bought in the slave markets of Leghorn and Malta by captains who owned and outfitted galleys and as mercenaries entered the service of the king. The volunteers were freemen who, in return for subsistence and a poor wage, served during campaigns. They outnumbered the slaves initially, but as economic conditions improved and better jobs became available, they were to shun the hard labor at the oars. By the end of the sixteenth century they had disappeared from the galleys. Only slaves and convicts remained until the fleet was decomissioned shortly before the Revolution.

During the three preceding centuries, the size of the French galley fleet fluctuated enormously depending on circumstances, such as the state of the royal purse, the frequency and length of wars, and the evolution of naval armament. At the end of the fifteenth century the fleet had twenty-four galleys. Half a century later there were forty, but by the close of the sixteenth century only a few, mostly unseaworthy, galleys remained. Still, convicts were being sent to them. That the galley captains were unable to absorb them may be inferred from the fact that in 1560 and 1561, letters patent ordered courts to make 400 criminals sentenced to galley slavery available to the Grand Master of the Order of St. John of Malta. In 1570 and 1582, similar orders authorized the Grand Master to take 400 and 200 convicts, respectively, from the French galleys, superseding an edict of 1562, which had forbidden the sale of rowers to foreign princes.[19]

Richelieu tried to produce a respectable fleet, but by his death in 1642, only 27 galleys were in service. His successor, Mazarin, neglected the navy. When the young King Louis XIV, in 1660, visited Toulon, where galleys had been temporarily moved from Marseilles, and saw the ruinous state of the fleet, he decommissioned all but 9 galleys. A few years later, Colbert, his secretary of the navy, began a program to make France a first-class maritime power. Galleys and men of war were constructed in record time at the arsenals and shipyards of Marseilles and Toulon, and by the end of the century the navy had 42 galleys, as well as 155 line ships, most of which mounted 40 or more cannons.[20]

The galleys had grown larger too, requiring more rowers. The standard galley of the sixteenth century needed 144 oarsmen, but the 42 galleys of Louis XIV required more than 10,000, or an average of 240 rowers per vessel. To meet this need, slaves were continuously bought and courts were importuned to impose galley sentences. Lifelong slavery at the oars had been a form of commutation of death sentences, but the practice of sending men to the galleys for petty crimes had also existed, as had the practice of galley commanders of retaining convicts far beyond the end of their terms. A decree of 1656 ordered a search for "all malefactors, bohemians [i.e., gypsies], vagrants, sturdy beggars, discharged soldiers, counterfeiters, salt bootleggers, and other disreputable fellows for commitment to the galleys." Five years later an edict noted that "considering that persistent begging engaged in by healthy people is the source of all crimes against God and man . . . we wish . . . that sturdy beggars . . . who have thrice been taken by the archers be punished by imprisonment and whipping and that if they are again caught begging, they shall be sentenced to the galleys for five years."* Army deserters, instead of being executed, were sent to the galleys for life to make their labor profitable to the state. A new type of convict appeared in the galleys after the revocation of the Edict of Nantes in 1685. For nearly a century, Protestants, though harrassed, had been reasonably free to exercise their religion; but Louis XIV was determined to rule over a unified Catholic people. Those found attending Protestant services, chiefly Huguenots, or attempting to leave the country, were sentenced to life in the galleys.[21] In spite of the greater tolerance during the next century, Huguenots were sentenced to galley slavery as late as 1752.[22]

According to law, influenced by ancient Roman legal concepts, not only execution but a life sentence to the galleys was also a capital punishment, afflictive and infamous, as was banishment for life. Such punishments automatically resulted in the confiscation or loss of the offender's property and in his civil death, which in fact meant that he took on the attributes of a chattel slave, a nonperson in the eyes of the law, because civil death "sunders completely every bond between society and the man who had incurred it; he has ceased to be a citizen but cannot be looked upon as an alien, for he is without a country; he does not exist save as a human being, and this, by a sort of commiseration which has no source in the law."[23] The auxiliary punishment was not abolished until 1854.

Sentences to galley slavery were handed down by courts in widely scattered places. The condemned man was exposed to public view, whipped, and branded. Branding began to be used in the middle of the sixteenth

---

*(Masson, *op. cit.*, pp. 271–72). Because of the active campaigning of the French galleys in the 1680s, the need for oarsmen to replace those who had died or become invalid led to vigorous efforts to buy or otherwise obtain slaves. In 1684 and 1687, for instance, the governor of French Canada received orders that "as the Iroquois were robust and strong, he should capture as many of them as possible and send them" to the French galleys (Francis Parkman, *Count Frontenac and New France under Louis XIV* [Boston, Beacon Press, n.d., reprint of 1880 ed.], p. 140). The story of the result is related by Bamford, *Fighting Ships and Prisons*, pp. 163–65. Negro slaves were bought too, but the experiment was short-lived because they proved unfit for the service.

century.[24] At first, a fleur-de-lis was burned into the shoulder by the public executioner, but later letters, such as V *(voleur)* for thief, were substituted. Soon the use of the letters GAL became common practice. After this ordeal, the convict was confined in the local jail to await his transfer to the galley port. This waiting period might last many months spent in chains in dungeons so filthy and vermin-infested that many died of diseases or became unfit to handle the oars.

Originally, the commanders of the galleys collected the oarsmen they needed, but little is known about the procedure. When the galley fleet grew and vast numbers of convict rowers were needed, a more rational system of delivery had to be devised; however, the date of its origin is obscure. Colbert gave it a firm organization. Private entrepreneurs, under contract with the government, were entrusted with transporting the prisoners. The system became known as the "chain," a term applied to a convoy consisting of from half a hundred to several hundred convicts and their escorts. A map of the routes[25] followed by the "chains" serving the Mediterranean ports of Marseilles and Toulon shows three, originating in Paris, Rennes, and Bordeaux, with tributary "chains" joining them along the way.

Preparing the "chain" for departure involved a grisly ritual. Marteilhe, the young Huguenot who had been marched from Dunkirk to Paris to join the "chain" for Marseilles, described it briefly.

> They took us all out of the dungeons and brought us into a spacious courtyard before the castle. They chained us by the neck, in couples, with a thick chain three feet long in the middle of which was a round ring. After having thus chained us, they placed us all in file, couple behind couple, and they passed a long and thick chain through all these rings, so that we were thus all chained together. Our chain made a very long file, for we were about four hundred.[26]

The prisoners walked to Marseilles, a month's journey from Paris. A few wagons were reserved for the crippled, the old, and the sick.

> The trip was exhausting because of the weight of the chains, the length of the marches, the insufficiency of the food, and the bad treatment. There were those who died en route, while many arrived at Marseilles in a feeble state, especially as they were often dispatched from the jails in a bad state. It even happened that these miserable wretches were goaded to hopeless rebellion, resulting only in death sentences for their leaders.[27]

In 1667, a squadron commander wrote Colbert that his efforts to increase the galley fleet were rendered almost useless because of the bad treatment received by the prisoners from those charged with transporting them. The two "chains" just received have, therefore, arrived in a weakened state, and the last from Guyenne [Bordeaux], besides losses during transit due to the oppression and avarice of the conductors, has arrived in such a ruinous condition that a part has perished and the rest not worth much more.[28]

Conditions gradually improved when strong regulations were passed to control the contractors, but the "chain" remained a harrowing experience.

After arriving at their destination, the convicts had the neck chains replaced by ankle chains; then they were distributed among the galleys. Chained to their benches in these floating prisons, they ultimately became part of the human engine that powered them.

Galleys came in different sizes. The average galley was about 140 feet long and 20 feet wide. Its gunwales rose about 3 feet from the water and it could navigate where sailing ships would run aground. Easily swamped, it was serviceable only in reasonably calm weather and usually did not venture far from shore, where a sheltering harbor might be found for a storm-driven vessel. From the captain's quarters at the stern to the platform at the prow, which carried a pointed ram and artillery, ran a narrow walk below and on each side of which were from 24 to 28 benches for the rowers. Each oar was manned by from four to six rowers, depending on the size of the vessel. The part inside the gunwale—about a third of its length—weighed as much as the rest and was so thick that handles for the rowers were affixed to it. Managing the oar required great skill. A strong slave, usually a Turk or a Moor well versed in the art, was given the inmost place on the bench; the place closest to the hull was reserved for the weakest man.

Rowing was hard labor at best, and brutal during campaigns, when the rhythm was doubled in order to catch or escape from an enemy and the rowers were urged on by lashes or blows of their boss who trod the walk between the rows of benches. Chained to their places, the rowers could not leave them. "They slept stretched out between the benches . . . in a space at most ten feet long and four feet wide. Without thinking of the discomfort of their position, one may imagine the evil odors emanating from this human mass, devoured by vermin and permitted no hygienic practices." [29] Poor and inadequate food, disease, and maltreatment made for high mortality and morbidity rates.

During the winter months the galleys were moored in port and disarmed, but the rowers were not idle. Some were set to work in the shops of the arsenal where convicts unfit for rowing labored the year round, or to cleaning up the port, digging canals, and strengthening the fortifications. Those having some skill might rent one of the small workshops in the sheds on the docks and, chained to their places, go into business for themselves. There one might find "tailors, hatters, shoemakers, lace makers, wigmakers, engravers, and even portrait painters; other men, more or less selftaught, worked at wood-carving, knitting, button making, or polishing coral and mother-of-pearl."[30] The product was sold to the many visitors or to shopkeepers in the city. There were even convict-entrepreneurs who kept a galleyful of men busy at some marketable handicraft.

Many convicts worked in the city by day. Chained in couples, a convict and a Turk or a lifer and a short-termer, and escorted by an armed guard, they were employed as domestic servants or in a variety of mercantile or industrial establishments. Some performed highly skilled work. Because the wages paid them by their private employers were only about a fifth of what free labor received, the businessmen of Marseilles resisted or criticized every plan to remove the galleys from their port. Small as the wages were, they helped make the convicts' existence a little more bearable. At times convicts rendered conspicuous service to the city, as in fighting fires, and especially in 1720–1722, when hundreds helped bury the victims of a plague epidemic. Freedom was to be their reward, but nearly all succumbed to the disease.[31]

Discipline, though harsh, was adapted to the need for conserving manpower. As a rule, an offending galley slave was whipped for his misdeeds, the punishment varying with the severity of his crime from a few lashes to hundreds and the feared bastinado, from which some victims never recovered. Naval courts-martial might, in certain cases, change a short sentence to one for life, inflict mutilating punishments like cutting off a nose or an ear, and for especially heinous crimes order the offender hanged.

As the galley fleet grew in size and the number of rowers increased, the administration became concerned about the cost of maintaining the growing number of oarsmen unfit for service. These men, old, sick, or invalid, lived in old decommissioned galleys. Beginning in the 1680's, about nine hundred were shipped to the French West Indies, but the practice was soon discontinued because of complaints that they were poorer workers than the black slaves and given to crime.[32] There were still about two thousand invalids at the base in 1693,[33] and the problem of how to make them profitable to the state rather than a drain on its resources led to a partial solution in 1700, when a large industrial prison was established in the arsenal. The *bagne* was born. (The history of this innovation will be told later.)*

---

*A large prison in Constantinople for the confinement of slaves was called a *bagno* by the Italians (Saint Edme, *op. cit.*, "Bagne"). The Provençal *bagna,* or floating prison, probably had the same derivation.

The demise of the French galley fleet in the eighteenth century was a long-delayed event. Galleys had played no significant role in naval warfare since the middle of the previous century because sailing men-of-war with heavy armament had proved superior in battle. When the Galley Corps was merged with the Department of the Navy in 1748, most of the fifteen remaining galleys were obsolete and useless. The majority of their four thousand rowers were sent to the base for men-of-war at Toulon, and about one thousand to the base at Brest to construct a prison in the arsenal of that port. The galleys were no more, but galley slavery survived until the Revolution, when its form changed but not its intrinsic character.

The Galleys of Spain

The other great maritime power of the western Mediterranean, Spain, began to use convict rowers even earlier than did France. Castilian war galleys were known to have been employed in the twelfth century to help drive Arab and Norse pirates from the northern coast, and during the following two centuries both Castile and Aragon established arsenals and shipyards, but the first mention of convict oarsmen is found in the Ordinance of Alcalá of 1384, which threatened certain offenders with galley slavery. However, since Alfonso X of Castile had a century earlier introduced penal slavery in the form of labor in the king's mines or in other works of his, it is possible that his war galleys fell into the latter category.[34] Nevertheless, slaves and volunteers were to constitute the mass of oarsmen, until the growing power and wealth of Spain after its colonial conquests made it a target of Moorish, English, Dutch, and French pirates and freebooters and of covetous rival nations, necessitating the construction of a large navy of ships of war to patrol the oceans and galleys for the protection of the coasts. Then the manpower squeeze began. The volunteers preferred to be sailors and marines; the recruitment of rowers became more difficult.

Early in 1530, the king of Spain, Charles I, who by that time had also become Emperor Charles V of the Holy Roman Empire, ordered that a man convicted of a crime meriting whipping, the amputation of foot or hand, exile, or similar punishment, have his sentence commuted to galley slavery for two years or longer unless the crime was so heinous as to merit death.[35] During the following century numerous offenses were made directly punishable by commitment to the galleys for terms ranging from three or more years to life, but it is noteworthy that nobles were not subjected to this degrading treatment.[36]

There is no need to give details about the life of the convict oarsmen of

Spain. The transportation of the men to the galley ports and their life asea and ashore were much the same as in France, and remained so as long as the galleys existed. In 1748, the same year the French Galley Corps ceased its function, Spain decommissioned its galleys. The oarsmen were transferred to the fortresses of North Africa or the mercury mines of Almadén.[37] Galleys were reactivated in 1784 and courts were ordered to supply rowers until 1803, when an ordinance put an end to the venture.[38]

—and Elsewhere

Other naval powers also employed convicts at the oars of their galleys. They were found in the fleets of Malta, Genoa, Savoy, and the Papal States. The great merchant republic of Venice, which had rarely used unfree oarsmen before 1545, was forced to adopt the practice when the supply of volunteers dwindled. By the end of the century nearly all of its many galleys were rowed by convicts. Hard-pressed to find enough convicts of its own to replace those who died or were crippled in the service, Venice appealed to the landlocked city states of northern Italy to send it their criminals for its galleys. A similar arrangement was made with the Duke of Bavaria.[39]

Galley slavery was not confined to the Mediterranean area. The Burgundian rulers of the Netherlands introduced it quite early, as evidenced by the fact that seven convicts were sent from Mechelen to the Antwerp galleys in 1452.[40] England, too, used this punishment. By a statute of 1598 "quarter sessions justices were given the alternative of sending incorrigible vagabonds of dangerous character into perpetual banishment or to the Queen's galleys." [41] When the Spaniards successfully brought galleys north for their war with the Dutch, the British were spurred on to build four galleys and man them with convict rowers, but they never saw active service. England's strength on the seas lay in her sailing ships of war.

Convict oarsmen were used in the Danish galleys in the seventeenth century.* Even the landlocked states of central Europe saw galley slavery as an attractive means of ridding the community of undesirables. In the middle of the sixteenth century, the Swiss canton of Lucerne had a galley for con-

---

*(Fr. Stuckenberg, *Faengselsvaesenet i Danmark 1550–1741* [Copenhagen, 1893], p. 15.) Sweden is said to have experimented briefly with it "when the Stockholm magistracy was ordered in 1670 to build and maintain vessels in which such 'rascals' who were not corrected by other punishments could be fastened by chains for towing ships between Stockholm and Dalaro" (Henrik Enström, *Om fångar och fångvård* [Stockholm: Norstedt, 1926], p. 26). The order was issued but never implemented (see Sigfrid Wieselgren, *Sveriges fängelser och fångvård* [Stockholm; Norstedt, 1895]). Galley slavery in Russia will be dealt with in a later chapter.

victs on Lake Lucerne, and Bern had one on Lake Geneva, but they soon became superfluous because the states with fleets in the Mediterranean, avid for oarsmen, importuned the Swiss and the German states and cities to send convicts to their galleys. Bern made a contract to that effect with Savoy in 1571. Basel sent convicts to the French, Baden to the Spanish, Württemberg to the Venetian, and Nuremberg to the Genoese galleys.[42] A contemporary chronicle of Schaffhausen frankly referred to these transactions as sales.[43]

We have noted that the war galleys of ancient Greece were rowed by the lowest class of freemen, that the Romans preferred to use former slaves for this task, that by the late Middle Ages the maritime nations of the western Mediterranean used slaves and mercenary volunteers at the oars, that as the supply of volunteers dwindled only slaves remained, and that when there were not enough of them to fill the crews of oarsmen, rulers made galley slavery a punishment for crime. It was never thought of as a means of reforming offenders and restoring them to the community better men; its aim was to remove the undesirable or dangerous from the community and put them to work for the profit of the state. It ceased to exist as a specific form of punishment when galleys no longer served any useful purpose. As a form of penal slavery it is but one illustration of the degrading influence of the social institution of slavery on the evolution of the penal system. Penal slavery in other guises was to become a feature of the treatment of serious offenders down to our times.

V: PUBLIC WORKS

The disappearance of the galleys did not end galley slavery. It was simply turned into penal slavery at naval bases, but continental states that had sent some of their worst criminals to Italian, French, or Spanish galleys were compelled to find retributive, intimidating, painful, substitute punishments. Housing was a problem. In states where capital and corporal punishment, fines, and banishments were the standard methods of repressing crime, prisons were used almost exclusively to confine the accused awaiting trial and the convicts awaiting the execution of their sentences. Dungeons in castles, court houses, city halls, or in the gates and towers of the walls of cities served this purpose, the only appropriate function of a prison according to the third-century Roman jurist Ulpian. This view was generally accepted by lawmakers and legal experts alike. The famous criminal code promulgated by Charles V for the Holy Roman Empire in 1532 mentions punitive imprisonment only once. A thief unable to make twofold restitution could be kept in prison for "some time." Indeed, because of the illegal practice of some courts of using imprisonment as punishment, the code explicitly ordered judges to desist. The Theresiana,[1] 1768, Art. 5, Par. 7, noted that imprisonment, thought not a primary punishment, could be granted by the ruler by way of commutation, but how or where it would be served was not specified. The code did allow town courts to impose brief jail sentences on bread and water for petty offenses. The Swedish code of 1734 likewise permitted imprisonment in local jails on bread and water as punishment in some cases, but normally only for nonpayment of a fine. Usually such confinement would be for a week and not longer than a month.[2] Consequently, it is not surprising that leading French eighteenth-century jurists like Daniel Jousse and Muyart de Vouglans agreed with Ulpian's dictum, although they were well aware that deprivation of liberty had long been used as punishment. The Church had used imprisonment, even life sentences for centuries. Monastic orders, bishops, and the Inquisition had used it to punish heretics and offending clerics or laymen, but since it was an instrument of canon law it fell outside the province of secular justice. Nor did the arsenal prisons at the galley ports challenge the dictum; they held convicts sentenced to slavery, not to imprisonment.

Forced labor or penal slavery was a distinct punishment, and the loss of freedom it entailed was but an incidental evil. It was generally regarded as a corporal punishment and was so listed in the Theresiana, which defined it as "the [punishment] which, apart from direct physical pain, subsequently causes suffering and torments the body by subjecting it to public labor."[3] The harshness of its execution made these sufferings and torments a constant reality at least to those who experienced the grossest forms of servile labor and whom official documents sometimes designated as "slaves," even as "galley slaves," though they never saw a galley. They were the criminals sentenced to labor "in irons" on fortifications, a form of punishment that had made its appearance in Germany in the seventeenth century and approximated the galley slavery used by the great maritime powers. It arose after the disastrous Thirty Years' War (1618–1648) which had ravaged cities and farmlands, broken the power of the imperial government, and led to the rise of some three hundred large and small more or less autonomous principalities and lordships ready to defend themselves against encroachments by rivals. The reconstruction of damaged and destroyed city walls, fortresses, and other strongholds, became important. The terrible loss of life caused by the war had reduced the labor force, and the great increase of the homeless, landless, and vagrant classes presented a problem which could not be solved by traditional methods. The use of convict labor on fortifications—criminals whose lives had been spared by arbitrary judgments or the mercy of rulers—offered a partial solution. Soon, however, more laborers were needed. In 1660, for instance, Saxony decreed that when courts imposed sentences of whipping and banishment, the government reserved the right to substitute fortress labor; in 1661, it was decided that banishment would be automatically changed to such labor,[4] and in 1744, banishment was abolished and labor on fortifications substituted.[5] In 1685, the East Prussian territorial code provided for such labor in only one instance, but in the revised code of 1721, about forty offenses carried that penalty. A significant wrinkle was introduced by Prussian rescripts of 1791 and 1809, which limited commitments to fortresses to "unreformable" criminals.[6]

Penal historians have paid little attention to the operation of the fortress prisons. A document entitled "P.M. about the labor of the cart-prisoners and the treatment of these slaves in Haarburg"[7] affords us a glimpse at how such a prison was managed in 1791 in Harburg, a walled city in the kingdom of Hannover. The citadel was garrisoned and had a prison called the "stockhouse"[*] in which the slaves were confined when not at work. The unskilled

---

[*]The word "stockhouse" does not appear in standard British and American dictionaries. So far as I can determine, German and Scandinavian sources use the terms "stockhaus" (Jacob and Wilhelm Grimm, *Deutsches Wörterbuch*), "stokhus," or "stockhus" to designate fortress prisons.

labored on the fortifications, carted earth, stone, lime, and sand, cleaned ramparts, walks, walls, and moats, and served as handymen to the more skilled convicts, who worked as masons, plasterers, stonecutters, and rapairmen of walls and implements. A few prisoners serving short terms for petty crimes might perhaps benefit from the fact that the commandant and the bailiff were entitled to select two of them to work in their gardens or cut their firewood. Furthermore, if a burgher needed a couple of slaves for haying or other labor, he could hire them if he guaranteed that they would be well guarded by himself or by someone paid by him. He had to pay the slave a small daily wage (probably about one fourth or one-fifth of the wage of free workers), of which the slave could keep one-third, the rest being added to the garrison's treasury. All slaves returning to the stockhouse after work were searched for contraband such as dangerous tools, weapons, or stolen goods.

On his first arrival in the stockhouse the convict was outfitted in coarse clothing consisting of a coat, two pairs of pants, two shirts, two pairs of stockings, two pairs of new shoes, and two pairs of worn shoes. This outfit was replaced annually.

The slaves were always shackled. Those serving life terms or ten to twelve years wore strong iron bands on both legs connected by a short chain, which prevented them from taking long strides. A leather strap attached to the middle of the chain and the waist kept the irons from sliding down during work. Others wore a chain connecting a handcuff to an iron band on one leg. The handcuff was unlocked and the chain wound about the waist when the slaves were at work. When John Howard had visited the citadel ten years earlier (1781), he observed that "thirteen slaves [were] working on the fortifications, with irons on one leg and chains supported by girdles around their waists" and that they were guarded by soldiers.[8]

Discipline was harsh. Beating with a bull's pizzle was the punishment for minor violations of rules. For more serious offenses, slaves were tied hand and foot to a post and beaten with rods "by their own comrades, each of whom must deliver a given number of strokes under the supervision of an officer or a sergeant."[9]

The daily ration of the slave consisted of one and a half pounds of bread like that given to soldiers. John Howard called it "ammunition bread" and estimated the cost of the ration at three half-pence. Water was free, and each slave was allowed five to ten farthings daily which he could spend at the canteen on returning to the stockhouse. The size of this allowance depended on the type of labor he performed and the diligence he showed at work.

In the stockhouse the slaves were locked in rooms holding ten to twelve men, the lifers being segregated from the rest. All slept in their clothes on barrack bedsteads with a sack of straw for a mattress and another sack for a pillow. Some were chained to their bedsteads. Each room had two buckets, one for water and one for excrement, and the slaves had to take turns in refilling the one and in emptying and cleaning the other daily. They also took turns at fetching the bread allotment. In winter, a fire heated and a lantern lit each room. A small opening in the door permitted the sentry assigned to the stockhouse to watch that the light was not extinguished.

Attendance at Sunday services in the garrison church was compulsory. In the event of accident or illness, a salaried physician or the garrison surgeon was summoned. The latter supervised the treatment, supplied trusses and bandages and, when needed, a crude casket. The cost of these supplies, medicines, and the soup given the sick was borne by the commissariat.

John Howard also visited other fortress-prisons in Germany in 1781. At Magdeburg, "the Prussian slaves were at work on the fortifications, serving the masons, digging sand, etc. Their allowance is two pounds of bread, and on the days they work they have also, in money, a grosche, about three farthings. The number was only fifty-one, for many had been taken to recruit the army." At Dresden,

the apartments for the slaves, being under the fortifications, must be unhealthy. I saw four sick and yet they had their irons on. Among those that were at work, one had an iron collar, by way of punishment for making an escape, besides the broad iron about his leg. Another was sitting and endeavoring somewhat to alter the place of his iron. He told me that the weight was marked on it *twenty-one* pounds and that he could not have it changed to the other leg without paying a smith.[10]

At Hanau, in Hesse-Cassel,

the galley slaves (so called) are distinguished into *honnètes* and *déshonnètes*. The former are condemned for three, four, seven, nine, fourteen years, according to their crimes, but the term is sometimes shortened on account of good behavior. These wear a brown uniform and a small chain from the girdle to one leg. The latter are such as have committed capital offenses. They wear a white coat with one black sleeve and have a chain from the girdle to both legs; they never work out of the town and are put to the most laborious and disagreeable employments in it.[11]

The Prussian code of 1851 dropped fortress labor as punishment, but a preparatory report of 1836 had recommended its use for terms of from eight years to life. That it was meant to apply only to the lowly may be inferred from the suggestion in another project of the same period that persons of "higher and educated" status should not be subjected to it.[12]

In France, the revolutionary penal code of 1791 introduced a punishment "in irons" as a substitute for sentences to the galleys. The convicts were to be "employed at forced labor to the profit of the state, either in a *maison de force* [maximum security prison] or in ports and arsenals, or in the extraction of ores, or in draining of marshes, or, finally, in any other painful labor which upon the demand of a department [administrative district] might be determined by the legislative assembly."[13] However, the males were sent to the navy's aresenal prisons at Rochefort, Brest, and Toulon; women sentenced to "irons" were sent to other prisons.

This French initiative was copied by the Swiss and the Bavarians. The Swiss national code of 1799 noted that the state would profit if the worst male criminals were made to work in mines, arsenals, drain marshes, or do any other excruciating work that the law might demand.[14] The Bavarian code of 1813 defined the punishment "in irons" as the most severe form of deprivation of freedom. Those subjected to it were declared civilly dead, and Article 8 of the code provided that "the state uses him [the slave] preferably in public labor draining swamps and marshes, and the like when such labor is possible; otherwise he will be imprisoned in the *Zuchthaus* [prison] and, segregated from other prisoners, employed in the most painful labor."[15]

Forced labor on fortifications was also in use in the Scandinavian countries. In Denmark, an ordinance of 1636 urged nobles, who possessed the "high justice"—i.e., the power to impose the death penalty on peasants and retainers—to consider the value of human life, refrain from hanging petty thieves and, instead, punish them with "irons" and labor.[16] If they lacked facilities for such punishment, it was suggested that they send the offenders to Bremerholm, the navy's arsenal prison in Copenhagen, which for a long time was to serve as the state prison for those sentenced to "irons." Imprisonment in fortresses became more and more common, however, partly because slave labor was needed in the construction or maintenance of fortifications and partly because Bremerholm was overcrowded. In 1739, an ordinance prohibited sentences to the navy arsenal and two years later the army was ordered to remove the slaves from Bremerholm to the stockhouse in Copenhagen, which was under the administration of the commandant of the citadel. Ninety-four lifers and a vagrant serving a term of six years were thus transferred. After 1764, most slaves in the Danish fortresses were moved to that stockhouse.

The slaves worked at a variety of tasks, at least at Bremerholm: in the bakery for the contractor supplying bread to the army, treading the bellows in the smithy, cleaning the hospital and yards, etc. John Howard described his visit to the stockhouse in 1781 as follows:

> Here criminals from the garrison and convicts from the different classes of people are condemned to slavery. . . . Here I saw a hundred and forty-three slaves, who were distinguished by a brown coat with red sleeves and breeches likewise of both colors. They never put off their clothes at night; and as they have new clothes only once in two years, and those very light, I did not wonder to find many of them almost naked. Some had light chains on one leg, some heavier chains on both legs; others had iron collars; one was chained by his wrists to a wheelbarrow. These, I understood, were punishments inflicted upon those . . . who had attempted to escape, etc. These slaves work on the fortifications and their time for working in summer is from five to eleven and from one to six. Their allowance is seven pounds of black bread every five days, besides a pay of one stiver a day in winter, and in summer, when they work more hours, a stiver and a half. They were attended by a guard of twenty soldiers. In returning from their work, I observed that some of them were chained to one another in pairs with loose chains. These I found were some of the worst, who had passed under the hands of the executioner and were branded.*

Most of the slaves were property offenders, thieves, and defrauders. Forced labor in irons had begun to replace the death penalty for these crimes in the seventeenth century both by ordinance and by the exercise of royal mercy. At first thieves were spared labor in irons until their fourth offense of petty theft or their second offense of grand larceny. In 1771, capital punishment for theft was abolished, and by an ordinance of 1789, forced labor on fortifications for a period of three to five years could be imposed for a second offense, and for life for a third offense. In either case, the thief would first be whipped and branded.[17]

As in Harburg, slaves could be leased to private employers who paid a per-capita price of six shillings a day. The employer had to fetch and return them safely, but if more than ten or a dozen slaves were so hired, a guard accompanied them. In spite of fetters and other security arrangements, escapes were frequent. An official report of 1802 noted that of 200 slaves in Copenhagen and the fortress of Kronborg, 36 had escaped, and added the observation that "slavery" had outlived itself.†

In Sweden, a major contestant in the Thirty Years' War, an ordinance of

---

*(Howard, *op cit.*, pp. 77–78.) He noted (p. 76) that whipping and lifelong slavery had been the punishment in Denmark for grand larcency since 1771. In his account, the *stockhus* is erroneously referred to as *Stockthause*.

†(*Ibid.*, p. 278) Advocates of furloughs for prisoners should note that an ordinance of 1790 allowed slaves soon to be discharged to go out during certain hours of the day in search of employment (Stuckenberg, *op. cit.*, p. 39).

1642 decreed that idle vagrants be "brought to the nearest castle to work in chains," [18] but fortress labor was first used as punishment when Sweden acquired its southern and west-coast provinces through peace treaties in 1660 and 1679 after her victory over Denmark. The new border had to be fortified, and the fortresses at Marstrand became the chief receptacles for those sentenced to "labor in irons." In 1682, official notice was taken of some prisoners who, "sentenced as slaves, are to work at the fortifications at Marstrand blasting rocks, in the smithy, in masonry or dragging stones and lime." They were heavily fettered, wearing iron collars, ankle irons, and heavy chains. Slaves were also used at the admiralty's smithy at the naval base of Karlskrona; in 1725, some were transferred there from Marstrand.[19]

The Swedish criminal code of 1734 specifically punished a few offenses with forced labor in a royal castle, fortress, or smithy, but this punishment could be ordered, and more and more frequently was, by the king's court, when it commuted capital sentences provided for by the code for sixty-eight crimes. Counterfeiting coins was punished with forty stripes with a rod or a month in jail on bread and water, followed by three years of forced labor. Falsifying court records or official financial records was punishable by a term of several years to life. A third offense of theft of less than a hundred dalers, was punished by whipping and three years of labor. A highly structured punishment faced the embezzling tax collector. He lost his job, had to return the money plus 6 per cent interest, and was fined forty dalers for each one hundred embezzled. If unable to make full restitution and owing less than one hundred dalers, he was sentenced to a year of forced labor and one year for each additional hundred. If he owed between one thousand and two thousand dalers, he received a life sentence. If he made full restitution but was unable to pay the fine, he was jailed for from eight days to a month, depending on the amount owed. Thefts of less than one hundred dalers' value from a church brought one or more years of labor. Brothelkeepers were whipped and given labor terms of three years for the first offense; a second offense drew a life sentence.

Another variant, reminiscent of medieval practice, appeared in the form of forced labor for the victim of theft or pilfering. If the thief was not sentenced to hanging or fortress labor and was unable to make restitution, he had to work for the victim at a specified daily rate until the value of his labor equaled the value of the property stolen.[20]

The penal system of Spain presents perhaps the best example of the power of survival of forced labor in fortresses and on fortifications. It may well have begun in the middle of the thirteenth century, when Alfonso the

Wise introduced penal slavery in the royal mines and other works of his. When North Africa was conquered, in the early sixteenth century, convicts labored on the fortifications of Oran and other coastal fortresses, and after 1580 at Ceuta. When Oran was abandoned in 1792, there remained Ceuta and Melilla, the two most important ones, as well as Peñon, Alhucemas, and the isle of Chafarina. All of them had stockhouses or *presidios* which remained in use until 1907–1911, when their inmates were transferred to prisons on the peninsula.[21]

The *presidios* were, of course, under military management and staffed by army personnel, as were some prisons established in Spain when the *presidios* became overcrowded. The peninsular prisons were taken over by civilian state departments in 1834.

The various forms of punishment provided for in the penal code of 1822 included hard labor for life or on public works with the convicts chained in pairs. The codes of 1848 and 1870 also listed the punishment of "irons" for life or for terms of years and those so punished were to carry a chain attached to the waist and foot and serve their terms in the fortresses of Africa, the Canary Islands, or overseas, which in practice meant Ceuta and Melilla. A census in 1895 found that 99 per cent of those under sentences to hard labor in chains for life, and 70 per cent of those serving shorter terms were confined in the African fortress prisons.[22]

In view of the arbitrary power of courts in fixing punishments for crimes, it is not always possible to distinguish the criminals who were sent to work on fortifications from those sentenced to forced labor like street cleaning, who presumably were less serious offenders, chiefly idlers, beggars, and pilferers. This type of punishment also came into use in the sixteenth century. Thus in 1532, the Parlement, or high court, of Paris decreed that "all persons able to work, men and women, yet live in idleness or beg in this city, shall be employed to empty and clean the cesspools, streets, and sewers, and work on the ramparts and on other public works needed to promote the welfare, profit, and utility of the city."[23] In 1577, Nuremberg began to put offenders to work cleaning streets; they spent nights in a prison, the Springer, in the *Bettelstock,* or beggars' block, in stocks or chained to a block to prevent escape.[24] Hamburg introduced such forced labor in 1609. Wearing gray clothes and pulling high two-wheeled carts, the convicts cleaned the streets and removed rubbish and garbage from houses. Two or three men were chained to each cart; others assembled the rubbish and cleaned the gutters. Each man carried on his shoulder a number of bells, fastened by iron bands, corresponding to the length of his sentence. At the end of each year, one bell was removed. Sentences ranged from one to twelve years, and the number of convicts varied between nine and twenty-nine. At night they were housed in dark rooms in an old tower.[25]

In the seventeenth century many Swiss cities created special houses for those condemned to forced outdoor labor. Such houses were called *Schallenwerke,* or bellhouses, because while at work the prisoners, always in chains, had bells attached to the iron neck bands they wore. Such bellhouses had been established in Solothurn in 1601,[26] in Bern (1614), in Basel (1616), in Freiburg (1617), in Zurich (1639), and in St. Gallen (1661), the last two former nunneries. All were designed to take care of "vagrants, beggars, profligate householders, idlers, workshy people, and malefactors,"[27] male or female. The men cleaned streets, dug ditches or wells, built bridges and dams, or did farm labor. In Freiburg and Basel they also worked in stone quarries. When John Howard visited the *Schallenhaus* in Bern in 1778, he noted that it contained 141 "slaves," most of whom were "employed in cleaning and watering the streets and public walks; removing rubbish of buildings; and the snow and ice in winter. . . . The convicts are known by the iron collar, with a hook projecting above their heads; weight about five pounds. I saw one riveted on a criminal in about two minutes." [28] The two full-page engraved illustrations accompanying his description show small groups of male and female convicts, some chained to carts, engaged in street cleaning. The strange iron collar is portrayed, but no bells are visible.

The Spanish penal code of 1822 for the first time included a new punishment of forced labor on public works. "Criminals sentenced to public works shall be promptly conveyed to institutions of this class. . . . They go out to labor in public and without exception on highways, canals, the construction of buildings and the cleaning of public thoroughfares." [29] In fact, the code merely redefined a punishment of old standing, since an official document of 1802 referred to public works prisons which then existed in Malaga and Madrid.[30] More such prisons were needed, and they were constructed here and there as permanent or temporary institutions, depending on the nature and duration of a public-works enterprise. Some of the work undertaken was under the direction of the prison administrators, but convicts were often leased to private firms under contract with the government. In 1834, some twenty-eight hundred convicts were leased to contractors building the canal of Castile and in 1867, the Home Office authorized the leasing of convicts to companies engaged in railroad construction.[31] Chain gangs of convict workers were not an unusual spectacle in Spain.

Beccaria's Penalty "Worse Than Death"

We have noted that galley slavery and penal slavery on public works of military importance were to a large extent substitutes for capital punishment, reflecting a growing reluctance to use that penalty. During the eighteenth century, called the century of Enlightenment, when philosophers were developing the political doctrines of democracy, the penal system did not escape their scrutiny. The foremost advocate of penal reform was Cesare Beccaria (1738–1794), a youthful Milanese noble, who published a tract entitled *Dei delitti e delle pene (Of Crimes and Punishments)* in 1764.[32] In this work, which was to have an enormous influence, the author called for the abolition of capital punishment and its replacement by another penalty. The one he recommended was, in his words, something "worse than death." It was deduced from his basic view of the aim of punishment and his conviction that the death penalty was not a deterrent.

> The aim of punishment is not to torment and afflict a sentient person. . . . [It is] none other than to prevent the criminal from doing more damage to his co-citizens and to deter others from doing likewise. Those punishments, then, and the method of inflicting them should be preferred which, while proportionate to the crime, will make the most effective and enduring impression on human minds and be least tormenting to the body of the criminal. . . . For a punishment to achieve effectiveness, it is enough that its painfulness only just exceed the benefits derived from the crime. Anything more is superfluous and tyrannical. Men regulate their conduct by the repeated effects of the evils they know and not by those of which they are ignorant. If there were two nations, in one of which the most severe penalty in the scale of punishments, proportionate to the scale of crimes, were slavery for life, while in the other it were [breaking on] the wheel, I say that the former will fear its most severe punishment as much as will the latter [fear the wheel].[33]

Beccaria could find no evidence that the death penalty possessed a deterrent force. Therefore, it was useless to execute criminals, except possibly when the death of a powerful leader already in custody would thwart an attempt by his followers to overthrow the government. Generally speaking, potential offenders did not expect to be caught in case they committed a crime. Witnessing an execution was too fleeting an experience to make a permanent impression. To produce "the salutary terror which the law wants to inspire," lifelong penal slavery would, by its *duration,* have that effect. It would be a constant reminder of the consequence of crime.

The strongest deterrent to crime . . . [would be] the long and painful example of a man deprived of his freedom and become a beast of burden, repaying with his toil the society he has offended. . . . No one today, in contemplating it, would choose total and perpetual loss of his own freedom, no matter how profitable a crime might be. Therefore that intensity of the punishment of lifelong slavery as substitute for the death penalty possesses that which suffices to deter any determined soul. I say that it has more. Many look on death with a firm and calm regard—some from fanaticism, some from vanity, which accompanies a man beyond the tomb, some in a last desperate attempt to cease to live or to escape misery—but neither fanaticism nor vanity dwells among fetters and chains, under the rod, under the yoke or in an iron cage, when the evildoer begins his sufferings instead of terminating them. . . . Were one to say that perpetual slavery is as painful as death and therefore equally cruel I would reply that . . . the former would be even worse.

Beccaria's proposal raises some interesting questions. Lifelong penal slavery as punishment for crime was no novelty. It had ancient roots and was found in all countries, where in the scale of punishments, it ranked just below the death penalty and was quite commonly imposed directly or by a commutation of that penalty. "Fetters and chains," the lash, forced labor "under the yoke," and confinement in the "iron cage" were commonly used devices and had not proved to be deterrent. Beccaria was certainly aware of this. He lacked any evidence that penal slavery for life was a greater deterrent than capital punishment. Therefore, his specious argument in its favor must have been due to his belief in Rousseau's theory of the social contract, in which the death penalty for common crimes had no place. Nevertheless, his argument was accepted widely and would encourage governments to employ horrible forms of deprivation of liberty. The best example is probably the Austrian empire of which Milan formed a part.

Beccaria had no more conscientious disciple than Joseph II. Coregent with his mother Maria Theresa since the death of his father in 1765, he may well have considered the penal code she promulgated in 1768—the Theresiana—outmoded, since it retained traditional customs which he would soon change. He may have been responsible in part for the abolition of judicial torture and for the reduction of the use of the death penalty decreed by his mother in 1776. When he succeeded her in 1780, he hastened to order a revision of her code, ready in 1787. It abolished the death penalty except under martial law, but since the emperor had stopped executions in 1781, Beccaria's "substitute" had already been in use for several years. It was forced labor or excruciating kinds of frightful imprisonment for life or long terms of years.

The popular forced labor on fortifications had been abandoned in 1783, when the war department stopped the construction of fortresses.[34] Then barge-towing up the Danube in Hungary was introduced, partly because prisons were badly overcrowded and maximum security prisons too few.[35] When John Howard visited the house of correction in Vienna in 1786, he noted that

the criminals sent off to Hungary are brought first to this prison. They are clothed in a uniform and chained by companies, five and five together, with *irons* around their necks and *on* their feet; besides a chain about ten inches long *between* the feet of each of them, and another chain about six feet long for fastening each of them to the person next to him. I was told that the hard work in which they are employed of drawing boats up the Danube wears them out so fast that few of them live in this state above *four* years.[36]

He did not mention how the prisoners were brought to Hungary; they probably walked there.

The military general-command post on the south Hungarian border described the life of the penal slave as follows: "Criminals, already emaciated, wasting away from hunger, harnessed in rows to the vessels, often to the waist or even to the neck in water, wading through swamps and constantly forced to labor,"[37] driven by the whips of their military guards, actually were subjected to a slow death, for of 1,175 slaves suffering it between 1784 and 1789, death claimed 721, or about 61 per cent.[38] "The unsound climate, the hard labor in foot and neck irons, the single meal evenings (by grace, a drink of vinegar water twice daily) led to certain death in about two years. Most prisoners died from 'exhaustion and bad fever,' " writes Hartl.[39] When the new penal code was promulgated in 1787, an imperial decree ordered that all prisoners sentenced to "hard imprisonment" be sent to towing "whether or not their health permits it," [40] and the procedural code of 1788 (Par. 180) provided that males convicted of murder, robbery, or arson and sentenced to hard imprisonment and public labor or, for other crimes, to long terms (eight to fifteen years) also be sent to towing. If the conduct of any one serving a prison sentence proved him to be incorrigble, he too could be sent to towing no matter what was his crime (Par. 191).[41]

Not all the worst criminals were sent to Hungary. Some were sentenced to "irons," an even harsher penalty. "The punishment of irons [*Anschmiedung*] consisted of chaining the criminal in the prison so closely that there was room for only the absolutely necessary movements of the body, and in annual canings publicly administered." [42] A sentence imposed in 1787 on a man in Vienna found guilty of robbery and murder required that "he shall on three successive days be exposed on the scaffold with a tablet hung on his chest and inscribed with the words robbery and murder, be given fifty strokes with a cane on the lower back the first and the last day, such caning to be repeated annually as a warning to the public, depending on his physical condition, and kept in severe imprisonment for thirty years, leaving him room only for necessary bodily movements." [43] In the most severe form of such confinement, the prisoner wore an iron band riveted to the wall around his waist and was loaded with chains.

When John Howard saw the Great Prison on his visit to Vienna, he

found very few of the dungeons empty; some had three prisoners in each dungeon; and three horrid cells I saw crowded with twelve women. All the men live in total darkness. They are chained to the walls of their cells, though so strong and so defended by double doors, as to render such a security needless. No priest or clergyman has been near them for eight or nine months." The new prison to which the prisoners were soon to be transferred had "twenty dungeons at the depth of twenty-two steps below the surface of the ground, boarded with thick planks, in which are strong iron rings for the purpose of chaining the prisoners.[44]

The Spielberg fortresses in Brünn, the then capital of Moravia-Silesia, the Schlossberg in Graz, Styria, and the Kufstein in the Tyrol were also used as state prisons.

The worst criminals, who according to pars. 186ff. of the procedural code were to be delivered to Schlossberg were housed in casemates or in the ten solitary cells. Of the two casemates, one had neither light nor fresh air, and in 1784, after an inspection visit by Emperor Joseph II, they were divided into twenty-one cells, walled with planks (so-called blockhouses), for holding the worst criminals sentenced to irons for life. A report by the government of Inner Austria, dated September 20, 1790, stated about the prisoners in the blockhouses that "the irons, weighing nearly fifty pounds, hinder them in working and sleeping. The confined air, the bread and water diet and the hard bed [they slept on bare planks] changed these wretches into semi-corpses and living skeletons. Consumption, dropsy and scurvy took their lives in a short time. Even the healthiest and strongest man could not last under this extreme kind of punishment more than four years."[45]

This was surely a punishment "worse than death."

Joseph II died in 1790 and was succeeded by his brother Leopold, who had for fourteen years ruled the Grand Duchy of Tuscany, where, inspired by Beccaria, he had commuted death sentences and, in 1786, abolished capital punishment "for ever." Leopold II was more of a humanitarian than was his brother. When he assumed the throne he promptly abolished the towing penalty and the punishment of "irons," as well as branding; burning a gallows like symbol into the cheek of the criminal. He also eased the lot of the prisoners by issuing them straw mattresses and blankets.[46] However, his fear of repercussions from the French Revolution led him to restore the death penalty for "all who dared to inflame the people and lead them to oppose the orders of the government by public violence." [47] After his death, in 1792, his brother Francis II made high treason as well as several other offenses capital crimes in 1795, and in his penal code, which took effect in 1804, we still find that under the most severe of three grades of imprisonment the prisoner was to receive only "that amount of light and room necessary for his health." He was to "wear heavy irons on hands and feet constantly and an iron band around his waist, by which, when not at work, he could be attached with a chain. Every other day he would receive a warm meal but no meat, and on other days only bread and water. He would sleep on bare planks, and no one could meet or speak with him." [48] Many decades would pass before such inhumane punishments were removed from the Austrian penal code, and since the death penalty had been restored, Beccaria's brand of penal slavery was less in demand.

VI: HOUSES OF CORRECTION

The first house of correction appeared in England during the second half of the sixteenth century in the city of London. Vagrancy had grown to alarming proportions since the early years of the reign of Henry VIII. To repress it, Parliament had tried corporal and even capital punishment, but without success. A statute of 1531 had provided that a vagabond should be "tied to the end of a cart naked and be beaten with whips . . . till the body be bloody," be made to take an oath to return promptly to the place where he was born or had lived the previous three years, and be forced to take employment there. Should he again be apprehended, he would "be scourged two days and the third day . . . put upon the pillory from 9 of the clock till 11 before noon of the same day and . . . have one of his ears cut off." Upon a third offense, the whipping and the pillory would be repeated and the other ear removed.[1] The thrust of the legislation was to place the onus of making the offender self-supporting on the community of his birth or legal residence.

The prescription evidently produced no cure, for in 1547 the statute was repealed and penal slavery substituted. Able-bodied idlers

> might be seized by their former masters, branded with a V on the breast, and made slaves for two years. These slaves could legally be chained, given only the coarsest food, driven to work with whips or subjected to any other cruelty. Vagrants for whom no master could be found were to become slaves of the Borough or Hundred which could employ them at road-building or any public work. If they ran away and were caught, they were to be branded S on the chest and made slaves for life. The punishment for a second running away was death as a felon.[2]

This statute proved to be unenforceable, and in 1549 it was revoked and the former one reinstated.

Had the vagabonds or vagrants—interchangeable terms—been mere social nuisances, the severity of the law would be difficult to understand, but they were, in fact, a real or potential danger to the community. The variety of their illegal occupations was described in the many "cony-catching" pamphlets reproduced by A. V. Judges in his *The Elizabethan Underworld.*[3] In a preamble of a later statute (1572), the "horrible murders, thefts, and other great outrages" happening daily in England were blamed on rogues, vagabonds, and sturdy beggars who pestered all parts of the realm.[4] Most of them would, for decades to come, suffer the severity of the law, but some excited the sympathy of charitable people who either found the traditional punishments excessive or believed that new methods had to be found to deal with the vagrancy problem. The first step was taken by London, a metropolis that attracted large numbers of vagrants.

The "Bridewells"

In 1552, the city fathers submitted a plan to the Privy Council "whereby the forward, strong and sturdy vagabond may be compelled to live profitably to the Commonwealth."[5] It was proposed to ask the young king, Edward VI, for the old palace of Bridewell and convert it into a "house of occupation," where vagabonds would be set to work at useful trades, the products of which would be used by the house and other charitable institutions or sold to the appropriate merchant guilds for distribution in the open market. The palace was given to the city, renovated, and opened in 1556. It was soon labeled the Bridewell, a name commonly applied to later houses of correction.

The institution received sturdy vagabonds and prostitutes. The women were set to carding, spinning, and similar tasks; the men worked in the bakery. The worst offenders were assigned to the treadmill grinding corn or to the smithy making nails. For a while some worked at a lime kiln in the yard and dredged sand for mortar, etc., but little is known about the actual operations in the house.[6] The pattern can be inferred realistically from what appears to be an imitation, namely a plan proposed in 1561 for a "house of occupations, or rather an house of correction" in Westminster "for repressing of the idle and sturdy vagabond and common strumpet."[7]

After noting that the house should be strong and airy and provide for separate quarters for men and women, its anonymous planner commented on the work program:

> The things that such people are to be trained and occupied in must neither be fine nor costly, for . . . you shall have to do with the most desperate people on earth, given to all spoil and robbery, and such as will break from you and steal. . . . Wherefore you shall not need to use any more than only these two things: a mill to exercise the vagabond, and a [spinning] wheel to exercise the common strumpet. . . . And this mill may you order in manner of task work, that so many appointed to the mill shall daily grind you so many bushels, and by this means shall you understand your gain or loss. And for the wheels, he may choose whether you will occupy them in woolen yarn or cotton wool. But the better is cotton wool, for that they may both most profit by and also can least steal.

71

Another useful thing would be "the setting up of a lime kiln," because any-body could work at it and "none of them can either steal or hinder you."

To manage the institution, at least six of the "gravest, wisest and wealth-iest" persons of the town were to be elected to serve without salary as Masters of the house.

[They would] have authority to use their discretion in the use and correcting of such vagabonds and idle people as shall be brought into the house. In like manner, the same persons must have authority to apprehend all such lewd and suspect per-sons, be they men or women, as haunt within their liberty; and the same to commit to the house of correction; and further to use and punish them as to their discretion shall seem mete.

Such actions needed the approval of at least two of the Masters.

The salaried staff was to include (a) a Clerk, paid four pounds a year, who was to keep an inventory of all that belongs to the house and a register of inmates, noting the reason for their commitment and the dates of arrival and discharge. He was to wait on the Masters and be present at their meetings which were to be held at least twice weekly. (b) An "honest, true and good man" as Keeper, responsible for the safekeeping of the inmates, and paid six pounds a year. (c) A Matron "who must have the order and government of the lewd women;" she should be paid nearly four pounds and be given an assistant. (d) A Miller "to keep your people on work and to put in sureties to answer for all such corn as shall be delivered to him to grind." His salary would be six pounds yearly. (e) Two Beadles, each paid five pounds a year, who would be out searching for vagabonds.

The plan did not mention the issuing of clothing, but the Masters were enjoined to see that the inmates were properly fed twice daily. At each meal, the women were to receive pottage, bread, drink, and one-quarter pound of beef. Men working in the mill should get the same fare except for one-half pound of beef. The bread should be baked in the house and each inmate given a sixteen-ounce loaf daily and at each meal a pint of thin beer, the mill workers getting a little more. Butter, cheese, herring, and the like would be substituted for meat on fish-days.

To insure discipline, the house was to have two pairs of stocks, one for the men and the other for the women, "and you must provide shackles of iron for the taming of the wild and lewd persons."

If beds were provided for the men, "you must hae good regard that they break not from you, for they will cut your beds and sheets and so escape. You must be careful of fire, for the people are desperate and care not what mischief they do."

The house might also receive disobedient servants sent there by their masters, and wives whom their husbands had committed "for lewdness." "They cannot labor and many times are of purpose kept secret and close for their punishment."

The Westminster house was never constructed, but the model, on a smaller scale, was that of the London Bridewell, where the "correction" of inmates was to be achieved by forced labor and physical punishment. Before arriving in the house, the vagrant had usually been whipped, but the whipping might be carried out in the house, and both the whip and the stocks were used to punish those who failed to meet their daily work quota or violated some rule. When Leopold von Wedel visited the institution for "whores and knaves" in 1585, he noted that some prisoners "have to tread a mill, which is so contrived that corn can be ground when the people are treading."* "They are also flogged twice a week. But the women, too, must work and they are also flogged twice a week until each has received the punishment proportionate to the crime."[8] An ex-convict who in 1703 described his reception in the institution and the work to which he was assigned wrote

> as soon as I came there, the word was strip. . . . My hands were put in the stocks, and then Mr. Hemings, the whipper, began to noint me with his instrument that had, I believe, about a dozen strings knotted at the end, and with that I had 39 stripes. . . . Then I was set at a block, a punny of hemp was laid thereon, and Ralph Compton (a journeyman in the shop) presented me with a beetle, bidding me knock the hemp with that as fast as I could. This beetle is of Brazil [wood] and weighed about 12 pounds.[9]

The regulations prepared in 1589 for the house of correction at Bury St. Edmund's throw a little more light on the matter. They were made for "the punishing and suppressing of rogues, vagabonds, idle loitering and lewd persons." On admission to the house, the offender was registered and "wel-

---

*This may be the first penal treadmill in England. The "Ordinances for Bridewell," believed to date from 1577, provided for "two treadmills, which will employ eighteen men of the vagabond class to grind corn for the use of all the hospitals" (O'Donoghue, *op. cit.*, p. 197). This contradicts the contention that the treadmill was invented about 1818 by William Cubitt of Ipswich, or by David Hardie *in 1803 (see* Sir John Cox Hippisley, *Prison Labour, etc.* [London, 1823], and James Hardie, *The History of the Treadmill* [New York, 1824]. In fact, Spiegel had suggested that one be used in the Amsterdam *tuchthuis,* and treadmills were not unknown in Germany. An illustration of the treadmill in the Mainz house of correction in 1743 is found in Hippel's *Deutsches Strafecht,* I, 592. John Howard found treadmills in other German prisons. Cubitt's mill was installed in the house of correction in Bury St. Edmund's in 1820. According to Hippisley, at least twenty-four British houses had treadmills by 1824. Hamburg installed a mill in 1825 *(see* Ed. Guckenheimer, "Gefängnisarbeit in Hamburg seit 1622," *Monatsschrift für Kriminalpsychologie und Straf-rechtsreform,* Beiheft 3, 1920, pp. 103–31).

comed" by from six to twelve strokes of a whip on the bare back and encumbered with some clogs, chains, iron collar, or manacle, at the discretion of the keeper. He was set to work from four to five o'clock in the morning, depending on the season, to seven at night, with breaks for two meals. Men and women were to be separated at all times. The regulations were silent about the kind of work done but detailed about the punishments in store for those violating rules, including transfer to the common jail to suffer the statutory penalty for vagrancy. The correction of the offender was presumably furthered by his compulsory attendance at prayers before and after work.[10]

The London Bridewell and later houses of correction, established after Parliament, in 1576, ordered counties to set up such houses, were among the agencies designed to reduce pauperism, and for decades they housed a mixed population of unemployed poor, juveniles being taught a trade, and the ubiquitous vagrant. They were meant to deal with misdemeanants, because other punishments also threatened rogues and sturdy beggars who were generally blamed for the rising tide of crime. In the county of Somerset, in 1596, for instance,

> 40 persons . . . were executed for robbery, theft and other felonies, 30 were burnt in the hand, 37 were whipped, 183 were discharged, yet the fifth part of the felonies in the county were not brought to trial, and the rapines committed by the infinite number of wicked, wandering people were intolerable to the poor countrymen and obliged them to keep a perpetual watch of their sheepfolds, pastures, woods and cornfields.[11]

Two years later an act prohibited begging, declared all beggars rogues, gave a long list of occupations which automatically marked their practitioners as rogues, and ordered every rogue, when caught, to be whipped from parish to parish until he reached his home. If he did not know where he was born, he was to be put in the house of correction or the common jail and kept at work until placed in some service. Rogues deemed dangerous or unreformable were to be detained in a jail or house of correction until the next quarter session of the court; they might then be exiled beyond the seas or sent to slavery on the galleys for life. If such an exile returned without permission, he was to be hanged.[12]

Especially during the early decades, a few of the bridewells seem to have had some success in restoring their inmates to an orderly life, but by the end of the seventeenth century they had become indistinguishable from the jails so far as management, discipline, and character of inmates were concerned.

The Justices no longer concerned themselves with the provision of . . . disciplinary employment for the sturdy rogues and vagabonds. They merely handed over to the Master a power to exact from his prisoners whatever labor he chose, partly as a means of relieving the county from the expense of maintaining them, partly as punishment, but in the main as the Master's own perquisite by way of supplement to a small salary.

Like the jails, the houses of correction "were, in effect, run as private ventures by their masters or keepers. . . . In many cases the jail and the house of correction were one and the same. In many others; though the two institutions were nominally distinct, they were kept in the same or adjacent buildings, under one and the same officer.[13] In 1865, they were merged into "local prisons."

The decay of the houses is well shown by John Howard who visited more than a hundred of them in 1775–76. His description of housing, furnishings, sanitation, fees, dungeons, etc, is fairly full, but he has remarkably little to say about employment. On the day of his visit, he found that 18 of the 105 houses had no inmates, 45 had from 1 to 5, 20 from 6 to 12, 6 from 13 to 20, and 7 had more than 20 inmates, the largest number, 34, being in the Exeter house. The London Bridewell had only 20 prisoners. No similar data were given for 8 of the houses. The turnover in the houses was very great, for the London Bridewell had received 1,084 prisoners in 1775. One house in Gloucestershire had only 6 inmates when Howard visited it, but had received 572 during a period of eight and a half years. Another, in Lincolnshire, with 4 prisoners, had in six years dealt with 236 prisoners. On the other hand, in the St. George's Fields house in Surrey, he found 29 prisoners, of whom 4 women were serving terms of ten years and 1, three years. Ten men had terms of one, two, or three years.

In twenty-three of the institutions no work was provided; this included three of the five houses with from twenty-one to thirty prisoners. Beating hemp, picking oakum, spinning, dressing flax, or weaving sacks were mentioned as occupations in five houses. The hard labor which justices had been authorized in 1609 to inflict as punishment had largely disappeared. In one house all five inmates were in irons; in another, the only prisoner, a woman, was at work in irons. In the Chester City bridewell, Howard found 30, 40, and 60 pound lead weights, which could, at the discretion of the Master, be fastened to the legs of refractory prisoners.

The houses of correction fell into discard with the resumption of the practice of sending vagrants back to their home parishes or transporting them to the American and West Indies colonies, as authorized by the 1598 act.

75

When that legislation was repealed in 1713, the colonies' need for workers persisted and was in part filled by the profitable trade in servants nurtured by the Virginia Company and carried out by sea captains who found the London Bridewell a particularly good source of supply. Therefore, unlike the continental houses, few houses of correction ever became prisons for major offenders sentenced to hard labor. Instead, England began to transport conditionally pardoned felons to the colonies during the seventeenth century, and in 1713 made transportation beyond the sea a legal punishment for most felonies.

The "Tuchthuis"

Scores of houses of correction sprang up throughout Europe during the seventeenth and eighteenth centuries. The most famous, and the forerunners of these houses, were established in Amsterdam some decades after the founding of the earliest English bridewells. There are no firm data to support a claim that the Dutch borrowed the idea from England, but circumstantial evidence suggests that they were not ignorant of what London, Ipswich, and Norwich had done, to mention some of the cities that traded with Holland.

Vagrancy and all its deleterious by-products was a social plague in Holland as elsewhere, and means of dealing with it were much sought after. In 1587, a distinguished religious leader, Dirck Volkertszoon Coornhert, published an essay on *Boeventucht*, i.e., the disciplining of rogues,[14] written twenty years earlier while he was a prisoner in The Hague. In it he proposed a plan for handling "dangerous vagrants," suggesting that each province should have a strong prison where vagrants could be put to hard labor, and that each city should likewise have a prison workhouse and depot for such as could be sent "chained in pairs, to be used on public works . . . such as driving piles, digging ditches, dredging canals, and other such labor."

Other voices were also heard decrying the harshness and ineffectiveness of the penal laws and stressing the urgent need for new ways of dealing with lawbreakers, especially the young. Magistrates were said to be "timid about sentencing anybody to death" and "greatly troubled and diffident about sentencing thieves to death in spite of the laws of the land and its traditions."[15] As good Calvinists, they knew that the Bible did not authorize capital punishment for theft. Their humanitarian sentiments and religious faith spurred them on to find an acceptable solution to the problem. The end result was the creation of an institution which peculiarly appealed to the thrifty burghers of Amsterdam, for whom a good investment was sound practice. The issue was squarely faced by the magistrates in 1589, when a sixteen-year-old thief and burglar appeared before them. They asked for a meeting with the city council "in order to discuss and establish some suitable means of maintaining such children of burghers at steady work so that they might be turned from their bad habits and induced to lead a better life."[16] The meeting was held, and later the council resolved to consider the possibility of providing a house "where all vagabonds, evildoers, rascals, and the like" could be put to work for periods to be determined by the court. One of the magistrates, Jan Laurenszoon Spiegel, was probably commissioned to prepare a plan for the administration of such a house. The resulting document was remarkable for its advanced ideas on prison management. The house was to be a *tuchthuis*, a house of discipline. The name won instant acclaim and appeared in Germany as *Zuchthaus*, in Denmark as *tugthus*, in Sweden as *tukthus*. The house was opened in 1596 in a former nunnery to care for male offenders.[17]

From the very beginning the inmate population was mixed. It consisted mainly of persons sentenced to terms which varied from brief periods to up to twenty years. Jan van Hout, who visited the house shortly after its establishment, even found some lifers there[18] and prisoners who had been whipped or branded before their arrival. Some had been committed for dissolute conduct on petition of their relatives to the burgomasters. Professional beggars abounded. Their "crutches, bandages, straps, trusses and wooden legs were prominently displayed on the wall of the courtyard near the whipping post."[19] Runaway apprentices could be found among the prisoners. Wealthy burghers could, with the court's permission, commit their incorrigible sons to the house; in 1603, these persons were completely segregated in a private section, spared the onus of labor, and supported at the expense of their families. Occasionally the number of prisoners rose above a hundred, although the house was not designed to hold more than about seventy. With the establishment of the New Workhouse in 1650, which took away the beggars, vagrants, and drunkards, and a juvenile reformatory in 1694, which removed the youngsters, the house became a prison for serious offenders. Even before 1650, so many property offenders, including burglars, were committed to the house that they outnumbered the beggars five to three.[20]

Spiegel had visualized an institution that would be a real reformatory, in which willing inmates would receive vocational training in a variety of trades and become healthy and content, used to labor, desirous of employment, capable of standing on their own feet, and God-fearing. All the inmates were to work, the obstreperous ones at crude tasks like beating hemp, "turning a wheel," or "treading a mill." A small share of the profit of labor should be paid as a wage to the inmate, and the diet should be simple. Violators of rules should receive only bread and water. Those most likely to escape should be kept in their cellrooms or chained.

The actual regime of the house was a gross distortion of Spiegel's far-reaching proposals. Thus, a weaving shop for vocational training was established, and in 1598, the regents who administered the house contracted with a master weaver to undertake its management. The young, the old, and the weak were employed in the shop and probably learned skills which they could profitably use on the outside after their release. But half a century later the shop was closed and remained closed for a century. What was left was an industry which became the mainstay of the institution and gave it its sobriquet—*Rasphuis,* or rasphouse—which came to be applied to many correctional houses regardless of the kind of labor program they introduced.

Before the production of synthetic dyes, the only dyes available to the clothing industry were vegetable dyes, which were extracted by boiling pigmented sawdust from trees imported mainly from Yucatan and Brazil. Holland's flourishing clothing industry provided a good market for dyes which had been supplied by private-enterprise mills that ground the dyewoods. The Amsterdam city fathers saw the chipping or rasping of the hardwood logs as just the kind of hard labor suitable for the "correction" of convicts. In 1599, they gave the house a monopoly, and three years later the States General, by letter-patent, extended this monopoly to cover all of Holland and West Friesland with the proviso that, if erected, houses of correction in towns of these provinces would enjoy the same privilege within town limits. Thus, ultimately the only "training" given inmates of the Amsterdam house was one they could not legally use once they were released.

To reduce a hardwood log to dust was backbreaking labor. The log was clamped in a vise attached to a work bench, and two convicts pulled a heavy cross cut saw with from six to twelve blades, across the end of the log. Each team had to produce between 40 and 60 pounds of dust daily, depending on the strength of the raspers. After 1656, when the regents set up a mill some distance from the house for the grinding of wood not suitable for rasping, weaker inmates chipped such wood and had to produce from 200 to 300 pounds of chips per day. Failure to meet these quotas invited punishment. The workers were paid a small wage, but they never received it because it was expropriated to cover the cost of their maintenance. Only if they were strong enough to exceed their quota were they paid a guilder for each extra hundred pounds. Two stivers of each guilder were withheld until the convict was released.

The labor was done under a contract system. The dyers who used the sawdust, which was weighed and packed in sealed sacks, furnished the logs which were stacked in the courtyard, and paid the regents an agreed price when the dust was picked up. The rasping was done in cellrooms which housed from four to twelve prisoners and also served as bedrooms. The raspers wore ankle irons connected with a chain, and the most refractory were also attached by both legs to a wall chain just long enough to permit them to move between their workbench, bed, and the toilet.

Violation of rules was harshly punished: restricted diet, the dungeon for days on bread and water, whipping with a bull's pizzle, rope or rods, and finally, the dreaded water cellar, a dungeon with a pump which the prisoner had to use to save his life when the room was flooded. The last of these was discontinued late in the seventeenth century, after a prisoner chose drowning over rasping.[21]

Youngsters in the house, at the end of a day's work, were given some instruction in reading and writing—by the weaving master. On Sunday mornings between six and eight, the preacher instructed them. The texts used were, of course, religious tracts and Bible selections. Raspers were considered too dangerous to participate in the instruction, nor where they admitted to the Sunday services. Instead, they were given religious texts to read and memorize in their cellrooms, and they had to say prayers at meals and before starting work or going to bed. It is hardly likely that these exercises improved their disposition. If they became seriously ill, a physician was called in, but all in all, their welfare, present or future, was given little thought, because the cardinal aim of the regents, merchants and manufacturers all, was to make the institution profitable by exploiting the manpower of the inmates, the cheapest available labor. And so the house became in effect, a municipal factory with a captive labor force. "In this scheme," says Hallema, "reform was wholly neglected."[27]

A *Spinhuis,* or spinning house, for women was opened in 1597 in a former convent. At first it received poor women needing work, but within a decade it had become a prison for adulteresses, prostitutes from the brothels, streetwalkers, drunks, professional beggars, and women who had been whipped for thefts and committed to serve terms, usually of short duration but at times several years in length. The inmates were set to spinning, but in later years, the sewing of linen cloth and the knitting of nets dominated.[23]

The "Zuchthaus"

Directly or indirectly, the Amsterdam establishments became models for similar workhouses in other Dutch cities and in the Hanseatic cities of Bremen, Lübeck, Hamburg, and Danzig, which in turn led to other imitations. By the end of the eighteenth century, there were some sixty of them in Germany alone. Hamburg provides an example of the larger ones. In that city a spacious combined workhouse and house of correction able to accommodate about five hundred persons was built and ready for occupation in 1620. In part, it was to provide work for willing paupers, but its chief purpose was to take beggars, drunkards, and idlers from the street and force them to earn their livelihood by hard labor in the institution, begging being a violation of the law, albeit not one which rendered the offender infamous.[24] The exclusion of infamous criminals, which characterized all early houses of correction, posed a problem for courts and pardon authorities when they did not wish an offender to suffer a capital or corporal punishment prescribed by law for his offense. One solution was the creation of a special institution for such offenders. This was done in Hamburg in 1665, Nuremberg in 1670, and Danzig in 1691. The Hamburg institution, a *Spinhouse* (!) or prison for men and women, erected next to the workhouse, received petty thieves, whores, and persons spared capital punishment. At the beginning of the eighteenth century, lower courts were sending prisoners there for terms of ten, fifteen, twenty, or thirty years for robbery and homicide. The house had four large work- and bedrooms for the men, and one workroom and one bedroom for the women.

The inmates of the *Spinhouse* worked at rasping dyewoods, weaving bombazine, carding wool, spooling, spinning, knitting, etc. A task-system was used: raspers had to produce 45 pounds a day (270 pounds a week), the weavers 1½–2 pieces weekly, the carders 3–4 pounds daily, etc. The men had to earn the equivalent of 12 shillings a week, the women 8. If their labor yielded more, they received the excess in cash and could buy shoes, caps, shirts, and neckcloths. In 1785, these amounts were doubled, but they still purchased very little. Their rations were scanty, barely enough to sustain life. Their treatment may be judged from a complaint they voiced in 1709 at having to bear chains and blocks weighing up to 100 pounds, deprived of fresh air, barred from seeing relatives or from access to legal counsel.[25]

The discipline was harsh. Refractory prisoners, unruly or reluctant to work, were starved. For a second offense they were also beaten. A third offense brought them to the whipping post, and a fourth to a ride on the wooden horse. Both these instruments were in the courtyard of the workhouse. The horse, on whose sharp-angled back the delinquent was mounted with fifteen-pound weights attached to his feet, was on wheels and was pulled around the courtyard three times while the house-master whipped the rider.[26] Hunger, the rod, fetters, hard labor, and sermons were the means used in all houses of correction to "reform" the offender.

Many of the houses of correction contained a mixed bag of paupers, vagrants, beggars, thieves, orphans, and, at times, the insane. These classes were occasionally, though never completely, segregated. The penal houses did attempt to classify their inmates. For instance, in the house of correction of Fribourg, Switzerland, an ordinance of 1757 divided its inmates into three classes: infamous criminals whose death sentences had been commuted to life imprisonment and who had to wear neck irons and foot chains; lesser criminals, also infamous, who wore neck irons; and minor offenders, who, when at work cleaning streets, were chained to the carts and, by couples, chained together by ankle fetters. In Basel, which had a similar system, convicts in the first two classes also had the capital letters S.W. stamped on their smocks.[27]

As penal institutions, the houses of correction were not thought of as places in which persons served sentences of imprisonment. They merely housed criminals sentenced to forced public labor. Indeed, a Prussian rescript of 1723 ordered the establishment of a house of correction for the reception of criminals sentenced to *opus publicum*.[28] This concept of the function of the houses was current throughout the eighteenth century and even later. The Theresiana and the Bavarian code of 1813 expressed this view, one also reflected in the "forced labor" punishment in France, the sentences to penal servitude in England, and, in disguised form, in the penitentiary sentences to hard labor "of the most servile kind" in American states in the first half of the nineteenth century.

The idealistic aim of the founders of the earliest houses of correction, to make them reformatories that would restore their inmates to society trained in useful occupations and Christian morals, was hardly realized even in the Amsterdam houses. As they spread over the continent they became state factories serving the mercantilistic policies of rulers more concerned with the balance of trade than with the reformation of criminals. To illustrate, Eberhard Schmidt relates that troublesome news about merchants of neighboring states who bought up all raw wool in the Electorate of Brandenburg and, after converting it into salable articles, controlled the Brandenburg market in such wares, led the Elector to establish the Spandau house of correction in 1687 "for the promotion of wool and silk manufactures and also for the improvement of the hitherto deficient spinning industry in our land." When the Brandenburg city of Küstrin submitted a report in 1738 on the local house, "no word was said about the moral reform of inmates and what had been done to promote it; stressed was that so far the house had been successfully maintained by the industries therein." The efforts by the authorities to avoid competition with free industry often led them to lease their houses to private contractors who were, of course, chiefly concerned with the profitable exploitation of the labor of inmates.[29]

But no matter who managed the houses, the regime was repressive. Upon admission, the inmate was often whipped, either because this was traditional practice or because it had been ordered by the court, and before he was discharged he was similarly treated. He was chained while at work, beaten for violating rules, and housed in overcrowded and often dark and unsanitary quarters. "Correction" was to be achieved by compulsory attendance at church services and prayer meetings, routine instructions in doctrinal religion, and forced labor. Insofar as that labor taught the convict a useful skill, he might gain something from his incarceration, but we know little about the attitude of employers toward the hiring of ex-convicts, especially where a rigid guild system governed trades and handicrafts. Thus, while the houses of correction signified a radical change in penal practice, they became a device for making prison labor profitable to the state.

VII: THE BAGNE

We are told that slavery originated when victors in war, instead of killing their captured enemies, enslaved them. Slavery, in other words, derived from military activity. When European states instituted slavery as punishment for crime in the late Middle Ages and substituted it for capital punishment of major offenders whose death sentences had been commuted or who had been given life sentences by courts, their confinement was under military control, as in the case of the stockhouses in army fortresses and the galleys at naval dock yards. These two variants of penal slavery have been discussed in earlier chapters, but galley slavery underwent a change which is well worth examining—the bagne.

When galleys became obsolete as naval combat vessels, slavery at the oars ceased, but in France this neither changed the laws nor affected judges, who continued to impose sentences to the galleys. Court records of Brittany, for example, show that in 1772 a man was sentenced to six years in the galleys and branded on the shoulder with the letters GAL. Two years later a man was given a term of three years for assault and battery, and in 1783 another was branded and sentenced to three years for breaking into a chicken coop and stealing a goose and six chickens. The same year three thieves were branded with the letter V (*voleur*), their property confiscated, and life sentences to the galleys imposed on them.[1] The law provided no alternative until 1791, when the revolutionary National Assembly legitimized the transformation of galley slavery begun at the dawn of the eighteenth century.

The construction of a prison at the navy yard of Marseilles where slaves— "Turks" and convicts—could be confined and put to work had been proposed to Colbert in 1669, and he ordered a study made of such institutions already in existence at Malta and Leghorn, but nothing came of it. The proposal was reexamined in the 1680s, because the government was becoming concerned about the rising cost of maintaining thousands of oarsmen unfit for rowing. To reduce their number they were sent to the West Indies to be sold, but this plan was soon abandoned. Another and partial solution to the problem was tried in 1700. The many shops of the great arsenal were organized into a state—i.e., royal—factory which was leased to a consortium of capitalists. The character of this lease system of prison labor may be seen from the principal provisions of the contract signed in 1707, nearly identical to the earlier contract of 1701. (a) The lessee would have for his use the entire main building of the new arsenal completed in 1690. (b) The lessee would accept up to 1,500 convicts and Turks assigned by the intendant—oarsmen, invalids, malingerers, or those rejected by the captains—so long as they were not manually crippled, blind, or too old or feeble for work. (c) The king reserved the right to recall them to galley service, except foremen and a hundred weavers. (d) The lessee would receive nineteen *deniers* per capita per day for the feeding of the prisoners, who would be clothed at the expense of the state. The lessee must give each prisoner twelve ounces of bread daily and the beans needed by the invalids not working in the shops, and he must pay wages to the prisoners according to their capacities and the quality of their work. (e) The lessee must not let the prisoners go to work in the city without the intendant's permission nor put them to work that would weaken them or injure their health. (f) The state would supply the guards, assume the care of the sick, and see to the spiritual needs of the prisoners. The state would also furnish the wooden barrack bedsteads, heating, needed utensils, etc. (g) All expenditures for feeding the prisoners and employees of the prison would be exempt from excise taxes. (h) At the end of each month, the state would take possession of all the textiles and other goods manufactured, at previously fixed tariffs. (i) The lessee would cut and sew all the clothing of the oarsmen and be paid by the piece. (j) The lessee would also make all the uniforms of the guards of the galleys. (k) The prisoners would be obliged to work for the lessee in preference to outsiders.[2]

The prisoners worked from dawn to dusk, ate their meals in the factory, and slept there on raised, slightly inclined wooden platforms, twelve by fifteen feet in size, accommodating four pairs of inmates. They were always chained together in couples by a long chain attached to a heavy iron anklet. During the night the chains were looped around a stout iron bar affixed to the foot end of the platform. The inmate could procure a coarse mattress for a fee. The small wage he received might allow him that comfort unless he preferred to spend it in the prison canteen run by a noncommissioned officer of the galleys.

The base at Marseilles was almost completely abandoned soon after the Galley Corps was merged with the Navy Department in 1748, and most of the roughly four thousand slaves were sent to the base at Toulon, where a bagne had been constructed in 1723. A thousand were sent to Brest to construct a prison in that port; it was to become the largest of the four prisons, called bagnes, operated by the Navy Department at Brest, Toulon, and Rochefort.*

When the National Assembly, in 1791, created the punishment of "irons" (*fers*), which in severity ranked after death in the catalogue of punishments, those sentenced to this penalty were to "be employed in forced labor (*travaux forces*) for the profit of the state, either within strong prisons (*maisons de force*) or in ports and arsenals, mines or in draining marshes, or at any other hard labor, which the legislature may determine upon a request from an administrative district (*département*)."[3] The highly repressive panel code of 1810 abolished "irons" and substituted forced labor for life or for terms of not less than five years. Those sentenced to this punishment must "be employed in the most grueling labor" and "drag an iron ball at their feet or, in couples, be chained together."[4] In practice, the bagne was to become their destination. After 1828, those with sentences of between five and ten years were sent to Toulon; the rest, including lifers, to Brest and Rochefort. This classification was abandoned in 1837. Thenceforth, the length of the sentence did not determine the destination of the convict slave.

The prelude to the convict's actual admission to the bagne remained substantially unchanged. Branding, which had been abolished by the code of 1791, was shortly thereafter readopted for recidivists, forgers, and arsonists, and was given a new status by the code of 1810, which required that all sentenced to forced labor for life (*travaux perpétuels*) be publicly branded on the right shoulder with the letters TP; those sentenced to terms of years were to be branded with the letter T. The letter F was added if the offender was a forger.[5] Branding was abolished in 1832, but the letters GAL continued to be stamped on the jackets worn by the convicts.

The delivery of the convicts to the arsenal ports also remained substantially unchanged, except that after the Revolution the marching "chains" practically disappeared. At the assembly depots, chiefly Paris and Bordeaux, the convicts were still being chained by couples, at the neck, with a master chain uniting groups of 20 to 30 convicts. Each group then mounted a wagon and seated themselves back to back, legs dangling, on a long bench on each side of a long wagon which was drawn by a team of six horses. The "chain" was abolished in 1837 and cellular vehicles substituted, but the practice of entrusting the transport to private contractors persisted.[6]

The bagnes were closed in 1854, when penal transportation to Guyana

---

*A bagne at Lorient, exclusively for military offenders, was closed in 1830 and its inmates transferred to the Toulon bagne.

and New Caledonia was substituted, except that the Toulon bagne was kept as a depot for prisoners awaiting transportation until the 1870s, when this function was assigned to the citadel on the isle of Ré, north of Bordeaux. Civil death in conjunction with a sentence to an infamizing and afflictive punishment was also abolished in 1854, thus ending penal slavery, at least in theory.

The transition from slavery at the oars to slavery in the bagnes at the navy yards was a natural development. Even in the days when galleys were functional vessels of war, their service was limited to the summer months. The rest of the year the slaves were put to work in the ports. At Toulon and Rochefort, most of them were held on decommissioned galleys or hulks when not at work, but at Brest a large prison was constructed. The building was 250 feet long, and each of its three stories had two large halls or dormitories housing about six hundred convicts each. The bagnes must have been the largest penal institutions in Europe. Those at Brest and Toulon held between three thousand and four thousand prisoners, and the one at Rochefort well over one thousand. By comparison, as late as 1850 the largest American penitentiaries—Auburn and Sing Sing in New York state—had fewer than seven hundred inmates each. A look at the bagnes, which employed prisoners in forced labor for the profit of the state, and at the treatment of the inmates, makes clear that these institutions were forerunners of industrial prisons for felons.

When a convict arrived at the bagne, the chains which he had worn during the transport were removed and he was fitted with new "irons"—an anklet of tempered metal affixed to a chain held up by a hook on his wide leather belt. He was bathed and shaved, his hair cut, and prison clothing supplied to him. Both his toilet and clothing marked the class of convicts to which he was assigned. This classification system was not used in the early years of the institutions. It seems to have originated early in the 1780s with Pierre Victor Malouet, intendant at Toulon, whose persuasive views on the matter were favorably received by Louis XVI, who was interested in prison reform. At the time, the Toulon bagne held military deserters, smugglers, and criminals, all of whom were subjected to the same regime and indiscriminately chained together by couples, "even though they were very different in basic character, in the consideration they merit, and in the real wrong they have done society."[7] Malouet suggested that since the Toulon bagne had four large halls, one of them could be used to house smugglers serving life sentences, another those serving definite terms, and the rest reserved for the criminals. The haircuts and clothing of the three classes would differ as would the type of labor assigned them. No criminal was to be chained to a convict of another class. These suggestions were officially adopted in 1782 in the hope that they would combat the moral contamination inherent in the old practices. An enlightened interest in the welfare of the convicts was also evidenced by some economic aid given to discharged prisoners with no personal resources.[8]

The bagne of Toulon rather impressed John Howard, who saw it in 1786 and described it at some length.

> The *Galleys,* formerly at Marseilles, are now removed to the arsenal at Toulon. Five were moored near each other. . . . In them were about sixteen hundred prisoners, who are obliged always to wear a bonnet or cap, on which is fixed a tin plate with a number. Their caps were grey–green–and red, to distinguish deserters—smugglers—and thieves. . . . These galleys had only one deck. Many of their windows in the roofs were open and, being swept twice every day, they were clean and not offensive. The slaves also were kept clean and their clothing was neat, even in that galley which is appropriated to the aged and infirm. Some of them had been confined forty, fifty, and even sixty years. All have a coat, waistcoat, trousers, two shirts and a pair of shoes, given them every year; and a greatcoat every two years. They had good brown bread, well baked, in loaves weighing a pound and three quarters. All had some little allowance in *money,* and to those who worked was granted an additional allowance of three sous every day for wine. In each galley there were two *cantons* (little rooms) [canteens], one for wine, for those who worked for government, the other for the sale of white bread, greens, etc. Many worked at their own trades, as shoemakers, basketmakers, etc., but none were allowed to keep shops on shore as formerly at Marseilles; nor have they the same convenience . . . for the sale of their work. Forty were at work at *La Place* (the Square) in the city digging and removing the soil for the foundation of a house for the intendant. These were chained, two and two, and when one wheeled the mould, the other carried the chain; but in digging, sawing, and other stationary employment, both worked. Many were at work in the *Arsenal;* and employed, some in moving, hewing and sawing timber; and others in the cotton and thread manufactory. The number engaged in the last of these employment was about two hundred. They were lodged in an adjoining hall; and I observed, that when they left off work they were searched to prevent their secreting any of the materials. All were loaded with chains of some kind or other. Those employed in the manufactory (and some owners in the arsenal) had only a ring on one leg; but this, and likewise the choice of irons, I found to be a distinction which might be *purchased*. The slaves who worked *out* of the arsenal were loaded with *heavy* chains; and few are able to escape; if any do escape they are punished, when retaken, in various ways—some by a confinement under *heavier* irons—some by a recommencement of their term of confinement—and such as have been condemned for life, by hanging.[9]

As institutions administering the punishment of forced labor, the bagnes were not subjected to critical scrutiny until the end of the Napoleonic era, when the American penitentiary movement began to arouse the interest, and ultimately the enthusiasm, of leading legislators, jurists, and publicists.[10]

Their writings, which appeared during the last three decades of the arsenal prisons, have helped us learn more about the management of the bagnes and the treatment of their inmates than did Howard. The description which follows is drawn from these sources and will deal primarily with the institution at Brest, although the other bagnes were substantially similar, since the ordinances and regulations governing them applied to all.[11]

The classification system, originated by Malouet, was standardized. There were three classes: the incorrigible, the ordinary, and the merit class. On admission to the institution, the convict slave was usually placed in the ordinary class unless he was a recidivist who had previously done forced labor or served long terms of imprisonment, in which case he was classified as incorrigible. This class also contained convicts sentenced by the special maritime court-martial to a term in heavy irons—the "double chain"—or, for crime, to a lengthy term or for life. Unmanageable or insubordinate convicts were also among those classed as incorrigible. In the larger bagnes the incorrigibles usually numbered about four hundred. The merit class was reserved for those who had distinguished themselves by good conduct and industry. The size of that class was limited to three hundred at Toulon and Brest and one hundred at Rochefort.

Just as it was possible for an "ordinary" convict to earn a transfer to the merit class after one year, so it was possible for him to become an incorrigible through misconduct. Some of the incorrigibles were always confined to their dormitory, chained to their sleeping platform, but recidivists and rebels might be returned to the ordinary class after two years, and those sentenced to heavy irons, after finishing that sentence.

The type of sentence a convict served and the class to which he belonged could be told from his dress and haircut. Those serving terms of years wore a red woolen bonnet with a tin number disc. The lifers' bonnets were green. The hair of convicts in the ordinary class was cut in furrows. The incorrigibles had their hair cut short, the merit men wore crewcut. All convicts were issued a yellow pair of pants, two coarse linen shirts, a pair of hobnailed boots, and a red woolen, buttonless coat. This outfit was renewed every two years. The merit man's coat, unlike that of the other classes, had a narrow red collar. The coat of the incorrigible recidivist had one yellow sleeve, and that of the rebel two. Merit men carried no chains or ankle irons, only an iron ring on one ankle.

When not at work for the navy outdoors or in the arsenal, the convicts of each class were lodged together in separate dormitory halls which, as already mentioned, numbered six at Brest, each with a six hundred–man capacity. There were fewer halls at Toulon because the ordinaries there were lodged in decommissioned galleys. The most conspicuous objects in a hall probably were the cannons mounted at each end of eight-foot-high platforms and enclosed by iron grills. They were loaded with grapeshot. Every hall at Brest had a line of twenty-five barrack bedsteads, each consisting of two sturdy wooden platforms joined together lengthwise and sloping from the joint to the foot. They were raised from the floor and each platform accomodated six pairs of convicts whose individual places were marked by numbers. Each place held a coverlet in which the convict, always fully clothed, could wrap himself. His individual chain was attached to an iron bar at the foot of the bedstead, permitting him to reach the night-bucket set between the bedsteads.

The punishment of forced labor was administered in the daytime. What other sufferings the convict would experience from his confinement—the meager diet, the burden of chains, the harsh discipline, etc.—were corollaries. The labor to which he was assigned depended on the class to which he belonged, and the variety of tasks made it possible to aggravate or lighten his punishment. The navy yards, where the bagnes were located, were huge establishments for the construction, repair, and equipment of vessels and for the manufacture and storage of supplies needed for these purposes. Many of the jobs involved required very skilled labor, and therefore as many as several thousands of free artisans from the locality were employed in the dockyards and the factories. Some convicts were skilled workers, and if they were merit men they were employed in the shops of the arsenal. The ordinaries worked in the warehouses and the shipyards at menial tasks, sheltered from the elements, while the incorrigibles were engaged outdoors, in all weather, in the most fatiguing and hard labor.

The bagne was only one of several departments or sections headed by commissioners serving under the commandant of the naval base. The commissioner of the bagne was responsible for the housing and feeding of the convicts, and, in general, keeping a tight prison and maintaining discipline with the aid of custodial officers. A similar custodial force guarded the gangs at work outside the bagne. The only labor the commissioner directly provided for convicts was at tasks inside the bagne in connection with the feeding of the inmates and keeping the institution clean and orderly. The really punitive labor resulted from requisitions by the sections of naval construction, the port, the hydraulic section, the warehouse, and the artillery section. Heavy logs had to be loaded and unloaded, dragged, piled up, and sawed into planks; docks and vessels had to be pumped; masts erected on or removed from vessels; ballast replaced; stone and lumber transported; cannons and anchors scraped, painted, mounted, and demounted; ball and shrapnel sorted; charcoal stored; metal weighed and piled, etc.[12] The ropewalks furnished supplies for the rigging of ships, and weaving shops the canvas for sails. There were forges and printing and stonecutting shops. Since the need for workers of the various sections varied from time to time or season to season, there were periods when the convict labor force was not fully employed. Then the convicts, confined to their dormitories, passed the time in various ways, often in the making of small articles for sale at a shop on the base.

The workday of the convicts began at daybreak. Marching in squads of ten or twelve, each supervised by an officer, they were taken to their assigned place of work. They were chained together, by couples, by a long chain, riveted to their ankle irons, consisting of nine or ten foot-long links like those in a surveyor's chain. The two convicts thus linked together by a tether, which was rarely removed until a man was promoted to the merit class, were compelled to enjoy or suffer each other's company perhaps for years, regardless of the differences in age, temperament, or criminal background.

At eleven o'clock, the squads were brought back to their dormitories for their midday meal and an hour of rest, followed by another five or six hours of labor. The workday was no longer than that of free artisans. Immediately on their return to the bagne, the incorrigibles were chained to their bedsteads, but the ordinaries were allowed to circulate in their halls after their supper until the whistle of an officer announced the time for their "lock-up." Another whistle at eight o'clock called for silence and a sleep disturbed by the clanking of chains and other night sounds.

The bagnes were state prisons operated by the navy department for the profit of the state. The lease system of labor, which had characterized the earliest bagne at Marseilles, no longer existed. A state-use system had replaced it. The convicts received a daily wage ranging from five to twenty centimes. Those paid at piece-rates might earn thirty centimes and those favored ones who worked in the shops elbow to elbow with free artisans, were paid fity centimes. Sers, writing in 1848, addressed the following question to the authorities: "Is it moral, is it suitable that branded men, men sentenced to infamizing punishments, be placed in contact with free and blameless workers and receive the same wage, when they are assigned to the shops?" [13] The paymaster's office credited the convict's wage to his account. If he was serving a sentence to a term of years, one-third was impounded and given him when he was discharged. Otherwise he could spend his earnings, usually in the canteen in a grilled enclosure in the middle of each dormitory that dispensed food and wine and was run by a convict.

The food of the convict was rationed, and its amount depended on whether he was working, sick, or idle, i.e., without an assigned task. The daily ration of the laborer was two pounds of fresh wheat bread or a pound of sea bisquit and an ounce of cheese, a pint of ordinary wine or a quart of beer or cider, a quarter pound of dried vegetables, a small dab of butter or a dash of oil, and a pinch of salt. The idle convict received the same ration except for the wine, cheese, and oil. Neither of them received meat. That item was reserved for the invalids in the hospital, who received half a pound of fresh meat and green vegetables four days a week. The other days they had only dried vegetables. They also were given a pint of wine, a pound and a half of bread, and miniscule portions of butter and salt. The diet was most inadequate for the working convict, whose only chance of getting meat was to purchase it at the canteen with his meager earnings. There bouillon could be bought at five centimes a liter and other dishes at top prices of twenty centimes.

The hot vegetable soup, to which the convicts had had to contribute several ounces of their bread, was brought from the kitchens by convicts assigned to that work. It was served in large wooden "troughs," around which half a dozen inmates would gather and eat the soup with their wooden spoons.

The convicts were given no moral or religious instruction. "There was no teacher except the rod of the guard or brief and sharply spoken orders."[14] Sick convicts were hospitalized. At Brest, they, as well as the permanently blind and crippled or aged invalids were housed in the large two-story hospital across a wide court from the bagne. It is claimed that the convicts received the same medical attention as the marines on the base, except that the former were chained to their beds. Merit men served as nurses and orderlies in the infirmary and enjoyed better food than that distributed in the dormitories.

The primary concern of the bagne administration was the safekeeping of inmates and maintaining order by strict discipline. The convicts were counted each time they returned to the dormitories, and their fetters were inspected and tested each time they left for work. In spite of all precautions, some managed to escape. A recaptured escapee who had been serving time had three years added to his sentence; a lifer was loaded with the double chain and fastened to his sleeping platform, day and night, for a like period of time. The same punishment awaited the thief who stole more than five francs' worth of goods. Criminal cases were adjudicated by special maritime courts-martial, and the commissioner of the bagne dealt with breaches of discipline and petty offenses. A convict who insulted a guard, refused to obey an order, or beat his partner was subject to whipping on the bare back with an inch-thick tarred rope. The number of blows ranged from ten to one hundred, depending on the offense. Other punishments included transfer to a lower class, lower rations, or confinement in a dungeon on bread and water for from one day to a month. Assaulting an officer, killing a partner, or inciting to rebellion was punished by the guillotine, with the execution taking place in the interior of the bagne in the presence of all the convicts, the incorrigible given ringside seats.

Between 1826 and 1850, some fifty-two hundred men sixteen to seventy years of age were sent to penal slavery at the bagnes for life; thirty-two hundred were committed for twenty or more years; seventy-three hundred for from eight to twenty years; and twelve thousand three hundred for less than eight years.[15] For the vast majority of them freedom would finally come, but the conditions attached would place almost insurmountable obstructions in the way of their social adjustment. Forbidden to remain in the cities where the bagnes were located, or to live in Paris or most other large centers or within twenty miles of the borders, the authorities assigned them a place of residence, until 1832, when they were allowed more freedom of movement in looking for employment, but always under police surveillance. They shared the experience of all ex-convicts—the difficulty of erasing the stigma of conviction and punishment. Finally, in 1851, a decree revoked their privilege to select their place of residence and gave the government the right to remove them to Guyana or Algeria as a measure of social defense.[16]

Spanish Bagnes

After the War of the Spanish Succession, which ended with the Peace of Utrecht in 1713–14 and left England master of Gibraltar, Spain began the construction of the great naval bases at Cadiz west of the Rock, Cartagena on the southeast coast, and El Ferrol on the northwest tip of the peninsula. The need for manual labor in that connection was largely met by diverting large numbers of galley slaves and prisoners from the fortresses to these ports.[17] After the galley fleet was dissolved in 1748, the worst criminals were sent to Almadén, where, as royal slaves, they labored in the mercury mines which had always competed with the navy for penal slaves. When, in 1770, a commission studying penal reform proposed that major offenders not sentenced to death be sent to arsenals, King Charles III acquiesced. His ordinance of the following year divided criminals meriting afflictive punishments into two classes. Those seemingly reclaimable would be committed for not over ten years to the African fortresses at Ceuta and Oran to labor on fortifications and for the garrisons. The second class consisted of those who had been guilty of "hideous and denigrating crimes, evincing in the offender a corruption and vileness of soul with total abandonment of honor." [18] They were to be sent to the bagnes at the three navy arsenals, chained in pairs, and put to pumping and other abject labor. The purpose of such punishment was to give the offender his just desert and protect the community by removing him from society.[19] The maximum term was fixed at ten years so that the convict would not lose all hope of ultimate freedom and commit desperate acts.

The Spanish bagnes were so much like the French that a description of their administration, the treatment of their inmates, and their labor program would be repetitive.* A very elaborate ordinance governing all these matters was issued in 1804,[20] after a brief period which saw the galley fleet revived, but other types of prisons would soon displace the bagnes. In 1807, there were still about a thousand criminals in each of them, but persistent complaints that these institutions were no longer profitable led to their decline. In 1818, there were only seven convict slaves left in El Ferrol, and ten at Cartagena.[21]

John Howard visited Spain and Portugal in 1783, but he saw no Spanish bagne. His tour of the Lisbon institution was described in the following words:

In the *Arsenal* are four large rooms for slaves or convicts, most of whom are Moors. Some work at the rope-walk, others fetch water, a few are closely confined, and three or four chained to one spot; one of whom (an *Italian*) told me he had been thus confined eight years; another four years. The rest were chained two and two together; and those that went out had a long chain between them, which was taken off as soon as they returned to the *arsenal.* Their allowance from government was one pound of biscuit a day, and some rice, and half a pound of meat three times a week. They were employed in carrying water to the prison, the infirmary and the great prison and guarded by the military. The *Infirmary* for the marines and slaves consisted of two remarkably good rooms, lofty, clean, and quiet. The slaves had *each* a bed with sheets and great attention was paid to them.[22]

---

*(Francisco Lastres, *Rapport*, pp. 407–19, II, part 1, *Actes du Congrès Pénitentiaire International de Rome . . . 1885* [Rome, 1888]). Lastres noted that the marching "chain" survived until 1881 as the method of moving convicts from jails to bagnes, and later from prison to prison. "The transportation of prisoners from one point to another in the country was made on foot on highways . . . and as the poor prisoners and the state police (gendarmes) who guarded them had to rest in the jails en route, a long time was consumed in making a journey, which caused great physical pains and moral sufferings." After 1881, the government contracted with railroad companies to convey the prisoners in cellular cars (p. 417).

The Bagnes of Italy

The maritime states of the Italian peninsula witnessed the same change from slavery at the oars to slavery in the bagnes. Some of these institutions were seen by John Howard when he visited the country in 1778. At Leghorn he found 132 slaves housed in the fortress, each wearing an iron anklet.

The prisoners are condemned to labour for thirty, ten or seven years, or for a shorter term, according to the nature of their crimes; and are chiefly employed on the public works. They are sent out every morning under a guard of soldiers and are chained two and two together with a chain of about eighteen pounds weight. An hour's relaxation is allowed them at breakfast and two hours in the afternoon, and at an hour before sunset they are reconducted to the prison. . . . When they are employed on the *works* by his *royal highness* [the Grand Duke of Tuscany], they are paid two crazzies (about three half-pence) a day, but if employed by other persons they are paid four or six crazzies, according to the nature of their work. . . . Their daily allowance is a loaf of thirty ounces, which is made two thirds of flour and one third of bran, and soup made from four ounces of pease boiled in water, with salt and oil. On each of the two *Easter* holidays they are allowed a pound of meat and three ounces of rice. Every two years they have a coat of gray cloth, a waistcoat of red cloth, and a red cap; every year a pair of shoes and a pair of drawers or breeches. Their drawers are shifted once a month, their shirts every week. For lodging they have a mattress filled with straw and a coverlet; the straw is changed and kept in good order. If one attempts to desert and be taken before sunset, he must wear a ring and chain of eighteen pounds weight; and he must pay his future earnings, till it amounts to a zechim, to those that apprehended him. If they, who are condemned for five years, desert, when retaken their term again commences; and for repeated desertions, they are more severely punished, and sometimes tortured.[23]

The slaves in the Pope's galleys at Civitavecchia were occupied in clearing the harbor, "sawing in the arsenal," as masons, or carrying stones and water, or in the "canvas and calico manufactories." Vagabonds were committed for three years, thieves for at least seven, and forgers for life. Lifers were chained two and two together, others wore a single chain until the approach of the end of their terms when they had to wear only an iron anklet.

For escapes, they are obliged to finish their *first* condemnation and then receive a fresh one for the same time as the former, and they receive from a hundred to two hundred lashes a day for three days after their arrival. None are sent to the galleys *under the age of twenty;* criminals of a younger age are kept at the hospital of *S. Michele*[24] in Rome till they are of age; and are there employed in spinning, and fed on bread and water.[25]

At Naples, in the Kingdom of the Two Sicilies, Howard found four galleys with a total of twelve hundred slaves, all chained by twos. They worked in the arsenal and on other public works but were confined to the vessels at night. Forty years later, in 1819, when Stephen Grellet visited Naples, this arrangement had changed, the slaves being housed in prisons ashore.

> The prisons for galerians [Grellet wrote], exceed in gloom, dirt, and damp everything I have beheld before. In the first, I found in one room, level with or below the ground, paved but covered with accumulated filth, and soft mud by the rain and damp, 670 prisoners, chained two and two; the light comes in from above, so that some parts are very dark and are rendered the more so by the walls and vaults, which are black by the smoke and cobwebs. The room is 72 yards in length and 11 in breadth; ten large pillars in the middle support the vault; the prisoners sleep on boards placed on benches, which cover the whole surface, so that when they lie down, the picture Thomas Clarkson has given of a slave ship is that of this prison also; for want of room, many of them have to sleep under the boards, which are about two feet from the ground, and to lie on the damp or muddy floor; 300 of these prisoners (murderers) never go out; the others are sometimes employed outdoors. I saw there about 15 boys chained with the men. The other prison . . . I expected to find . . . something better, but it is literally the same; the size of it is 58 yards by 6 yards and it contains 340 prisoners. They work in the ship yards. There are shutters but no glass to the windows; they had a filthy yard about 6 yards square. The prisoners look sickly and there are many boys among them.[28]

The unification of Italy in 1870 had little effect on the bagnes. As late as 1885, there were 39 bagnes in 28 fortified ports which, at the end of 1882, had a total of 17,715 inmates. In a report to the International Penitentiary Congress in Rome in 1885, Senator Count Adolfo de Foresta stated:

> In these numerous bagnes, the punishment of forced labor is expiated almost like once in the ancient system of bagnes, i.e., with life in common day and night, forced labor indoors or outdoors, according to circumstances, the convict carrying a chain riveted to an ankle iron and attached to the waistband, wearing the traditional red jacket of the galley slave and working in accord with rules of forced or galley labor, which existed not long ago in France.

He observed that a royal decree of 1878 had established rules for the bagnes.

> According to this regulation the convicts carry the chain, wear red jackets and on their bonnets the identification of the four classes in which they are divided, are subject to labor in the open air or inside the bagne, and are under a severe discipline. The four classes are: first (white border on bonnet), military offenders and those guilty of unpremeditated crimes of passion; second (yellow border),

thieves; third (yellow-black border), robbers; fourth (black border), assassins, parricides and all condemned for the most atrocious crimes. Based on their conduct, the convicts are divided into three classes, identifiable by the coat collar: black for the third, yellow for the second, and blue for the first class. On arrival in the bagne the convict is first subjected to a month of cellular isolation, after which he is assigned to the third class. Six months later, barring a record of disciplinary punishment, he is promoted to the second class and two or three years later to the first class, if his conduct merits it. First class men can be made foremen and employed as clerks and in domestic services. Convicts are called and known by their number which, in large figures, are worn on the left sleeve of their jackets. Disciplinary punishments, inflicted by the council of discipline, are: warning, the double chain, cell with double chain at bread and water, the same but chained to wall of cell, the same and a bread and water diet, the same but in solitary confinement from forty days to six months.[27]

The bagnes were not closed until 1889, when the first national penal code of the unified kingdom of Italy substituted cellular prisons called *ergastolo,* a name which the ancient Romans gave to the prisons for offending slaves on their large plantations.[28]

VIII: THE BAGNES OF ENGLAND AND THEIR AFTERMATH

The French bagnes were supplanted by transportation to penal colonies beyond the seas. The reverse of this process occurred in England when the American War of Independence put an end to the transportation of felons to the colonies—chiefly Maryland and Virginia—and what the Webbs characterized as "virtually a branch of the slave trade."[1] The shipping of criminals to America had begun early in the seventeenth century. In 1615, the Privy Council ordered that unless convicted of willful murder, rape, witchcraft, or burglary, a felon could be sent to the American plantations.[2] Forty years later, executive pardons began to be issued to capital offenders on condition that they would accept transportation for long terms, and this practice was approved by the Habeas Corpus Act of 1679.[3] In 1718, courts were authorized to impose sentences to transportation, usually for seven or fourteen years. The combined effect of these provisions was that in the eighteenth century most convicted felons were transported to the American mainland or the island colonies of Barbados, Bermuda, Jamaica, and the Leeward Islands. This is evident from the fact that 1,121 felons were sentenced to death at the Old Bailey, London, between 1749 and 1771, and 678 were executed, while 5,199 were sentenced to transportation. In addition, 401 were granted conditional pardons and transported. Between 1750 and 1772, courts of the Norfolk and Midland circuits executed 233 felons and sentenced 2,239 to transportation.[4] In other words, transportation had become the standard punishment for about 90 per cent of convicted felons, and courts continued to impose it although the destination was uncertain. Perhaps it was assumed that the American rebellion would soon be crushed and the market for convict labor reopened. In the meanwhile the jails were becoming overcrowded with transportees, and soon a temporary relief measure became imperative. And so the bagnes came into being in 1776. Collectively they became known as the Hulks, because when not at work their inmates were housed in decommissioned men of war moored at dockyards.[5]

The idea of using felons for hard labor at dockyards had been broached a quarter of a century earlier, but a bill to that effect was defeated in the Parliament. Now a statute provided that males "lawfully convicted of great or petty larceny or any other crime for which he shall be liable by law to a sentence of transportation to any of His Majesty's colonies or plantations in

America . . . shall be punished by being kept to hard labor in the raising of sand, soil and gravel, and cleansing the river Thames, or any other service for the benefit of the navigation of the said river."[6] Promptly, the first floating bagne was established at Woolwich, a few miles east of London, the site of the oldest shipyard and the largest arsenal of England.

Three years before this event, John Howard had become sheriff of Bedfordshire. What he discovered about conditions in the Bedford jail was to start him on his famous campaign for prison reform. Legislators were impressed by his report on the *State of the Prisons*, published in 1777, and in 1779 Parliament passed a bill (19 Geo. III, c.74), drafted by Blackstone and Eden, with Howard's assistance, creating two national penitentiaries, one to house six hundred male and the other three hundred female convicts. The drafters hoped that "if any offenders convicted of crimes for which transportation has been usually inflicted were ordered to solitary confinement, accompanied by well-regulated hard labor, and religious instruction, it might be the means, under Providence, not only of deterring others, but also of reforming the individuals, and turning them to habits of industry."[7] The act incorporated recommendations made by Howard in his report, but it reflected a view of convict labor that was shared by tough-minded conservatives. Convicts were to be assigned "to labor of the hardest and most servile kind, in which drudgery is chiefly required, and where the work is little liable to be spoiled by ignorance, neglect or obstinacy, and where the materials or tools are not easily stolen or embezzled, such as treading in a wheel or drawing in a capstern, for turning a mill or other machine or engine."[8] The act also created a new punishment—direct sentences to hulks for some crimes previously punished by transportation, "imprisonment in the hulks from one to five years being the equivalent of seven years' transportation, and (not exceeding) seven years in the hulks the equivalent of fourteen years' transportation."[9] As for the penitentiaries, decades were to pass before they were built, but a few county prisons were constructed on the model.

The failure of the government to implement the Penitentiary, or Hard Labour, Act was partly due to the burden it would impose on a nation which had just lost an expensive war with the American colonies and was facing a prolonged war with France, but it was also due to a deep-rooted attachment to the traditional punishment of transportation which rid the country of "atrocious and dangerous" offenders.* Penitentiaries were seen by conser-

---

*England's barbarous criminal laws in force until well into the nineteenth century made the phrase "atrocious and dangerous" incongruous. The hundred convicts sent from a hulk at Chatham in 1829 to New South Wales included persons sentenced to life for stealing an apron, bacon, or

vatives as institutions that mollycoddled criminals not deserving of pity. In 1784, therefore, an act was passed which empowered courts "before whom a male felon shall be convicted, to order the prisoner to be transported beyond seas, either within His Majesty's dominions or elsewhere; and his service to be assigned to the contractor, who shall undertake such transportation."[10] The act also provided for commitments to the hulks either preliminary to transportation or as a separate punishment.

The final solution was found in 1787, when the government decided to establish a penal settlement on the eastern shore of Australia at Botany Bay in New South Wales. From then on until 1867, when the last shipment of transportees left the United Kingdom for Western Australia, more than 163,000 convicts were sent from their homeland.[11] In the meanwhile the bagne system had expanded. In addition to the one at Woolwich, they had been established at Portsmouth (Langston Harbour and Gosport) and Plymouth in the 1780s and at Sheerness in 1810, as well as at Bermuda in 1823 and Gibraltar in 1842. They served as floating bagnes, in which transportees with seven-year sentences were likely to remain, and as depots for those with longer sentences up to life, who would ultimately be sent away. Their importance began to ebb in 1843, when Millbank Prison in London, a large cellular structure completed in 1821, was made the "depot for the reception of all convicts under sentence or order of transportation in Great Britain, in lieu of their being sent as heretofore to the hulks."[12] By that time, the system itself was being challenged by the colonies, which had begun to object to being the dumping grounds for criminals, and by reformers, who were trying to devise either a system of preparatory trade training for those destined for Australia or a national prison system to supplant transportation.

In 1840, the very year that New South Wales decided to accept no more convicts, a new prison was planned for London—Pentonville. Opened in 1842, it was a "model prison" on the principles of the Pennsylvania system of separate confinement, and designed to receive up to six hundred convicts from all of Great Britain between the ages of eighteen and thirty-five with sentences to transportation for fifteen years or less for a first offense. Pentonville was to be "the portal to the penal colony;" the convict would spend eighteen months—later reduced to nine months—in a solitary cell learning a useful trade like weaving, shoemaking, or tailoring before being shipped to Van Diemen's Land, which still accepted convicts until 1852, when that outlet was closed, leaving only Western Australia, where convict labor was

---

worsted material, and others sentenced to fourteen years for stealing two pounds of potatoes, a pair of shoes, or a bottle of spirits. (W. Eden Hopper, *History of Newgate and the Old Bailey* . . . [London: Underwood Press, 1935], pp. 115–16.)

still useful to the free colonists. Anticipating the end of that enterprise, the government constructed a cellular bagne ashore at Portland harbor in 1850, followed by others at Portsmouth and Chatham harbors. The hulks were doomed; the last burned at Woolwich in 1857, the year in which the definitive act was adopted instituting the punishment of penal servitude for most crimes previously punishable by transportation. After nine months of "separate confinement" in Pentonville or an appropriate local prison, the penal "slave" was assigned to associated labor in the bagnes or in Dartmoor (a former prisoner-of-war camp reconstructed into a cellular prison in 1850),[13] now called Public Works or Convict Prisons, employing their inmates in stone quarries or in manual labor in dockyards and arsenals.[14]

Prisons Afloat

The first floating bagne was moored at the Woolwich dockyard and the first hulk was the 260-ton, *Justitia,* an old convict ship that had made several voyages to Virginia transporting felons. Its owner, Duncan Campbell, was a veteran in that trade. He was appointed overseer by the justices of Middlesex and given a contract to house, feed, clothe, and guard the convicts sent to him. He purchased an old frigate, the *Censor,* from the Admiralty and filled the two ships with prisoners "brought thither from all parts of the country, chained two and two by the leg."[15] Their reception was probably much like that which greeted a young boy, William Day, who was committed to the *Justitia* (a second ship brought from Chatham in 1829) in the late 1830s with a ten-year transportation sentence for stealing a waistcoat. Decades later, when he had achieved a respected position in Australia, he wrote in his memoirs:

> Before going aboard we were stripped to the skin and scrubbed with a hard scrubbing brush . . . and plenty of soft soap, while the hair was clipped from our heads as close as scissors could go. . . . We were then supplied with new "magpie" suits—one side black or blue and the other side yellow. Our next experience was being marched off to the blacksmith, who riveted on our ankles rings of iron connected by eight links to a ring in the centre, to which was fastened an up-and-down strap or cord reaching to the waistbelt. This last supported the links and kept them from dragging on the ground. Then we had what were called knee garters. A strap passing from them to the basils and buckled in front and behind caused the weight of the irons to traverse on the calf of the leg. In this rig-out we were transferred to the hulk, where we received our numbers, for no names were used.[16]

The law establishing the bagnes prescribed that the labor of the convicts would be concentrated on making rivers more navigable, especially the

Thames. The prescription was observed at Woolwich, judging from a report which appeared in the *Scots Magazine* in 1777.

Some [convicts] are sent about a mile below Woolwich in lighters to raise ballast and to row it back to the embankment at Woolwich Warren. . . . Others are employed in throwing it from the lighters. Some wheel it to different parts to be sifted; others wheel it from the Skreen and spread it for the embankment. A party is continually busied in turning round a machine for driving piles to secure the embankment from the rapidity of the tides. Carpenters, etc. are employed in repairing the . . . hulks that lie hard by for the nightly reception of those objects, who have fetters on each leg with a chain between that ties variously, some round their middle, others upright to the throat. Some are chained two and two; and others, whose crimes have been enormous, with heavy fetters. Six or seven are continually walking about with them with drawn cutlasses to prevent their escape and likewise prevent idleness.[17]

The needs of ports in which hulks were moored required the performance of other tasks as well. When John Howard visited Portsmouth in 1788, he found that of 557 convicts lodged in two hulks, 434 were at work on Cumberland Fort, 19 as masons, 6 as carpenters, and the rest as laborers. "Most of them were unloading the ships and carrying stones to different parts of the new works.[18] At Woolwich, as time passed, the jobs done by the convicts became diversified. William Day was assigned to

the turfman's gang [and] our first business was repairing the butts, a large mound of earth against which the guns were practised. After completing this we were employed some days at emptying barges, and then at a rocketshed in the arsenal cleaning shot and knocking rust scales from shells, filling them with scrap-iron, etc. as great preparations were going on for the China war. At other times we would be moving gun carriages or weeding the long lanes between the mounted guns. . . . During all this time I was never for a moment without the leg irons, weighing about twelve pounds.[19]

The heyday of the bagnes came in the years immediately before New South Wales closed its ports to convicts. The government had a dozen hulks at Bermuda, Gibraltar, Portsmouth, Plymouth, and Sheerness, and between 1823 and 1844, one at Chatham for juvenile convicts. The four Bermuda hulks had about a thousand inmates, the Gibraltar bagne—barracks ashore and a hospital hulk—a few hundred, and the English hulks at times more than four thousand. The character of the convicts in the English hulks can be inferred from some data for the year 1841, when 3,265 convicts were received in them. Three were under ten years of age, 213 from ten to fifteen, 458 from fifteen to twenty, 1,612 from twenty to thirty, and 839 were thirty years old or older. Forty per cent were first offenders; the rest had served prison terms before, and 52 of them had already been transported at least once. Most, or 55 per cent, were unskilled laborers, but 32 per cent were "mechanics and persons instructed in manufactures, for whose skills there was little or no employment in the hulks. Seventy per cent were single." [20]

The convicts' lot was a miserable one. The food they received was generally insufficient for men doing heavy labor. Discipline was harsh and the rod and cat-o'-nine-tails in frequent use. Self-mutilation in order to escape the exhausting labor was not uncommon. Cholera, the "gaol fever," and other infectious diseases took a heavy toll, and morbidity and mortality rates were high. In 1841, when 638 convicts were housed on the *Warrior* hulk at Woolwich, there were 400 admissions to the hospital hulk and 38 deaths. This hospital was described in 1849 as follows:

> In the hospital ship, the *Unité*, the great majority of the patients were infested with vermin and their persons, in many instances, particularly their feet, begrimed with dirt. No regular supply of body-linen had been issued; so much so that many men had been five weeks without a change, and all record had been lost of the time when the blankets had been washed, and the number of sheets was so insufficient that the expedient had been resorted to of only a single sheet at a time to save appearances. Neither towels nor combs were provided for the prisoners' use, and the unwholesome odor from the imperfect and neglected state of the waterclosets was almost insupportable. On the admission of new cases into the hospital, patients were directed to leave their beds and go into hammocks, and the new cases were turned into the vacated beds, without changing the sheets.[21]

But the worst feature, as seen by reformers, was the indiscriminate commingling of the convicts, especially in the hulks, where they were herded together in large compartments between decks. John Howard saw such a room on the *Dunkirk* at Portsmouth in 1788. It was 67 feet by 18 and 6 feet high and held 68 convicts. He assumed that at night such a room would be "very offensive."[22] Indeed, it was a danger to both health and morals.

> There are still officers in the Woolwich hulks [wrote Mayhew] who remember a time when the *Justitia* . . . contained no less than 700 convicts, and when at night these men were fastened in their dens—a single warden being left on board ship in charge of them! The state of morality under such circumstances may be easily conceived—crimes impossible to be mentioned being commonly perpetrated.[23]

It was the evils of the congregate jails of England that had led to the passage of the Penitentiary, or Hard Labour, Act of 1779, and the same conditions in the hulks had helped to spur the establishment of the state prisons of Millbank and Pentonville, where convicts were separately confined and taught a trade. But, to the despair of the reformers, the hulks, which were to be only a temporary expedient, survived for half a century and nullified whatever good the discipline of the state prisons may have achieved. Unfortunately, so long as the transportation system prevailed, these prisons were conceived to be merely "portals to the penal colony." The hulks, from which the transports departed, were a kind of half-way house, where the convicts, after transfer from the state prisons, often remained until the end of their sentence, especially after the early 1840s, when the decline of the transportation system set in.

The separate confinement and trade training in the state prisons, followed by the commingling of the convicts in the hulks, was a mixture both illogical and misdirected, which evidenced "the inertness of government as well as . . . its utter callousness as to the fate or reformation of criminals." At the hulks, the convict was "thrown among brutal companions, whom it was before [at Pentonville] considered perdition to allow him to associate with and even to *see.*" Furthermore, having been given some training in tailoring, shoemaking, or weaving at the prison, "he has to lay aside the craft that he has only just learnt and is set to scrape the rust from shells or else stack timber" at Woolwich, doing "the lowest description of labor—in some instances at the muzzle of a guard's carbine—and impressed with the idea that it is the very *repulsiveness* of this labor which is his punishment." Nor was the previous training in a craft of much use to him who after 1853 was sentenced to a term of penal servitude and sent to the public-works prisons (the bagnes at Portland, Portsmouth, and Chatham) "to dig, drag, break stones," or to labor in the stone quarries and peat bogs of Dartmoor.[24]

With the disappearance of the last English hulk in 1857, the Bermudan hulks in 1862, and the hospital hulk at Gibraltar in 1875,[25] state reformers would continue the thankless task of improving correctional methods in the public works prisons and the many county and municipal jails and houses of correction of England.

Penal Servitude

The transportation penal system with its adjuncts of hulks and forwarding prisons was operated by the national government. The jails and houses of correction under county or municipal rule constituted a separate system that enjoyed local autonomy until the second half of the nineteenth century. These local institutions, which John Howard had surveyed and condemned, contained prisoners awaiting trial or execution, debtors, those committed to short terms or imprisonment at hard labor for crimes not meriting death or transportation, and, before the establishment of the bagnes, those awaiting transportation. For a century between the passage of the Hard Labour Act and their takeover by the state in 1878, they were the main target of penal reformers; after that takeover, some of their worst practices would, for years to come, remain part of national policy. However, what happened when "atrocious and dangerous" criminals could no longer be shipped across the seas for life or for terms of seven or fourteen years, the most common sentences?* Such offenders would now have to be imprisoned and perhaps later let loose at home. In view of the stories of rapine and other depredations committed by unregenerate convicts in Australia, this prospect aroused anxiety and even fear. Penal colonies might of course be created in other parts of the far-flung British possessions. Vancouver Island and Hudson Bay, for instance, were considered and shelved.

Finally, a suitably harsh and repressive substitute was found—penal servitude. It was not only thought to be an effective deterrent of the "criminal class"; it accorded well with the philosophy of punishment embraced by the aristocracy and landed gentry, who controlled the legislative, judicial, and executive branches of government, and by the upper-middle classes of merchants and manufacturers, who firmly believed that the only way to combat crime was to make punishment terrible. This sentiment was well expressed by one of their eloquent spokesmen, the Reverend Sydney Smith, in the *Edinburgh Review* of 1822. "It is a mistake," he wrote, "and a very serious and fundamental mistake, to suppose that the principal object in jails is the reformation of the offender." Commenting on the annual report, 1821, of the Society for the Improvement of Prison Discipline (organized in 1816), which praised the educational and industrial programs in a few local institutions, he added:

We again enter our decided protest against these modes of occupations in prisons... they are not the kind of occupations, which render prisons terrible. We would banish all the looms of Preston jail and substitute nothing but the treadwheel or the capstan or some species of labour, where the labourer could not see the results of his toil—where it was as monotonous, irksome and dull as possible—pulling and pushing, instead of reading and writing—no share of the profits—not a

*Between 1827 and 1833, for instance, 3,871 persons were transported for life from England, Wales, and Ireland; 4,467 for terms of fourteen years, and 21,995 for terms of seven years. Only 21 transportees had received sentences of different lengths: thirty-five years, twenty-eight years, ten years, and nine years. (William Crawford, *Report on the Penitentiaries of the United States* [Montclair, N.J.: Patterson Smith, 1969; reprint of 1835 ed.], pp. 187, 191.)

single shilling. There should be no tea and sugar—no assemblage of female felons round the washing tub—nothing but beating hemp and pulling oakum and pounding bricks—no work but was tedious, unusual and unfeminine. Man, woman, boy and girl should all leave the jail unimpaired, indeed, in health but heartily wearied of their residence and taught by sad experience to consider it the greatest misfortune of their lives to return to it. We have the strongest belief that the present lenity of jails, the education carried on there—the cheerful assemblage of workmen—the indulgence in diet—the shares of earnings enjoyed by prisoners are one great cause of the astonishingly rapid increase of commitments.[26]

These views echoed the provisions of the Hard Labour Act and were to dominate the British system of dealing with convicts and ordinary prisoners until the end of the nineteenth century.

The first penal servitude act was passed in 1853. Sentences to transportation for less than fourteen years were replaced by penal servitude for not less than three years. Ticket-of-leave, a kind of "parole" which for a decade or more had been granted to worthy convicts in Australia before the expiration of their sentences, was abolished. Experiments had also been made there—and especially at Norfolk Island, where Alexander Maconochie[27] was governor of a prison for recidivists for a few years in the 1840s—with the conversion of time sentences into labor sentences expressed in so many work units or "marks,"* which permitted a well-behaved, hard-working convict to move by stages toward a license—ticket-of-leave—to be at large. The omission of this provision in the penal-servitude act soon proved to be unwise, and in 1857 an act was adopted which provided that this punishment be applied to all convicts previously subject to transportation, that the length of sentences be the same as the old sentences to transportation, and that the ticket-of-leave be restored.[28] The first nine months of the sentence were to be spent in cellular confinement in Pentonville or in cells rented by the government in large local prisons. Then followed a period of congregate labor in a Public Works prison "divided into three equal 'progressive stages,' carrying increasing privileges and gratuities so that the convict might have a definite stimulus to work hard and behave well.[29] A release on license terminated the incarceration. An act of 1864 increased the minimum sentence to five years, adopted Maconochie's "mark system" to enable a convict to alleviate his situation by good behavior, and provided more drastic corporal punishments for misconduct.

---

*Making the length of imprisonment dependent on the amount of labor performed by a prisoner was first proposed by William Paley in 1785. (*See* Thorsten Sellin, "Paley on the Time Sentence," *Journal of Criminal Law and Criminology,* 22 [1931], pp. 264–66.)

The 1864 act was the work of a Select Committee on Prison Discipline of the House of Lords, which also took steps to regulate and consolidate the administration of local penal institutions where maximum two-year sentences to "imprisonment with hard labor" were served. The result was embodied in the Prison Act of 1865, which did not apply to convict prisoners. It "led to a drastic tightening up of the administration under which not the 'professional criminal' only, but all the unfortunate inmates of the goals, suffered for a whole generation."[30] The act eliminated the distinction between jails and houses of correction, referring to all of them as "prisons." It practically erased the distinction between penal servitude for convicts and "imprisonment at hard labor." Local authorities lost their treasured autonomy and were required to establish cellular prisons in which the prescribed punishments would be administered. The model for such institutions already existed—Pentonville. Two categories of labor were prescribed for all prisons. Prisoners would have to spend at least the first three months in "first-class" labor, which the Select Committee designated as "hard labor."[31] All other bodily labor fell into the "second class," except that the Committee regarded oakum picking as an intermediary form. Seen as a means of taming the offender and filling him with fear of imprisonment, first-class labor was made revolting and degrading, especially by making it unproductive and, in the main, useless. It was penal slavery at its worst, the treadwheel, the crank, and shot drill being its chief instruments. These were not new devices, but since they continued to be used after the government nationalized local jails and, with oakum picking, became almost the exclusive forms of hard labor in these institutions, they merit attention.

The Treadmill

The invention of the penal treadmill, also called the stepping-mill or treadwheel, is usually credited to William Cubitt, an Ipswich engineer who, while on a visit to the Suffolk County jail at Bury in 1815, was urged to find some way of giving employment to its many idle prisoners. He designed a machine which was installed in the jail early in 1820. That year, the governor of the jail reported to the Prison Discipline Society that

> the Discipline Mill . . . recently erected . . . is capable of grinding wheat and dressing flour with any number of hands, from 16 to 30, at one time. It will grind and dress from 20 to 30 quarters [160 to 240 bushels] per week at ten hours each day. The machinery consists of two pairs of stones, each capable of grinding four

bushels per hour; one dressing mill, which dresses two sacks of flour per hour, and one pair of malt rollers, which grind twelve bushels per hour.

He noted that the purpose of the mill was

the adoption of a kind of labour to which every one would have a natural dislike, and yet such as every one could perform without previous instruction" and that such mills could serve different needs. "The operation of the convicts would be precisely the same as that . . . of wind, water, steam, or horses . . . there would be no difficulty in establishing a mill or manufactory near the boundary wall of a prison, through which a single shaft or axle would have to pass and thus communicate the power."[32]

The rotation of the millstones was made possible by a set of shafts and gears connected with the axle of a tread*wheel* turned by manpower or, perhaps more accurately, by leg-and-foot power. The usual form of such a wheel "was something like that of a very wide mill-wheel, such as is turned by water power, containing twenty-four steps. Each prisoner held on to a wooden bar or ladder rung above his head and kept on treading as the steps went around. The body or barrel of the wheel was mostly about five feet in diameter.[33]

Mr. Cubitt's idea caught on. One after the other, local jails or houses of correction installed treadmills for the grinding of corn or the pumping of water. By 1832, eighty-seven of the ninety-three English local institutions had them,[34] but why they were considered Cubitt's innovation is a mystery, since they were found in the very first London house of correction in the 1580s and in use in various German prisons seen by Howard a century later.[35] Furthermore, the Hard Labour Act of 1779 had mentioned "treading in a wheel" as a suitable form of convict labor "of the hardest and most servile kind . . . for turning a mill or other machine or engine." The terminology treading *in* a wheel rather than *on* it may have been deliberately chosen. In the Leicester house of correction the wheel had a diameter of twenty feet and the prisoners treaded it from the inside like a squirrel cage. It was discarded some time before 1824 because of two fatal accidents.[36]

As time passed, the treadwheel became the most common method of administering the punishment of imprisonment at hard labor in local institutions; in some of them women and even untried prisoners had to tread it. In 1832, 32 per cent of the inmates of English local prisons worked on the treadwheel, and 24 per cent at other employments.[37] The rest, or 44 per cent, presumably were either idle, held for trial, debtors, or invalids. The treadwheel was the most important component in "first class" labor. When the government, in 1877, discovered that "other expedients for enforcing first class labour, such as cranks, capstan, shot drill, etc. were in use in many prisons," an advisory committee recommended that "the treadwheel should in future be the recognized machinery for the purpose."[38] It remained so until 1899.

The best illustration of this perversion of convict labor is a description of the treadwheel at the Middlesex House of Correction (Coldbath Fields) in 1862, the largest local prison in England, housing some twelve hundred prisoners.

There are six treadwheels . . . four in the felons' and two in the vagrants' prison. . . . Each wheel contains twenty-four steps, which are eighteen inches apart, so that the circumference of the cylinder is sixteen feet. These wheels revolve twice in a minute, and the mechanism is arranged to ring a bell at the end of every thirtieth revolution, and so to announce that the appointed *spell* of work is finished. Every man put to labour at the wheel has to work for fifteen quarters of an hour every day. . . . The entire length of the apparatus was divided into twenty-four compartments, each something less than two feet wide, and separated from one another by high wooden partitions. . . . The boards at the back of these compartments reach to within four feet of the bottom, and through the unboarded space protrudes the barrel of the wheel, striped with the steps, which are like narrow 'floats' to a long paddle-wheel. . . . When the prisoner has mounted to his place on the topmost step . . . he resembles the acrobat . . . at a circus, perched on the cask he causes to revolve under his feet.

The men supported themselves

by a handrail fixed to the boards at the back of each compartment, and they move their legs as if they were mounting a flight of stairs; but with this difference that instead of their ascending, the steps pass from under them, and . . . it is this peculiarity, which causes the labour to be so tiring. . . . Only every other man, out of the twenty-four composing the gang on the wheel, work at the same time, each alternate prisoner resting himself while the others labour.

All the wheels to which 142 men were assigned daily were connected with

an immense machine situated in the paved court, which leads from the main or felons' prison to that of the vagrants. In the centre stands a strong iron shaft, on the top of which is a horizontal beam some twenty feet long, and with three Venetian-blind-like fans standing up at either end, and which was revolving at such a rapid pace that the current of air created by it blew the hair from the temples each time it whizzed past. This is what is called the regulator of the treadwheel. But this apparatus the resistance necessary for rendering the treadwheel *hard* labour is obtained.

A device attached to the revolving shaft made it possible to close "the fans at the end of the beams, thus offering a greater resistance to the air, and, consequently, increasing the labour of the prisoners working at the wheel."[39] That labor produced nothing except sweat and fatigue, and sometimes physical ailments or injuries. The prisoners used to say that they were "grinding the wind." They had been doing that ever since the wheels were installed in this prison in 1821.[40]

The treadwheelers in the Middlesex house worked a seven-and-a-half-hour day. Half of this time was spent on the wheel, during which they "climbed" 7,200 feet, although stationary. Exhausting as this climb was, other prisons were even more taxing. In the early 1830s, for instance, the workday was longer and the tasks harder, as seen from the following table.[41]

INSTITUTION	HOURS ON WHEEL		DAILY "CLIMB" (In Feet)	
	Summer	Winter	Summer	Winter
Durham Jail	9	6	10,867	7,560
Exeter House of Correction	8	7	9,860	8,612
Knutsford House of Correction	10	7	14,000	9,800
Reading Jail	8	8	12,564	12,564
Worcester Jail	10	8	13,600	10,880

In some prisons the rest periods were much shorter than in the Middlesex house.

Treadwheel labor was "vehemently attacked by humanitarians, not only as cruel, but also as ineffective in working any reform in the convict; and no less obstinately defended by Justices in search of a punishment at once cheap and easy of application, and potent as a deterrent."[42] Some opponents, however, whose main objection to the wheel was that it was a health hazard, believed that they had found a safer means of inflicting hard labor: the crank.

The Crank

When the system of separate cellular confinement became the national policy of prison discipline, the penitentiary of Pentonville, opened in 1842, became the model to be imitated. But the adoption created a problem. The small cell in which a convict had to spend even his working hours put a limit on the kind of labor he could perform. He could work at shoemaking, tailoring, weaving, mat-making, and the like, but this was hardly "labor of the hardest and most servile kind, in which drudgery is chiefly required," to quote the Hard Labour Act which made work rather than the deprivation of liberty the real punishment. What was needed was a machine that a convict could operate in his cell and that would be as effective a deterrent as the treadwheel was thought to be. Such a machine was promptly invented by one Gibbs, attached to Pentonville. It was spawned by the cellular system and it introduced a new form of completely unproductive and punitive hard labor. In that respect it differed from hand-cranking machines operated by prisoners in groups, in use at Millbank to power mills or pumps since the early 1820s.[43]

Cranks came in different models. At Coldbath Fields, the machine was

a narrow iron drum, placed on legs, with a long handle on one side, which on being turned causes a series of cups or scoops in the interior to revolve. At the lower part of the interior of the machine is a thick layer of sand, which the cups, as they come round, scoop and carry to the top of the wheel, where they . . . empty themselves after the principle of a dredging machine. A dial plate, fixed in front of the iron drum, shows how many revolutions the machine has made.[44]

The turning of the crank handle could be made harder or lighter. In one type of crank, weights were used, in another a metal band which could be tightened and acted like a brake on the axle inside the drum. The officially approved type, according to the Prison Commissioners' annual report of 1879, consisted of a drum turned by a crank handle. "Clip-brakes of various construction were applied [to the drum] so as to retard its motion by friction."[45]

The daily task of cranking varied, depending on local practice. The usual requirement was for 10,000 revolutions to be completed in ten hours, but in 1848, when the justices of Leicester County ordered that all adult male prisoners in their prison be put to work on the cranks, the daily task was fixed at 14,000 revolutions. Since many prisoners were physically incapable of meeting this quota in the allotted time, the punishment cells or flogging were in frequent use. To cope with the situation, the justices invented the scheme of denying food to the prisoner who failed to meet his quota. He would have to make 1,800 turns of the crank before getting his breakfast, 4,500 before dinner, and 5,400 before supper, leaving a balance of 2,700 turns for dessert. This made the workday of many prisoners much longer than the ten-hour maximum prescribed by law. Furthermore, the regime was very injurious to the health of the inmates. The government finally intervened in 1852. Similar practices in the Birmingham jail produced a scandal in 1853 arising from the suicide of a youth who had been brutally punished for his failure to finish his work assignment on the crank.[46]

Like the treadwheel, the crank was a controversial punishment. Its opponents objected to it because it had no educational value, gave the prisoner no training in a trade, made him hate his work, injured his health, and enabled spiteful prison officials to make a hard task more difficult by manipulating the internal controls of the machine. These objections seemed to have little effect on the judiciary and the legislature. The Prison Act of 1865 included crank labor as a suitable kind of "first class" labor for convicts. It also endorsed a third form of punitive labor: the shot-drill.

The Shot-Drill

This punishment obviously originated with the armed services. Making a prisoner carry heavy cannon balls from one place to another could only have been invented in fortresses or bagnes. The manner in which it was administered at the Middlesex House of Correction in 1862 has been described as follows.

> This most peculiar exercise takes place in the vacant ground at the back of the prison, where an open space, some thirty feet square and about as large as a racket-court, has been set aside for the purpose. . . . Along three sides of this square were as many rows of large cannon balls, placed at regular distances, and at the two ends were piled up pyramids of shot. . . . The shot drill takes place every day at a quarter past three and continues until half past four. All prisoners sentenced to hard labour, and not specially excused by the surgeon, attend it. . . . Prisoners above forty-five years of age are generally excused, for the exercise is of the severest nature and none but the strongest can endure it. . . . The number of prisoners drilled at one time is fifty-seven. . . . The men are ranged so as to form three sides of a square and stand three deep, each prisoner being three yards distant from his fellow. . . . The exercise consists in passing the shot, composing the pyramids at one end of the line, down the entire length of the ranks, one after another, until they have all been handed along the file of men and piled up into similar pyramids at the other end of the line; and when that is done, the operation is reversed and the cannon balls passed back again. But what constitutes the chief labour of the drill is that every prisoner, at the word of command, has to bend down and carefully deposit the heavy shot in a particular place, and then, on another signal, to stoop a second time and raise it up. It is impossible to imagine anything more *ingeniously useless* than this form of hard labour.

Lifting up the cannon ball, each prisoner carried it sideways to the right three yards, deposited it, and returned to his original position ready to lift up the ball placed there by his neighbor on the left. The ball weighed twenty-four pounds.[47]

Oakum Picking

Picking oakum, which had always been a favorite occupation in the earliest bridewells, continued to be an important form of hard labor in the local prisons after 1865, especially since protests of manufacturers and their free workers had forced the legislature to curtail various profit-making enterprises in these institutions.

> The disagreeable and monotonous task of picking old rope to pieces, which needed no instruction, which might be imposed upon prisoners of any physical strength or mental capacity, which could be performed in silence in absolute cellular isolation, and which was rendered all the more "penal" in character because of its very unprofitableness, became under the Du Cane regime, after the hated treadwheel and crank, the favorite form of prison labor.[48]

The centralization of the prison system in 1877 brought all local prisons under the control of the Home Office, operating through a Prison Commission, chaired by Colonel Edmund Du Cane, a strict militarist who shared Sydney Smith's views on prison discipline. In 1951, Sir Lionel Fox, then occupying the same chair, wrote: "Our prisons for twenty years presented the pattern of deterrence by severity of punishment, uniformly, rigidly, and efficiently applied. For death itself, the system had substituted a living death. It became legendary . . . even in Russia."[49] Significant progress toward a more enlightened system was to be reserved for the twentieth century.

IX: PENAL SLAVERY IN RUSSIA

The peculiar character of Russian slavery and its imprint on the penal system that evolved in Russia were shaped by the vastness of the country, the composition of its population, its class structure, and its economic institutions. Elsewhere in Europe, the ancient type of chattel slavery gradually disappeared with the passage of time, but not in Russia, where initially such slavery played a relatively minor role. It gradually expanded until by the late eighteenth and early nineteenth centuries, Russia was the largest slave state in the western world.

It is claimed that in Kievian Russia of the ninth, tenth, and eleventh centuries, "the only bondsmen were . . . either foreigners captured in war or purchased or criminals deprived by law of citizenship, together with their descendants,"[1] but there were also other roads to slavery, because the first code of laws, the *Russkaya Pravda,* compiled during the rule of Yaroslav the Wise (1015–54), recognized three kinds of slaves: those who sold themselves into slavery; those who married female slaves and automatically became slaves of their wives' owners unless prior permission had been granted; and those who unconditionally accepted posts in the households of nobles.[2]

The lands of the princes and knights (boyars) were cultivated by indentured laborers who were free to leave the land when their terms of service expired, by free peasant sharecroppers who were in the majority, and by chattel slaves. Slavery, in its primitive form, did not actually disappear until the seventeenth century. Blum notes that

> of 5,615 homesteads listed in the cadaster of Tver for 1539–40, 9 per cent were those of slaves. . . . Slave labor was particularly important in the steppe. On many of the small [land grants held by nobles in return for military service] . . . of that zone, there were no peasants at all, but only slave workers. In one of the districts there, the proportion of slave homesteads in 1587–89 was 23.4 per cent; in another in 1587–89 it was 35 per cent, and in a third there were as many slave homesteads as there were of peasants.

In addition there were landless slaves who worked for their owners as artisans or field hands.[3]

Chattel slavery as a distinct legal institution was finally absorbed by another institution which had its roots in the Middle Ages and had grown to encompass all but a fraction of the population, namely serfdom, which gradually had reduced a largely free peasantry to the servitude that in the eighteenth century culminated in chattel slavery.

The erosion of the freedom of the poor became apparent in the twelfth century and took the form of debt slavery, for Vladimir, Prince of Kiev (1113–25), tried to "prevent enslavement of indentured laborers and other low-class workers caught in the financial web of landlords and money lenders."[4] Poverty and the exactions of landlords drove more and more peasants into dependency, a process speeded by rulers in need of military manpower. Tsar Ivan IV—the Terrible—intent on assuring the armed might of a strong autocratic state, reduced the boyars to vassals holding their lands in return for military service. They, with their peasants, were subject to a call to arms by the Tsar, and to facilitate this obligation, the freedom of movement of the peasants was curtailed. In 1580, the Tsar decreed that peasants could not exercise their traditional right to move except in years designated by him. During the next two decades about half of the years were so designated, but no proclamations were issued after 1603. Thenceforth the peasants were bound to the land. Their freedom had turned into serfdom. The serf who left his homestead without permission of his master became a fugitive from justice.[5]

During the rest of the century, the nobility increased its power. Its members occupied all military and civil administrative posts in state and local government, including the administration of justice. Coincidental with this was the further depression of the peasantry and the extension of serfdom. By the end of the seventeenth century, ninety per cent of the homesteads of Russia were occupied by serfs.[6]

The era of Peter the Great (1682–1725) saw significant changes in the status of the serfs and their masters. Instead of being bound to the land, as had been the serfs of western Europe, the Russian serfs were made the personal property of their masters, who could sell them like other chattel. In 1754, a provision in a proposed code stated that "the nobility has over its people and peasants, male and female, and over their property full authority without exception, save the taking of life and punishment with the knout and infliction of torture on them."[7] Catherine II—the Great—denied peasants the right to file complaints against their owners, and the Charter of Nobility of 1785 "implicitly recognized . . . [their] status as chattel slaves."[8] That status would remain substantially unchanged until 1861, when Alexander II emancipated them, except that the advertising of public auctioning of serfs and the splitting up of families had been prohibited. Shortly before the emancipation, official statistics recorded nearly eleven million serfs privately owned and nearly thirteen million "state peasants," whose status was almost as base as that of the privately owned serfs. These numbers refer only to registered males at a time (1858) when the total population of the empire, women and children included, was about seventy-four million.[9]

The earliest code of Kievian Russia, the *Russkaya Pravda,* was shaped by a ruling class whose Scandinavian ancestors saw the blood feud and indemnification as the proper means of dealing with interfamilial conflicts and injuries. With the code, society had advanced to a stage where the state had assumed the prerogative of dealing with criminals while relying on a system of fines and indemnities. It provided for neither capital or corporal punishment *except for slaves.* Such punishments were to be adopted in the fourteenth century under German and Mongol influence. The country had been conquered by Genghis Khan in the 1230s and remained under Mongol domination until the 1480s. And it was the Mongols who introduced judicial torture.[10]

Once freed from foreign control, the Russian realm was gradually extended, united, and brought under the rule of autocratic tsars supported by a landed aristocracy lording it over the mass of subject serfs. Judicial torture became standard procedure in the manorial and state courts. Beheading, hanging, impalement, burning, breaking on the wheel, and suspension by a hook anchored in the rib cage were favored methods of execution, and running the gauntlet and flogging by the knout often achieved the same ends, whether accidentally or deliberately.* Mutilating punishments and

---

*Running the gauntlet was used primarily in the armed services. The offender was forced to walk slowly between two long lines of men who, armed with rods, beat him on his bare back as he passed by. Abolished in 1845 as a primary punishment, it was retained in the code for crimes punishable by life-long penal servitude when committed by a convict already serving a life sentence in the mines. In that case the court was required to order the administration of from five thousand to six thousand blows. (*See* A. Solomon, *Rapport,* in *Actes du Congrès penitentiaire international de Rome.* 1885, II, 489–557, 519; George Ryley Scott, *The History of Corporal Punishment* [London: Torchstream Books, 1948], pp. 81–82.) "The punishment by the knout was an atrocious punishment of Tartar origin. Suffice it to say that one hour was required for administering twenty blows by the knout. The number of blows was not fixed by law, but was determined *by the court. Basically, the life or death of the condemned depended on the executioner" (Solomon, op. cit.,* p. 513n). On his visit to St. Petersburg in 1781, John Howard saw a man and woman suffer that punishment. Afterwards Howard was told by the executioner that he had been ordered to beat the man violently enough to cause his death, and that such orders were not unusual. (*See* John Howard, *The State of the Prisons* . . . [3d. ed.; 1784], p. 86, and James Baldwin Brown, *Memoirs of the Public and Private Life of John Howard, the Philanthropost* [London: 1818], p. 359). Howard described the knout as a whip "fixed to a wooden handle a foot long and consist[ing] of several thongs about two feet in length twisted together, by the end of which is fastened a single tough thong of a foot and a half, tapering toward a point and capable of being changed by the executioner when too much softened by the blood of the criminal." Abolished in 1845, the cat-o'nine-tails took its place.

penal labor on public works were introduced. Peter the Great's vast program for a strong navy gave rise to galley slavery in the eighteenth century; his construction of fortresses and fortifications on the borders, including his city of St. Petersburg, led to the use of convicts as forced laborers; and the need of the state for military and naval armaments and stores brought the rise of state factories employing convict labor. The exploitation of the state's rich gold, silver, copper, and iron mines in the Urals and in Siberia was heavily dependent on penal slave labor. In 1765, Catherine the Great gave the landholding nobles the right to sentence their serfs to lifelong penal slavery in Siberia, a right which they were to enjoy until 1802.[11] Since Peter the Great had begun to draft slaves and serfs into the army, even army service came to be used as a punishment by the gentry wishing to get rid of rebellious or work-shy serfs. At first army service was for life, and until the nineteenth century for at least twenty-five years. To the draftees and their families it seemed almost like a deferred death sentence. Until the emancipation, the army was composed of serfs and commanded by nobles, which may, in part, account for the ferocious discipline imposed on the soldiery.

In a society where less than two per cent of the population belonged to the privileged classes exempt from judicial torture and corporal punishment ("persons belonging to the nobility and the clergy, honorable citizens, and merchants of the two top guilds")[12] and where the mass of the population was in bondage, it is not surprising that penal slavery became the distinctive feature of the penal system. Siberia was to become its chief theater of operation; its annexation began when Boris Goudonov, in 1586, established fortresses at Tyumen and Tobolsk. In addition to political and religious dissidents exiled there to fend for themselves, and other obnoxious persons—vagrants, petty offenders, serfs expelled by their masters or village communes—to colonize the land under police surveillance, common criminals of the worst kinds were sent to slave in the mines. A part of this flow was due to judgments by state and manorial courts, but a large part resulted from the arbitrary decisions of police authorities without judicial intervention.

The government's desire to populate Siberia with Russians and its wish to exploit the area's natural resources, especially minerals, by convict labor had one interesting by-product—the disappearance of capital punishment except for treasonable crimes against the state. Empress Elizabeth (1741–61), against the advice of her councillors, abolished the death penalty for common-law offenses in 1744; no executions occurred during her reign. Catherine II (1762–96) reinstituted it for crimes against the security of the state (treason, violation of quarantine laws during pestilence epidemics, certain military crimes), which was not completely incompatible with her great admiration for Beccaria's arguments for abolition which she stated in identical terms in the famous instructions[13] that she began to compose in 1765 for the guidance of the recently appointed penal-code commission. Later rulers showed the same aversion to the death penalty. From 1796 to 1825, no capital sentences were passed by civil courts, though some were imposed by courts-martial. During the reign of Nicolas I (1825–56), the inept Decembrist coup by liberal young army officers in 1825 led to the hanging of 5 of the leaders originally sentenced to be quartered, but 116 were condemned to hard labor in Siberia, including 31 lifers whose death sentences had been commuted.[14] These offenders had threatened the security of the state, as did the Polish insurrectionists in 1830, of whom a score were executed. None of the rulers objected to the liberal use of the knout or the running of the gauntlet which so often resulted in the death of the victim.

The spirit of revolution hovered over nineteenth-century Russia. The lessons of the French Revolution, later political revolts in Europe, and the writings of foreign liberal philosophers and political pamphleteers were not without influence on the students and intellectuals of Russia. During the second half of the century, their growing opposition to autocracy found expression in clandestine societies, an underground press, and terrorism taking the form of the political assassination of high public officials, including that of Tsar Alexander II in 1881. Still, the policy of sending political offenders into Siberian exile and serious criminals to penal servitude persisted, and until the revolution of 1905 civil courts refrained from using capital punishment. That event brought the reintroduction of the penalty in 1906. By the end of 1909, there had been 2,825 executions, and in the year 1907 reaching a peak of 1,139.[15]

It would take more than a brief chapter to describe the complete evolution of Russia's penal system. Therefore, we shall focus attention on the elements which served to deal with felonious criminals condemned to penal servitude in Siberia. This punishment has usually been likened to England's transportation of criminals to Australia and France's to Guyana and New Caledonia, even though the Russian transportee never left the confines of his country. Placing this limit on our inquiry means that we can make only a few brief allusions to other aspects of the penal system, although some of them were, in fact, aimed at using the forced labor of offenders for the profit of the state.[16]

Two centuries would pass before Russia introduced the kind of houses of correction which England created in the last half of the sixteenth century. In 1775, Catherine II ordered each province to establish a bureau of public charities, which among other things was charged with setting up a house of correction for disorderly, dissolute, and idle persons committed there by courts, administrative authorities, or by the parents or masters of delinquents, for periods up to life. Except for the hours spent at meals or sleeping, inmates were to be put to work in the house. Each violation of rules would be punished by three lashes, three days' confinement at bread and water, or cellular isolation for a week. By 1816, twenty-six such houses were in use.

In 1783, the Empress also ordered the establishment of workhouses for thieves and defrauders whose crimes were responsible for a loss of at most twenty rubles. The length of imprisonment was correlated to the loss involved, and the inmate had to make good that loss and meet the cost of his maintenance by his labor. There were twenty-eight such houses in 1816. A plan for regulations governing all kinds of prisons was drafted by the Empress in 1787. One type of prison included in the plan would be a maximum security institution serving as a depot for criminals sentenced to penal slavery before they were sent to Siberia or to fortress prisons.

Deportation, or exile, to Siberia—not to be confused with transportation to penal slavery—began in the seventeenth century with the dual purpose of restricting the use of mutilating and capital punishments and of establishing colonies in that vast outpost of the empire. The latter aim was neglected during the reign of Peter the Great because he needed convict labor for the construction and servicing of the navy and the construction of ports and fortifications on the borders. His successors resumed the exiling of their offending subjects, many of whom were used in road-building and other public works. "Between 1761 and 1765," for instance, "thousands of exiles were sent to the steppe of Baraba to lay out roads between the towns of Tobolsk and Irkutsk, which previously communicated only by water. This enterprise cost the lives of a considerable part of the colonists worn out by labor often surprassing human strength."[17]

Numerous efforts were made during the nineteenth century to populate Siberia with exiles, but they failed, generally speaking, because of lack of financial support, the corruption of local officials, and the opposition of the growing free population victimized by criminal exiles. From 1807 to 1899, the deportees from European Russia totaled 864,549, including their families. In 1898, about 300,000 remained, half of whom under court sentences and the other half by executive order.*

_____

*Such orders originated with the political police which had existed in some form during most reigns, beginning with that of Ivan the Terrible. After the Decembrist revolt of 1825, it was organized as a division of the imperial chancellery, directly responsible to Tsar Nicholas I. The Third Department, with its corps of gendarmes and secret agents stationed in key cities, engaged

A third of this mass, 100,000 men, have escaped all control, the police not knowing their whereabouts. They are known, however, because they are the ones who rob on the highways and in the villages or beg or extort money from the natives by all manner of means. They hide in the Siberian forests, and in summer sleep under the open sky. In winter they enter the cities and use every means to get a berth in the local jails. Another third are also on the move, but change residence in search of work. If they have not lost the habit of industry and have retained remnants of honesty, they succeed, but otherwise they join the ranks of vagabond criminals. Of the remaining third, about 30,000 are farmers. . . . It is remarkable that this figure corresponds to the number of married deportees. The rest, or 70,000, are laborers. As long as they are young and healthy they earn their daily bread, but when infirmity comes many of them begin to beg and very often end their existence in a prison they had so far been able to avoid.

Deportees constituted five per cent of the population of Siberia, but fifty-eight per cent of the inmates of Siberian prisons.[18]

In 1900, deportation was partially abolished, to be replaced by imprisonment of from eight months to two years, or confinement in a workhouse of from one to six years. The law retained exile for political offenses and for offenses against the laws and the institutions of the Orthodox Church, but no longer limited the place of exile to Siberia. It also provided that vagrants (mostly escaped penal slaves) who refused to identify themselves would be transported to the penal colony on Sakhaline Island after serving four years in prison. The law did not abrogate transportation to hard labor, i.e., penal slavery.[19]

Toward the end of the eighteenth century a large number of prisoners were employed on construction in ports and fortifications. When John Howard visited Russia in 1781, he saw in the Peter and Paul fortress of St. Petersburg

twenty-five slaves with logs fastened to both their legs . . . [and] lodged in four rooms, which were . . . close and offensive. . . . At Cronstadt, the principal station for shipping, the slaves were lodged in several rooms enclosed by palisades, and guarded by an officer with a hundred soldiers, who attended them while at work . . . removing the ballast flung out of the ships. . . . The number of slaves, malefactors and debtors is in general about two hundred, but in November, 1781, their number was only one hundred and fifty-one, viz. slaves indebted to government and malefactors, thirty-four; debtors and peasants sent by their lords for crimes and misdemeanors on their estates, one hundred and seventeen.[20]

---

in many types of political surveillance. An order issued by the department "admitted of no protest, no defense and no appeal. . . . Persons guilty of nothing more than minor indiscretions of conduct were arrested, imprisoned and exiled" (P. S. Squire, The Third Department: The Political Police in the Russia of Nicholas I [Cambridge: University Press, 1968], pp. 227, 236). A map of the districts and station of the gendarmery is found in Martin Gilbert, Russian History Atlas (New York: Macmillan, 1972), p. 51.

Howard did not suggest that these prisoners were organized in companies, on military models, under naval command or the command of the corps of engineers. Nicholas I established such labor companies assigned to public works and under civilian direction. The criminal code of 1845 recognized two categories of prisoners in these companies: prisoners sentenced by the courts and those committed by executive order, such as serfs at the request of their masters. The prisoners received no wages, but might, upon their discharge, receive a bonus not to exceed one-sixth of the sum earned by their labor. They were not put to work Sundays and holidays; instead they had to attend religious services. After two years, prisoners of the first category, and after one year those of the second, could be promoted to a merit class wearing special dress and working separately, and have a third of their earnings placed in a savings account. Half of the savings was given them on discharge, the other half a year later by the police of the locality of their assigned residence. A kind of "good-time" law provided that ten months in the merit class counted for a year's service in the company. Besides disciplinary punishments, such as reprimand, two days in a dark cell, two to four days on bread and water, or up to thirty lashes, gross nonviolent refusal to obey orders could incur a hundred lashes, and shaving of half the head, and fettering. Each new application of these more serious punishments added six months to the term of the sentence.

Six months before the end of the prisoner's term, the chief of the company informed the provincial administration which, in turn, inquired if the prisoner's commune or master would accept him. If the reply was negative, an attempt was made to find a residence for him in a rural or urban commune in some province far from European Russia. If that failed, the prisoner was transported to hard labor in Siberia. All discharged prisoners were subject to four years of police surveillance and were forbidden to leave the locality assigned them without special authorization. They were not allowed to live in the capitals or chief cities of a province.

Labor companies were moved to wherever public works needed them. They were housed in local prisons, leased houses, or in temporary barracks raised at the work-site. In 1883, the maximum term of service was reduced to four years.

The nineteenth century saw the removal of corporal punishment from the criminal law. The code of 1832 still listed such punishments *for serfs and lower-class freemen.* Nobles, clergy, honorable citizens, and merchants belonging to the two top classes were exempt. Others might suffer the knout, whipping, birching, or running the gauntlet. The code of 1845 abolished the knout and, after the emancipation, Alexander II, in 1863, abolished branding, substituted whipping by the "cat" for the gauntlet for certain military offenses, and removed corporal punishments from the criminal code. Some of them remained in use, however, by the peasant courts in the villages and in disciplining the inmates of penal institutions.

Penal Slavery

As already noted, Siberia became the dumping ground for a variety of people whose conduct violated the law or was otherwise offensive to state or local authorities or owners of serfs. Some were sent away for five or more years, after which they might be allowed to return, but there were some who were condemned to spend their lives in the faraway parts of that vast land to which they had been assigned by the court that sentenced them for major crimes. They were the *kátorshniki* sentenced to hard labor, and the *poseléntsi* condemned to forced colonization. Both were by their sentences deprived of all civil rights. In the eyes of the law they were nonpersons; their property was distributed to their heirs; their wives could remarry since all family relations had been annulled by the sentences. It is the *kátorshniki* to whom special attention will be given in the following pages. *Katorga* was, next to death, the most severe punishment known to Russian law. It came into use during the reign of Peter the Great in the form of galley slavery, the construction of fortifications, and the extraction of precious metals, after the discovery in 1700 of the rich silver and gold deposits in eastern Siberia. Considering their legal status, one can fairly claim that the *kátorshniki* and the *poseléntsi* were slaves of the state—public slaves—as much as were the convicts sent to the bagnes of western Europe.

According to the penal code of 1845, *katorga* was imposed for terms of four years to life. If the offender did not belong to a social class exempt from branding and corporal punishment, he also was given from 30 to 100 strokes by the "cat" and the letters KAT were tattooed on his cheeks and forehead,* until these indignities were abolished after the emancipation. Both the severity of the beating and the length of the sentence depended on whether the offender was to be sent to labor in the crown factories, fortresses, or, most terrible of all, the mines.† A sentence to *katorga* was only the first stage of a

---

*The skin was punctured and gunpowder rubbed into the wound.
†Life at the fortress prison at Omsk was graphically described by Dostoevsky in his autobiographical novel *The House of the Dead*. Beginning in 1849, he spent four years there as a political prisoner serving a sentence to hard labor.

punishment which was lifelong but changed its character if the convict survived the initial term of confinement imposed by the court.

The first concern of the government was to transport the convict to the distant parts of Siberia where his punishment was to be executed. Thus arose a system similar in many respects to the "chain" France used to bring the galley slaves to Marseilles, but more dreadful because of the vast distances that had to be traversed and the much greater hardships caused by the severe subarctic climate. After 1858, when it was decided to send convicts from St. Petersburg to Moscow by rail, the prisoners had to walk from the latter city about forty-seven hundred miles to reach the mine fields east of Lake Baikal, and about fifty-two hundred to reach Yakutsk. Some possibly were destined for Verkhoyansk above the Arctic Circle and to Nizhni Kolymsk on the Arctic Coast, another fifteen hundred miles.[21] Even before he reached the place of his punishment, the convict might have spent from two to three painful years on the road and in filthy and overcrowded stations and forwarding prisons. The death toll was very high.

After the 1860s, the starting point for the "chain" was Tomsk, to which city the convicts had been brought in cattle cars by rail and in barges when feasible. The walking "chain" moved, by stages, from way station to way station. These stockaded depots, which had been erected in 1817, housed soldiers stationed there for the purpose of escorting the convicts from one point to the next. The distance between the stations was about fifteen miles, long enough for a day's trek by a "chain" of three to four hundred prisoners on muddy, slushy, or dusty roads, depending on season, weather, and wind. "The convicts wore irons: those condemned to hard labor wore them on hands and feet, the others only on their hands, but all were chained by couples and, in addition, each three couples were joined together by an iron bar, later replaced by a chain,"[22] which was discarded in 1881. The procession was led by the *kátorshniki*. Before it set out early in the morning, their leg fetters had been inspected by the blacksmith. Then came the *poseléntsi,* exiled for life, and the simple exiles who after a term of years could hope to return to their home communities and most of which had been banished by the police, not by court order. The marching party was completed by the women and children who had elected to follow their husbands and parents into exile, and wagons carrying baggage, the sick, and the infirm. Each third day was spent in rest at a way station.

"Chains" of hard labor convicts and penal colonists moved the year round, but from May to September the pressure on the transport system was greatest. It was then that the way stations and the great forwarding prisons of Tyumen, Tomsk, and Irkutsk were bursting with prisoners in transit. The Bureau of Exile Administration, the keeper of records of all categories of exiles was located in Tyumen. The prison had been built to accommodate 550 inmates and enlarged by means of barracks to hold 850. When George Kennan visited it in June, 1885, its inmates numbered 1,741. In the yard of the prison he noted a barrack, 35 by 25 by 12 feet, in which he found 160 men. Its walls were of hewn logs, its rough plank floor black with dried, encrusted filth.

Down the center of the room, and occupying about half its width, ran the sleeping bench—a wooden platform 12 feet wide and 30 feet long, supported at a height of two feet from the floor by stout posts. Each longitudinal half of this low platform sloped a little, roofwise, from the center, so that when the prisoners slept upon it in two closely packed transverse rows, their heads in the middle were a few inches higher than their feet at the edges. These sleeping platforms are known as *nári*, and a Siberian prison cell contains no other furniture whatever except a large wooden tub for excrement. The prisoners have neither pillows, blankets, nor bedclothes and must lie on these hard plank *nári* with no covering but their overcoats.

The room had air space for forty persons, and the "air was so poisoned and foul that I could hardly force myself to breathe it. . . . Scores of men slept every night on the foul, muddy floor, under the *nári* and in the gangways between them and the wall." [23] The main building had many cellrooms, the kitchen, workshops and a hospital. The cells varied in size from eight by ten to ten by fifteen feet and housed from a half dozen to thirty persons each. In one cell there were eight or ten nobles, and Kennan noted that in that cell the warden, who accompanied him, took off his hat, not the only sign that criminals or exiles from the privileged classes were treated with greater consideration. The workshops consisted of two small cells, 8 feet square. "In one, three or four convicts were engaged in cobbling shoes and in the other an attempt was being made to do a small amount of carpenters' work. The workmen . . . had neither proper tools nor suitable appliances." The basement kitchen was dark and dirty. A few men were boiling soup and baking black rye bread. The soup was good, the bread sour and heavy and of about the same quality as that eaten by peasants generally. The daily ration was a two and a half pound loaf of bread, six ounces of boiled meat, two or three ounces of coarsely ground barley or oats, and a bowl of *kvas* mornings and evenings. The hospital had several wards, somewhat lighter than the cellrooms, but wholly unventilated, no disinfectants apparently were used in them, and the air was polluted to the last possible degree. . . . In each ward were twelve or fifteen small iron bedsteads . . . each . . . furnished with a thin mattress consisting of a coarse gray bed-tick filled with straw, a single pillow, and either a gray blanket or a ragged quilt. . . . The most common disorders seemed to be scurvy, typhus fever, typhoid fever, acute bronchitis, rheumatism, and syphilis. Prisoners suffering from malignant typhus fever were isolated in a single ward.

But otherwise the sick were commingled except that women were separated from the men. The hazard to life which the transportation system presented may be seen from the fact that the hospital records of the Tyumen prison showed that between 1876 and 1887, the annual death rate varied between 23.8 and 44.2 per cent; in 1884 it was 29.5 per cent, and in 1885, 23.1 per cent.[24] Kennan thought the Tomsk prison even worse in every respect, and in the Irkutsk prison, built in 1861 to house 450 prisoners, he learned that the inmate population often rose to 1,500 and even 2,000.

Kennan graphically described the enormous hardships suffered by prisoners on the march for years—the verminous, run-down, overcrowded way stations with their sleeping platforms pre-empted by the strongest, the meager rations, the harsh discipline. Finally, the chain would reach its ultimate destination, which for the *kátorshniki* would most likely be the mining districts of Kará and Nérshinsk east of Lake Baikal. They were the property of the Imperial family.

The Kará mines consisted of "a series of open gold placers situated at irregular intervals along a small rapid stream called the Kará River" but the name Kará was applied "to the whole chain of prisons, mines and convict settlements that lie scattered through the Kará valley."[27] They included five prisons administered by a governor with headquarters in one of them, and two prisons for "political" convicts, administered by a state police officer reporting directly to St. Petersburg. Guards were supplied by a Cossack battalion stationed in the area. At the time of Kennan's visit there were about eighteen hundred convicts, half of whom were housed in the prisons; the rest were living close by. This arrangement evolved from the manner in which sentences to penal servitude were served.

As mentioned earlier, such sentences ranged from four years to life. The first part of the sentence was spent in close confinement lasting one year for those with terms of from four to six years, up to eight years for those with sentences twenty years or longer, and lifers. In-between, the period varied from one and a half to five years, depending on the length of the sentence. The convict was labelled a "probationer." At the end of this period, a convict who had behaved himself was promoted to a "reform" class, and after one to three years discharged and sent to eastern Siberia for the rest of his life as a forced colonist under police surveillance. Those in the "reform" class wore no irons, worked apart from the "probationers," and could be supervised by foremen instead of by the military. They had a few more rest days annually, could live in barracks with other persons of their class and even in a home of their own with their family. In exceptional cases, they might be allowed to settle close to the factories or mines where they had worked instead of being sent off to distant parts.

The rule of silence and the practice of shaving half the head of the convict were not abolished until 1901. Discipline was harsh. As late as 1905, lifers who erred might be "fastened to a small miner's wheelbarrow by a chain attached generally to the middle link of his leg-fetter. This chain is long enough to give him some freedom of movement, but he cannot walk for exercise nor cross his cell without trundling his wheelbarrow before him. Even when he lies down to sleep, the wheelbarrow remains attached to his feet." [26] According to a circular of 1908, lifers could be disciplined by solitary confinement for up to twenty days, others for up to ten days or up to a hundred blows by a rod and have their terms extended by one to two years. Probationers might be made to stay a year longer in their class and again put in irons. Those in the reform class might be given a year, a prolongation in that class, put in fetters for weeks or months, or for a year if the offender was under a life sentence. Those allowed to live outside the prison might be reincarcerated for a year.[27]

The convicts at work in the gold placers labored from 7 A.M. to 5 P.M. in the winter and from 5 A.M. to 7 P.M. in the summer.

[Because] the auriferous sand in the valley of the Kará lies buried under a stratum of clay, gravel, or stones, varying in thickness from ten to twenty feet, the hard labor of the convicts consists in the breaking up and removal of this overlying stratum and the transportation of the "pay gravel" or gold-bearing sand to the "machine," where it is agitated with water in a sort of huge iron hopper.[28]

The Nerchinsk silver-mining district was "scattered over a wild, desolate, mountainous region, thousands of square miles in extent, bordering on Mongolia." Discovered in 1700, "by the end of the century nine shafts had been sunk in more than twenty places and eight smelting furnaces had been established." Hard labor convicts began to be sent there in 1722.[29] At the time of Kennan's visit about nine hundred and fifty convicts were at the mines, half of them idle; the rest were working with primitive tools in deep, poorly ventilated shafts trying to complete the daily task imposed on them. Those not working were confined in overcrowded, verminous, unsanitary prisons which Kennan found to be so repulsive that he concluded that "the worst feature of penal servitude in Siberia is not hard labor in the mines; it is the condition of the prisons."[30]

The abolition of serfdom deprived noble landowners of their disciplinary power over the former serfs, and the abolition of corporal punishment shortly thereafter compelled the government to rely chiefly on imprisonment in dealing with offenders. Old government buildings in many Russian cities were converted into central congregate prisons where overcrowding soon made it necessary to use rooms intended for workshops as dormitories. Even convicts sentenced to penal servitude found themselves kept in these prisons in chains and with half-shaved heads but without occupation, because they could not all be sent off to Siberia where there was no work for them because the penal servitude system was showing signs of breaking down. The productivity of the crown mines and factories was declining, leaving many convicts idle. Some of the factories and gold placers were sold to private firms who for years were allowed to use convict labor. Those still operated by the Crown were managed by the Ministry of Finance and the Imperial chancellery and run by people more interested in getting convicts to work willingly and well than in making their punishment harsh and feared. Discipline had become so lax that men committed to labor companies in European Russia committed new crimes in order to be sent to penal servitude in Siberia.[31]

To remedy this situation, commissions were appointed to find a solution. It was decided to ship eight hundred convicts from eastern Siberia to the Sakhaline Island to work in its coal mines, build roads, clear forests, and work in agriculture. This was accomplished in 1869. Three years later an order was issued to rehabilitate the Nerchinsk mines and construct prisons near them.[32] From then on, the hard-labor convicts who could be absorbed in Siberia were sent either to Sakhaline or the Transbaikal mines.[33] The rest remained in the central prisons in idleness until they had served their "probationary" period and could be sent east as forced colonists.

The revolutionary activity in Russia in the 1870s, which in 1881 culminated in the assassination of Alexander II, and the severe repression that followed, greatly increased the number of sentences to penal servitude.

The hard labor cases [wrote Kropotkin] are provided for in 17 central prisons. Of these there are seven in Russia with accommodation for 2,745; three in Western Siberia with accommodation for 1,150; two in Eastern Siberia with accommodation for 1,650; and one on Sakhaline with accommodation for 600 (1,103 inmates in 1879; 802 on January 1, 1884). Other hard labor convicts—10,424 in number—are distributed among the government mines, gold-washings and factories in Siberia;

namely at the Kará gold-washings, where there are 2,000; at the Troitsky, Ust-Kut and Irkutsk salt works, at the Nikolayevsk and Petrovsk iron-works, at a prison at the former silver-works of Akatui and one on Sakhaline island.[34]

More and more penal slaves were sent to the island. More than fifty-five hundred were confined there in 1889,[35] but that penal colony was closed in 1906 by the Tsar, because after Russia's defeat a year earlier by Japan, the southern half of the island had been annexed by the victor.

The year 1905 also witnessed a widespread revolution in Russia; it was subdued but for years to come resulted in an increase in sentences to penal servitude. At the beginning of 1909 there were 6,143 hard-labor convicts in the Siberian mines and central prisons. Of these, 433 were lifers; 229 had sentences of 20 years or longer; most were serving terms of 12 years or less. Among them were 2,054 homicides, 861 robbers, 513 condemned for aggravated assault, and 584 "state criminals," i.e., political offenders. "Privileged" social classes contributed 109 convicts.[36] Soon the outbreak of World War I and the subsequent revolutions of 1917, which ended in the establishment of a Communist state, would raise penal servitude to a level not rivaled by any tsarist government. Only the bare outline of the story of that development can be given here.

In Soviet Russia

The penal system that gradually emerged in Soviet Russia after the October revolution was meant by its creators to be radically different from its predecessor, but its aim and function were basically the same. The tacit purpose of the tsarist penal code had been to safeguard the interests of the politically dominant upper classes. The early penal codes of the Communist state (1922 and 1926) frankly proclaimed that they were designed to protect the interests of the now politically dominant proletariat of workers and peasants. In order to achieve the construction of the classless socialist state envisaged by the Communist Party, which regarded itself as the custodian and tutor of the proletariat, those who did not share this vision had to be rendered harmless. Therefore, a strong police force, revolutionary tribunals, and penal measures were needed. Most of these agencies were imitations or adaptations of tsarist institutions. The All-Russian Extraordinary Commission—the *Cheka*—set up two months after the revolution, replaced the tsarist *Okhrana*, or political police and gendarmery. Exile and forced settlement in Siberia and penal servitude remained the prime means of dealing with political opponents and incorrigible criminals.

Thus arose a repressive system designed to eliminate elements which by word or deed endangered the security of the new order or who likewise were "enemies of the people" because they did not belong to the working class—the nobility, the tsarist bureaucracy, the clergy, big landowners, manufacturers and merchants, and the intelligentsia. During the early years of the "Red Terror,"* the police summarily shot tens of thousands of them and dispatched many more, with or without trial, to concentration camps,† which for decades to come would provide significant manpower for the drive to industrialize the nation and also successfully liquidate a large number of their inmates who were unable to bear the harsh living and working conditions near or above the Arctic Circle where most of the camps were located.

Most acts ending in commitments to concentration camps were counter-revolutionary crimes. The 1926 penal code (Art. 46) divided all crimes into those "directed against the foundations of the soviet regime established in the Union of Soviet Socialist Republics by the power of workers and peasants, and therefore declared to be most dangerous," and "all other crimes." The latter class included crimes against persons and property which did not strike at the foundation of the Soviet regime, i.e., most homicides, assaults, rapes, robberies, burglaries, thefts, disorderly conduct, and the like. The offenders were mostly workers and peasants who were believed to have been driven to crime by poverty, ignorance, or the survival of capitalist notions. The penal law dealt gently with these criminals. Thus, for instance, the 1926 code provided a maximum term of ten years for aggravated murder.[37]

The institutions created by the state to treat plebeian criminals were regulated by the Corrective Labor Codes of 1924 and 1933 which provided for a variety of more or less open agricultural, workshop, and factory colonies or communes and institutions for "strict confinement." The basic aim of all these institutions was to give the inmates vocational training and cultural education and make them good citizens fit to participate in the communal life

---

*"We are no longer waging war against separate individuals, we are exterminating the bourgeoisie as a class. Do not seek in the dossier of the accused for proofs as to whether or not he opposed the Soviet government by word or deed. The first question that should be put is to what class he belongs, of what extraction, what education and profession. These questions should decide the fate of the accused. Herein lies the meaning and the essence of the Red Terror." (Statement by a high official of the Cheka, in *Pravda*, December 25, 1918, cited by Karel Hulicka and Irene M. Hulicka, *Soviet Institutions, the Individual and Society* [Boston, Christopher Publishing House, 1967], p. 281; Robert Conquest [ed.], *The Soviet Police System* [New York: Praeger, 1968], p. 42; A. I. Solzhenitsyn, *The Gulag Archipelago I-II* [New York: Harper and Row, 1973], pp. 96–97.)

†Such camps were first mentioned in a decree of September 5, 1918, which stated that the protection of the Russian Soviet Republic from class enemies required their isolation in concentrations camps. (Conquest, *op. cit.* p. 77.)

and enterprises of the communist state. In the process, inmates of working-class origin were given preferential treatment as required by the codes.[38]

Before World War II and the subsequent cold war shut the Soviet frontiers for years to come, foreign visiting specialists from the Western world were greatly impressed by what they saw of these institutions. Remarkable colonies for young offenders—Bolshevo, for instance*—the programs of training and education in other colonies, the research institutes, and the experimental prison of Moscow led them to believe that Soviet Russia was an innovator in the realm of correctional administration.[39] They would have been rudely shocked if they had been allowed to inspect the concentration or "corrective labor" camps where the old tsarist penal slavery, or *katorga,* flourished in practice if not always in name.

Established by the *Cheka* in 1919 near Archangelsk and on the Solovetsky Islands in the White Sea for the purpose of putting some thousands of members of political parties opposed to the Bolshevik regime behind barbed wire, the number of corrective-labor camps rapidly increased to accommodate the constant stream of white-collar middle- and upper-class persons, whose existence was seen as a threat to the new society, and the real, suspected, or imaginary counterrevolutionaries, herded into the camps by the courts, or by the police without trial. By 1930, the "Northern Forced Labor Camps for Special Assignment," a state police organ, included seven camp establishments with a total inmate population of 662,000,[40] chiefly counter-revolutionaries and an admixture of common-law criminals committed for terms of five or more years; the Corrective Labor Code of 1924 applied only to those serving shorter terms in the labor colonies. Camps were constructed north of the Urals, especially in the inhospitable Arctic zone of Siberia, to receive the mounting waves of prisoners—prosperous peasants (kulaks) who resisted the government's decision to collectivize farms; the victims of the massive purges of the late 1930s; unreliable or antagonistic elements of the population of areas annexed during or after the war in the 1940s; citizens from the areas previously under German occupation and charged with collaboration with the enemy; soldiers returning from captivity and accused of desertion, etc. Before Stalin's death, in 1953, millions had entered the camps, nearly all males. Estimates vary from three and a half to seven or more millions.[41] By comparison, the number of prisoners sentenced to hard labor in 1913 was 32,757, including about 5,000 politicals.[42]

---

*Paradoxical as it may seem, this colony, the first of its kind, was founded in 1924 by Yagoda, the dreaded chief of the Cheka, who was genuinely concerned with the welfare of delinquent children and youths. (*See* Mary Stevenson Calcott, *Russian Justice* [New York: Macmillan, 1935], p. 220; William Reswick, *I Dreamt Revolution*[Chicago: Henry Regnery & Co., 1952], p. 106.)

The camp system was regulated by a statute of 1930[43] and managed by the Chief Administration for Corrective Labor Camps (GULAG), a division of the Unified State Political Administration—i.e., the political police—until 1934, when GULAG was transferred to the Union's Commissariat of Internal Affairs. The camps were scattered over several immense territories or zones[44] each containing from a few thousand to tens of thousands of inmates. Those of the Siberian North East Zone, with headquarters at Magadan on the Sea of Okhotsk, had a total population of half a million in 1935, and over three million five years later.* Altogether, the camps contained a formidable labor force which from 1928 on became an important instrument in meeting the goals of the successive Five-Year Plans designed to make the Soviet Union a great industrial power. The camps supplied manual labor for the construction of the White Sea–Baltic and Volga-Moscow canals and of railways, like the Kotlas-Vorkuta line. Prisoners built highways, barracks, cut timber, mined ores (gold, chromium, etc.) and coal, produced oil and cement, and labored in fisheries on the Arctic coast, rivers, and islands, all at a heavy cost in lives. It is claimed that of more than 200,000 who worked on the 142-mile long White Sea canal, over 50,000 died in a year and a half.[45] According to one author, "it is calculated that on the railways every sleeper cost one dead man and that in the mines there were two dead men for every yard dug underground.[46] Long work days, inadequate clothing, food, and health care, and the harsh and often brutal discipline combined to produce the very high death and morbidity rates described in the writings of inmates who survived their sentences (in 1937 the maximum sentence was raised from ten to twenty-five years).† It is evident from such documents that the *katorga* of tsarist days which George Kennan had so graphically described half a century earlier was practiced in the camps before it was formally legalized in 1943 and specifically applied to "collaborators with the enemy"‡

---

*(Barton, *op. cit.,* pp. 52–53). Vorkuta, a camp zone, "was a complex of camps north of the Arctic Circle on the boundary between Europe and Asia. There were 105,000 prisoners [in 1953] distributed among thirty camps of about 3,500 men each; most of them worked in the mines that supplied the coal for Leningrad" (Roland Gaucher, *Opposition in the USSR, 1917–1967* [New York: Funk and Wagnalls, 1969], p. 397).

†Autobiographical or eye-witness accounts of life in the camps proliferated after Stalin's death, as seen from the bibliography in Barton, *op. cit.* A recent example is Alexander Dolgun, with Patrick Watson, *Alexander Dolgun's Story: An American in the Gulag* (New York: Knopf, 1975). The most famous is *One Day in the Life of Ivan Denisovich* by A. Solzhenitsyn, who spent eight years in camps in the Arctic and Karaganda zones. A good account of the camp system is found in Barton's work, and a graphic presentation in Solzhenitsyn's *The Gulag Archipelago, III-IV* (New York: Harper and Row, 1975).

‡"On April 19, 1943, the Presidium of the Supreme Soviet decreed that collaborators with Germany may be sentenced to death by hanging (this too was a restoration of pre-revolutionary law, since only death by shooting had been permitted since 1917), or, in lesser cases, to exile to katorga for

and in practice to major common-law recidivists. The *katorgists* wore chains while in transport. Known only by a number and letter sewn to their caps and clothing, they were assigned to the hardest labor. In the mines they worked in the deepest pits and for longer hours. Their work done, they were confined in barrack dormitories, except at mealtime. They slept in their work clothes on plank bedsteads without mattress and covers. If they behaved well for three years, they gained a right to a coverlet. They were supposed to be totally isolated from other prisoners and have no contacts with the outside world.[47]

The gradual transformation of the camps and their ultimate absorption into the corrective labor colony system began in the late 1940s and was hastened by the death of Stalin, March 5, 1953, ending a bloody dictatorship. Three weeks after his death "the Presidium of the Supreme Soviet decreed an important amnesty giving immediate freedom to all sentenced to less than five years imprisonment . . . all condemned for administrative or economic crimes regardless of the length of sentence, certain military offenders" and some other categories of prisoners such as pregnant women, women with very young children, women above fifty, and men above fifty-five years of age, and the incurably ill. "However, the amnesty did not apply to 'persons sentenced to five or more years as counter-revolutionaries or guilty of grand theft of socialist property, banditry, or murder.' "[48] This and the repatriation of prisoners of war from the camps greatly reduced the population of the institutions. The following year, a decree reduced many sentences by from two-thirds to one-third. The most important decree was that of September 18, 1955, which amnestied all "collaborators with the enemy." In 1956, military personnel charged with surrendering to the enemy were also amnestied.[49] The same year, the camps were officially abolished and the Soviet Union began a return to a somewhat more conventional system of forced labor in dealing with "socially dangerous" offenders. One may assume that the widespread and large-scale strikes and revolts* by the inmates of the camps at Vorkuta, Norilsk, and elsewhere after the announcement of the 1953 decree may have played some role in producing this change of penal policy, but other circumstances probably played a great-

---

fifteen to twenty years. . . . The reform completed the reversion to old Russia in the terminology of penal law" (David Dallin and B. Nicolaevsky, *Forced Labor in Soviet Russia* [New Haven: Yale University Press, 1947], p. 275; V. Gsovski and K. Grzybovski, *Government, Law and Courts in the Soviet Union and Eastern Europe* [2 vols.; New York: Praeger, 1959], p. 931).

*These events were apparently triggered by the government's amnesty policy by which common criminals but not political offenders were pardoned (Gaucher, *op. cit.,* chapt. 23.) But judging from the detailed account of the Norilsk strike (Barton, *op. cit.,* pp. 467–83), the convicts had many other grievances.

er role. More and more of the labor formerly done in the camps was being performed by discharged convicts forced by law or poverty to settle and accept jobs within the camp zones, or by free citizens enticed by high wages or practically drafted by the government.* Convict labor in the camp zones no longer played a dominant role.

With the incorporation of the camps into the corrective-labor colony system, all sentences, regardless of length, were to be served in colonies. The criminal code of 1960 reduced the maximum of such sentences from twenty-five to fifteen years. Colonies of different types and different regimes were called for and, since history demonstrates that penal systems are hidebound and evolve at a snail's pace, we may assume that the colonies with "punitive" and "strict" regimes have not rid themselves of all the abuses and repressions that characterized the old camps.†

---

*After the 1953 amnesty, the population of Norilsk city and surrounding country consisted of 45,000 prisoners, 225,000 discharged prisoners, 15,000 functionaries, and 60,000 immigrants. It was estimated that the population of the Vorkuta region was composed of 105,000 prisoners, 120,000 discharged prisoners, and 12,000 guards, administrators, and technicians. (Barton, *op. cit.*, pp. 368–69.) One is tempted to assume that the present population of distant inhospitable regions of Siberia consists largely of former prisoners, mostly politicals, and their families.
†Evidence supporting this assumption is found in Anatoly Marchenko's memoirs of his stay in Mordovian camps and the Vladimir prison in 1961–66. (*See* his "My Testimony: Soviet Prison Camps Today," *Reader's Digest,* No. 48 [August, 1969], pp. 195–232.)

X: THE ANTEBELLUM SOUTH

By the time the discovery of America opened the continent to colonization, ancient domestic punishments originally reserved for slaves had long been accepted in Europe as appropriate legal punishments for criminals generally, unless they belonged to privileged classes exempt from the infamizing punishments thought proper for persons of low status. It was only natural that those who established settlements in the New World would bring with them not only their possessions and skills, but also their social and legal institutions, including the traditional penal methods of their homelands— Spain, Portugal, France, and England. Old World notions of criminal justice were thus transplanted together with all their implements—the whipping post, the stocks, the pillory, the stake, the wheel, the gallows, the gibbet, the branding iron, and instruments of torture and mutilation.[1] In the seventeenth century British colonists introduced them into what is now the United States, and the survival of some of them into the mid-twentieth century—the whipping post and the gallows, for instance—shows the power they have held over the minds of men. Once settled, these colonists even revived a punishment long since abandoned in their mother country—penal slavery—and fashioned a social institution which would put an indelible stamp on the penal systems of later centuries. That institution was chattel slavery, an outgrowth of servitude by indenture.[2]

The indentured servant, in part, filled the need of the colonists for manpower to aid them in their labors and free them from menial tasks. Usually, the potential servant was brought over by some enterprising ship's captain who furnished free ocean passage on condition that he could defray his cost by selling him or her to a colonist who, in turn, would be compensated by the labor of the servant during a period ranging from four to seven years, or even longer in the case of a child. This "labor contract" was known as the indenture.

During that "contract" period, servants could be sold or given to other masters. They had no control over how they would be treated. Theirs was a life not unlike that of a slave, and at times perhaps even worse, since once they reached the end of their term of servitude and were free, their masters were no longer responsible for their welfare.[3]

It is possible that the first blacks brought to Virginia in 1619 were treated like indentured servants, but soon the Negroes who followed them became transformed into the property, real or personal,* of their masters. It is evident from records of Maryland and Virginia that after 1640, blacks were being sold into lifelong slavery and that children born to them became slaves.[4] Thus, chattel slavery became entrenched in the colonies and flourished especially in the South, where the master class of tobacco, rice, sugar, and cotton planters found slave labor an invaluable, unequaled source of profit. By 1790, when the first national census was taken, Virginia had 292,627 slaves, South Carolina, 107,034, Maryland 103,036, and North Carolina 100,572. Seventy years later, on the eve of the Civil War, there were almost 4 million black slaves in the United States, all but 115,000 in the South, with Virginia in the lead with 491,000, closely followed by Alabama, Georgia, Mississippi, and South Carolina, with from 402,000 to 462,000 slaves each. In Mississippi and South Carolina, slaves constituted 55.1 and 57.2 per cent of the population, respectively.[5] The liberation of these blacks, formerly the private property of their masters and as such legally on a par with domestic draft animals, produced penal systems in the South that perpetuated the worst features of slavery.

The treatment of slaves by their masters or overseers has often been described as harsh, even brutal, but there were also lenient masters and well-treated slaves. On the large plantations where hundreds of field hands were forced to work under the whip of drivers, the life of the slave was usually hard, but in families owning only a few domestic servants, his life in the main was probably tolerable. Here we are concerned with only one aspect of his treatment, namely the punishment awaiting him if he incurred the wrath of his master and exposed himself to domestic discipline, or if he committed a crime punishable by law which might bring him to the attention of the courts. Both the culprit's status as chattel lacking personal rights, and as a being whose color marked him as a member of what was generally believed to be an inferior race, "born for slavery," influenced the nature of his punishment.

Domestic Discipline

Bondage could not extinguish aspirations, feelings, passions, and desires of the slaves. Some would steal, assault overseers, drivers, each other, and even their masters, shirk tasks, disobey orders, run away, or violate some

---

*"Slaves had the attributes of personal property everywhere, except in Louisiana (and Kentucky before 1852), where they had the attributes of real estate. . . . In states where slaves were

other rule governing their conduct. Unless such offenses seriously affected outsiders, they were dealt with by the master, whose disciplinary power over his slaves was virtually unlimited. Even the use of deadly force was usually tolerated. In Virginia, the Assembly in 1669 stipulated that if a slave were to die as a result of the "correction" applied to him, no felony had been committed "since it cannot be presumed that prepensed malice (which alone markes murther a felony) should induce any man to destroy his own estate." [6] An act of 1705 did forbid "immoderate correction" resulting in the slave's death, but unless "a lawful and credible witness" would testify on his oath that the slave was "wilfully, maliciously or designedly" killed, no felony had been committed. If a prosecution for the murder of a slave ended in a conviction for manslaughter, an act of 1723 provided that no penalty would be imposed.[7] Since slaves could not testify against a white defendant, and judges and jurors were themselves slave-owners, it was rare indeed to find a master convicted of murdering his slave. In 1739 and 1775 instances were recorded of masters being hanged for such offenses,[8] and it must be assumed that their crimes had been uncommonly outrageous.

The summary justice meted out to the slave is best illustrated by the practice on the large plantations which employed hundreds of slaves. The punishments inflicted by the slave-owner were mostly those in current use by the criminal courts—the whip, the stocks, the pillory, the brand, mutilation, jail—and they would survive as slave punishments until the Civil War, even after they had begun to disappear from the criminal law in the early part of the nineteenth century. The rawhide whip, which might be said to symbolize the power of the master, was used not only as a goad to speed the labor of field hands, but also as the most common penal instrument. Most plantations had stocks and pillories for confining runaway slaves when they were not at work chained by twos or with leg fetters. Such rebels against the master's authority might also be made to wear curious devices unknown to criminal law, such as buck's horns fastened to a neck collar, iron clamps and rods which prevented the slave from flexing his legs, or iron bands around waist and neck connected at the back with a metal rod projecting high above the head and with a cow bell on its curved end. Even the *furca* carried by offending slaves on the plantations of ancient Rome, was in use. It consisted of a pole about three inches thick and long enough so that when the center of it was attached to a neck ring, the culprit's wrists could be bound to its ends.[9]

---

generally considered as personality, they were treated as realty for purposes of inheritance. In Louisiana, where they were supposedly like real property, they retained many of the characteristics of 'chattel personal' " (Kenneth M. Stampp, *The Peculiar Institution*. [New York: Vintage Books, 1956], p. 197).

Some large plantations also had jails, reminiscent of the ancient Roman *ergastulum.* One such jail has been preserved on the Yellow Bayou Plantation in Chicot County, Arkansas, and may have served to confine both offending slaves of the plantation and those from neighboring ones.

[It] is about thirty-two feet long by twenty-four feet wide, constructed of six-inch-square rough-sawed oak timbers notched at the corners and fastened together with large iron spikes. Interior partitions and ceilings are of the same construction. There are four compartments in the jail: two small cells at one end, a narrow entrance hall running the width of the building in the center, and a large cell at the other end. The interior subdivision evidently was to permit segregation of male and female slaves, and also to provide a place for the guard. Small, square windows between the center hall and each of the cells permitted passage of food and water without opening the cell doors. Each cell has iron rings fastened to the walls for use in chaining prisoners. The few small exterior windows are double iron-barred, one set of bars recessed into the logs and the other bolted to the outside; the wooden-barred entrance door is also double, giving greater security.*

The Offending Slave and the Law

Slave-owners dominated the legislative assemblies in the South. They legitimized their domestic disciplinary powers and protected their property rights by law. They made crimes by slaves subject to public punishments not applicable to whites, and they ensured that slaves would find it difficult to defend themselves against accusations brought by whites and impossible to appear as witnesses against whites charged with crime. They created special courts to deal with slaves whom they could not, or preferred not to, punish by domestic discipline. Composed of county justices and, sometimes, slave-owning assessors, these courts, acting without a jury, dispensed summary and speedy justice, even in capital cases, before the nineteenth century, when regular courts gradually were given jurisdiction over such cases—in Georgia as late as 1850.

For misdemeanors and in some states for crimes not punished capitally, the summary processes of "Negro courts" survived until the abolition of slavery. Louisiana tried slaves for non-capital felonies before one justice and four slaveholders, Mis-

---

*(Orville W. Taylor, *Negro Slavery in Arkansas* [Durham: Duke University Press, 1958], p. 212.) Whitelaw Reid saw the slave jail on the Mississippi plantation of Jefferson Davis: "A band of iron, four inches wide and half an inch thick, with a heavy chain attached, was one of the relics found in the house. It had been used for the most troublesome slaves. During the day they had to wear it in the fields; at night a padlock secured it to a staple in the wall of the jail" (*After the War; a Tour of the Southern States, 1965–1966* [New York: Harper and Row, 1965; reprint of 1866 ed.], p. 283).

sissippi before two justices and five slaveholders, and Georgia before three justices. Alabama tried slaves for minor offenses before a justice (who could assign a maximum penalty of thirty-nine lashes), and for non-capital felonies before the judge of the probate court and two justices of the peace. The states of the Upper South generally subjected slaves accused of misdemeanors to similar informal and summary trials.[10]

The protection of the public required that both slaves and freemen suffer punishments for their crimes, but slaveholding legislators did not find the traditional criminal law adequate; it was made for freemen. Slave-owners needed laws assuring the help of public law-enforcement agencies in keeping the slave-labor force intact and docile on the one hand, and, on the other, terrify it by punishments harsher than those applied to freemen and befitting "social outcasts of an inferior breed." Such supplementary laws were, of course, adopted, and as the slave population grew and slavery became diversified—slaves being leased to or owned by factories, mining operators, railroad and canal corporations, etc.—they multiplied, especially after 1831, when the slave rebellion led by Nat Turner and the intensification of Northern abolitionist propaganda added to the fears of the master class. Altogether, they formed the South's "black codes," which were largely similar because the nature of chattel slavery gave rise to identical problems everywhere. Slaves were forbidden to leave the plantation without a pass; they had to be in their quarters by a certain hour at night, usually nine o'clock. If more than five gathered together away from home without a white man present they were guilty of illegal assembly. They could not own firearms or animals, buy liquor, trade or gamble, give medication to a white, work in drug stores or printing shops, etc.[11] The runaway slave who figuratively stole himself from his master faced a bleak future. As early as 1705, Virginia outlawed him; he could be killed with impunity. If recaptured alive, the county court for slaves could order him punished "either by dismembering [castration] or any other way [e.g., amputation of foot], not touching his life, as they in their discretion shall think fit, for the reclaiming any such incorrigible slave, and terrifying others from the like practices." [12] After 1769, castration was reserved for the slave "convicted of an attempt to ravish a white women." [13]

As noted earlier, a slave charged with crime was prosecuted in a special court and denied the trial by jury to which freemen were entitled. Judged by members of the master class whose decision was final, he was defenseless. The punishment meted out to him was more severe than that given whites. Because he owned nothing, death or corporal punishments were usually his fate. Whipping, from time immemorial considered proper for slaves, was the most common penalty, but death awaited him for many offenses which in the case of whites were punished less severely. Slaves were executed for criminal homicide, regardless of its degree; whites only for murder. Before the Emancipation, Virginia, for instance, decreed penitentiary sentences, varying from minima of six months, one, two, five, or ten years, to maxima of four, ten, twenty or twenty-one years for whites, but death for slaves convicted of one of a dozen or more felonies, from rape to knowingly buying or receiving a stolen horse.[14] To induce respect for masters and whites in general, a slave was killed if convicted for the third time of striking a white, and if, forgetting his lowly status, he "struck his master, a member of the master's family, or the overseer, 'so as to cause a contusion, or effusion or shedding of blood.' " [15] This was Louisiana law. These are merely samples; similar and often identical provisions were found in the laws of other states of the South.

This penal system, devised by slave-owning legislators, met their needs. It was administered by county and local authorities—judicial and police—which imposed and executed the punishments. If a slave was hanged, his owner was compensated from public funds for his loss of property. If he was corporally punished, he was promptly returned to his owner. So far as blacks were concerned, the local jail was a place for their detention before trial, or to house runaway slaves until their owners could be located, failing which the runaway could be sold. Imprisonment was not a suitable punishment because it would have deprived the owner of the labor of his slave.

The Penitentiary Movement

Before the Revolution, capital, corporal, and monetary punishments were commonly invoked for crimes committed by members of the master class, which even the lowliest whites in the South felt part of; but before the end of the century a radical innovation began to change this penal system. It was stimulated by Cesare Beccaria's famous tract *Of Crimes and Punishments,* published in 1764, and by the writings of the libertarian philosophers of France and England who shared his views. Beccaria advocated the abolition of the death penalty and the substitution of life imprisonment at hard labor. Indeed, imprisonment would not only be a fitting punishment for all who treasured freedom but one which, better than any other could be proportioned to the gravity of the offense.

American opinion leaders were quite familiar with these ideas and with the subsequent reforms of the penal laws in Europe. As early as 1776, the Commonwealth of Pennsylvania's first constitution

138

directed the state legislature to reform the penal law and make punishments "in some cases less sanguinary, and in general more proportionate to the crimes." To this end "houses ought to be provided for punishing by hard labour those convicted of crimes not capital; wherein the criminals shall be employed for the benefit of the public, or for reparation of injuries done to private persons: And all persons at proper times shall be admitted to see the prisoners at their labour." The aim was to "deter more effectually from the commission of crimes, by continued visible punishments of long duration." [16]

An additional impetus to reform came from John Howard's remarkable survey of British and foreign prisons, published the following year, and the English Hard Labour statute of 1779. After a disastrous experiment with the use of prisoners to clean the streets and privies of the city, a small "penitentiary" section was added to the Walnut Street Jail in Philadelphia in 1790, permitting the solitary confinement of convicts, and in 1794 the death penalty was abolished except for first-degree murder. The courts of all the counties of the state were authorized to commit felons to the Philadelphia institution where at least one-twelfth and not more than one-half of their sentences should be spent in the solitary cells, unless they were sentenced to life or twenty-five years for a second offense, previously capital, in which case they might have to serve their entire term in solitary. This statute was to be substantially reproduced by Virginia, Kentucky, and Maryland, as was the greatly admired and well-publicized regime of the Walnut Street Jail[17] when these states began the construction of state prisons or penitentiaries.

In Virginia the moving force was Thomas Jefferson, who, in 1776, headed a small committee appointed by the legislature to revise its code of laws. He undertook to prepare the penal code. It was submitted to the legislature three years later. He proposed that only treason, murder, and a second offense of manslaughter be made capital offenses, that rape and sodomy be punished by castration (he called it dismemberment), that the *lex talionis* apply to the crimes of maiming and disfiguring, that pretended witches, etc. be ducked and whipped, and that all other felons be sentenced to public labor for from one to seven years, depending on the gravity of the crime. Arsonists, robbers, burglars, and thieves should also indemnify their victims for their losses, and thieves should also be pilloried. The indignity of gibbeting, after hanging, should be the lot of the challenger who killed an opponent in a duel.[18]

The Revolutionary War and its aftermath delayed the debate on Jefferson's proposed penal code for two decades. When it was resumed, the legislature greatly reduced the number of capital offenses for whites, made solitary confinement—instead of the *opus publicum*—the standard form of imprisonment for felons, and authorized the construction of a state penitentiary in Richmond. It was begun in 1796 and opened in 1800. The penal philosophy responsible for this development was stated in the preamble of the statute passed in 1798.

> Experience . . . has shown that cruel and sanguinary laws defeat their own purpose by engaging the benevolence of mankind to withhold prosecutions, to smother testimony, or to listen to it with bias, and by producing in many instances a total dispensation and impunity under the names of pardon and benefit of clergy; when if the punishment were only proportioned to the injury, men would feel it their inclination as well as their duty to see the laws observed.

Capital punishments "weaken the state by cutting off so many who if reformed might be restored sound members to society." Finally, a sentence to hard labor would render the prisoners "useful to the community" and also make them "living and long continued examples to deter others from committing the like offenses."[19] There was no need to point out explicitly that the penitentiary was to house criminals from the master class. Criminal slaves were hanged, mutilated, or flogged. Free blacks of whatever hue who had committed serious crimes but had not been hanged were flogged, sold as slaves, and deported. The free black was an anomaly, a contradiction in terms, since blackness and slave status were considered synonymous. All the slave states sought to expel them or so circumscribe their civil rights that their status approached that of slaves.[20]

The penitentiary movement spread. Following Pennsylvania's example, Kentucky, which before 1792 had been a part of Virginia and thus subject to its sanguinary laws, abolished the death penalty except for murder, making the establishment of a penitentiary imperative. Two years later, a state prison was opened at Frankfort. Maryland opened a penitentiary at Baltimore in 1812 and, like Kentucky, adopted the mixed solitary confinement and congregate labor system of the Walnut Street Jail.[21] Only one other southern state would establish such an institution before the strident debate on the respective merits of the so-called Pennsylvania system of solitary confinement and the Auburn system of separate night cells and congregate labor under a rule of silence affected developments in the South. That state was Georgia, which opened a prison on the congregate plan at Milledgeville in 1817. A building with 150 cells was added in the 1830s; in 1841 it housed 159 white prisoners, four of them women, plus one mulatto.[22] Tennessee opened a penitentiary at Nashville, on the Auburn plan, in 1831; two years later it had 200 night cells. In 1841, a visitor reported that it held 173 white and 6 black male prisoners.[23] The Louisiana penitentiary was opened at

Baton Rouge in 1835, and the Missouri penitentiary at Jefferson City in 1836. The state prison of Mississippi, at what is now Jackson, received its first prisoners in 1840. The Arkansas penitentiary was opened at Little Rock in 1841, the Alabama penitentiary at Wetumpka in 1842, and the Texas penitentiary at Huntsville in 1849. Prior to these dates, convicts had been dealt with by the counties in the various states. This practice was never abandoned by the Carolinas and Florida before the Civil War, in spite of the pleas of executives and religious leaders who favored the establishment of state prisons.

The need for these institutions grew as legislators replaced sanguinary punishments with imprisonment for felons. In 1836, for instance, Alabama "abolished the death penalty for white persons for burglary, robbery, arson, counterfeiting and forgery, for which punishment was fixed at imprisonment not to exceed two years and 39 lashes on the bare back."[24] The reformatory value of punishment was also stressed by its proponents. In 1827, for instance, Governor Brandon of Mississippi, in recommending to the legislature the building of a penitentiary, said, "Punishment through a spirit of revenge for the infraction of penal laws . . . ought to be unknown in a civilized community. The object is to reform offenders, to protect society from the repetitions of offenses. . . . To inflict punishment with no effort at reformation only prepares for the commission of more crimes." [25] Therefore prisoners— white, of course—should be taught a trade, and this would make a penitentiary self-sustaining rather than a burden on the taxpayers. Making a profit was to become the prime objective of these institutions, and when they failed to realize it some of the states devised plans that in effect turned the prisoners into penal slaves. Thus the lease system was born.

Kentucky led the way. After years during which the Frankfort prison had been a drain on the treasury, the legislature, in 1825, "handed the prison over bodily to the newly appointed keeper, Joel Scott," who was to "employ the convicts at hard labor, treat them humanely, pay the state half of the net profits accruing from the labor of the convicts, and keep the other half . . . in lieu of a salary." [26] A new lessee-keeper was appointed in 1832; the prison continued to be a profitable venture for him and the state. The prisoners worked from dawn to sunset, with time out only for meals. When Crawford visited the prison in 1835, he found the ninety-two prisoners engaged in eighteen different occupations: They worked as blacksmiths or in cutting stone; making wagons, plows, chairs, barrels, brushes, or sleighs; spinning or carding wool, dressing cloth, weaving broadcloth, jean, carpeting, and flannel; spinning twine for bagging and weaving bagging; making hats and shoes, etc.[27] In 1844, the lucrative keepership was awarded to the firm of

Craig and Henry. The same year, a legislative committee "recommended that . . . the manufacture of rope and bagging, noncompetitive industries, be extended to employ as nearly as possible all prisoners." [28] Organized labor and manufacturers had protested against the competition of prison-made products.

The Missouri penitentiary was being operated by lessees in 1841, judging from a description of that institution and its regime in a work authored by one of three northern preachers committed late that year on sentences of twelve years for "stealing slaves." [29] After their delivery to the prison, they were stripped, examined, registered, one side of the head shaved, dressed in yellow-and-white clothing, put in chains, and conducted to a cell, which was "twelve feet by eight—arched—brick and plastered—a window, on hinges, in the corner at the top, defended by two large iron bars—an iron door, about four feet by twenty-two inches, with a thick wooden door on the out-side . . . there were two beds, one double and one single," covered by "small, very poor and thin Indian blankets." [30] The prison had eighty cells for about one hundred seventy inmates, most of whom were "in chains—some with one, fastened to the ankle and suspended from the loins—some with two, one on each leg and suspended in the same manner, and others with large fetters on the feet, besides two heavy chains, one on either side, obliging them to take very short steps."[31]

Most prisoners worked in the prison, which had a brickyard with a kiln, a smithy, a ropewalk, a cooper shop, a carpentry shop, and a "hackle house," but there was also outside work. Parties of inmates, supervised by from one to four guards armed with pistols and muskets, were led to work in the city to help masons in building ice houses or dwellings, or marched several miles to chop wood and split rails. The workday lasted from dawn to dusk. New lessees took charge of the penitentiary in 1843 on a ten-year lease.

Louisiana, which could have become a leader of penal reform if it had adopted the "code of reform and prison discipline" prepared by Edward Livingston in 1824,[32] did establish a cotton mill and a shoe factory in its penitentiary, opened in 1835, "not only to manufacture essential articles for slave wear but to train machine operatives and to fight the high prices of northern capitalists."[33] Within a few years, however, the prison ceased to be self-supporting, and in 1844, the legislature, eager to cut its losses, generously—since it asked not a penny in compensation—presented the prison, so to speak, to a private firm of manufacturers for a term of five years. Subsequent leases were granted until the war.

The operation of the Alabama penitentiary proved to be so costly that in

1846 the legislature authorized the leasing of the establishment, convicts and all, to a private firm for six years, free of charge. The lease was renewed twice, but the state received no rental for twelve years. It resumed control of the prison in 1862 from the lessee, Burrows, Holt & Co., manufacturers of "sash, blinds, doors, russet, brogans, cabinet furniture, wagons, wheat fans, well buckets, five and ten gallon kegs."[34] which suggests the kinds of work in which the prisoners had been employed. During the war the convicts were used in the construction of fortifications at Mobile, and in the penitentiary producing war supplies for the Confederate army, until the Union invaders occupied it in 1865 and released the convicts. The prison was returned to the state the following year.

Jefferson had finally urged the establishment of a penitentiary to supplant public labor by convicts on the highways and canals of Virginia, because such labor degraded instead of reformed the convict. In the legislature he argued that "exhibited as a public spectacle, with shaved heads and mean clothing, working on the highroads produced in the criminal such prostration of self-respect, as, instead of reforming, plunged them into the most desperate and hardened depravity."[35] Advocates of the penitentiary in other states also hoped that it would be a means of restoring felons to an orderly life in freedom. That hope was not to be realized. Life in these institutions was governed by a regime unable to produce that effect. Some of the institutions did provide some training in mechanical trades which might enable a convict to find honest employment upon his release, but the treatment of the inmates was generally counterproductive, especially in the penitentiaries leased to private contractors whose only aim was to work the convicts "like slaves." What a lessee was interested in was maximum financial profit from his management of the institution. This meant keeping maintenance costs at a minimum by feeding and clothing the convicts as cheaply as possible, hiring guards willing to work for substandard wages or using prisoners in that capacity. It meant working the prisoners from dawn to dusk and extracting their best efforts by the threat or use of the ever-present whip of the overseer.

Discipline was severe. In the Missouri penitentiary, disobedience of orders or violations of the lessee's strict rules were punished by flogging with the strap or the paddle, the number of strokes varying from ten to a hundred or more, depending on the nature of the violation or the caprice of the overseer.

The strap was of thick leather, about one inch wide and two feet long, sometimes tied to a short handle. It did not break the skin, but bruised and mashed it till it

143

turned black and blue. The paddle was a board about two feet long, six inches wide, one end shaved to a handle, the other bored full of holes, every one of which would raise a bloodblister, where it struck the flesh. It was very severe . . . this is a common instrument of torture among the slaveholders.

Another device was the ducking chair.

The ducking apparatus is a large armed chair, in which the sufferer is tied, hand and foot, so that he cannot move. Then there is a box, which fits close round the neck below, and open at the top, into which they pour a basin or pail full of water, directly into the man's face. Not being able to avoid the water, he is strangled, choked and almost killed.[36]

Variants of these disciplinary methods were used in other penitentiaries. In Mississippi, solitary confinement in a dark cell on bread and water was ordered used in 1841 after a legislative committee had found that a convict had died after being brutally beaten.[38] Whipping or solitary confinement were used in the penitentiaries of Virginia, Kentucky, and Maryland, but in Tennessee the law prohibited whipping. Stocks or pillories were also in use in some prisons. In other words, the disciplinary punishments employed were much the same as those used by slaveholders on the plantations or prescribed by law as primary punishments for crime before penitentiaries were invented.

The antebellum penitentiaries of the slave states were meant to confine criminals from the master class, slaves being otherwise disposed of. In 1850, for instance, there were 167 white males, 1 white female, and 4 free colored persons in the Alabama penitentiary.[38] It was rare to find blacks in the institutions, although there were exceptions. In Maryland, "slaves were sentenced to the penitentiary" until a law of 1819 provided that if they were not hanged they must be sold "out of the limits of the State." Prior to that time, 60 slaves had received penitentiary sentences between 1812 and 1819, and so had 466 free blacks and 514 whites.[39] Thenceforth, only free persons were committed to the institution. At the end of 1860, the Louisiana penitentiary, in addition to 236 white and 11 free colored males contained 96 slaves—82 males and 14 females—of whom 83 were serving life sentences for murder.[40]

Then came the Civil War. When it ended, the master class of the South would have to cope with a new and vast problem—the criminality of the ex-slaves, which was to produce an entirely new class of convicts.

XI: THE CONVICT LEASE SYSTEM

The defeat of the Confederacy, in April, 1865, was a traumatic experience for the master class; its ex-slaves were no longer subject to the domestic discipline which for so long had been the chief instrument for dealing with miscreant slaves. The liberation of the blacks began with President Lincoln's Emancipation Proclamation of 1863, which freed the slaves in the seceded states, and was completed with the ratification of the Thirteenth Amendment in December, 1865, which abolished slavery throughout the nation. Consequently, the penal laws of the southern states became applicable to all offenders regardless of race. This was a distressing prospect for states which had created industrial penitentiaries for offenders from the master class and now faced the rapidly growing criminality of poor, unskilled, bewildered ex-slaves cast into a freedom for which few of them were prepared.

Burdened with heavy taxes to meet the expenses of rebuilding the shattered economy, and committed to the traditional notion that convicts should, by their labor, reimburse the government for their maintenance and even create additional revenue, the master class, drawing on its past experience with penitentiary leases, reintroduced a system of penal servitude which would make public slaves of black and poor and friendless white convicts. In some states they in fact became the temporary or lifelong slaves of private employers or corporations to whom the government delegated the right to exploit them for private profit. The revived convict lease system would for decades place the stamp of slavery on the penal systems of the South, postponing substantial reforms until far into the present century and offering a good illustration of the debasing effects of the "peculiar institution" on the evolution of penal systems for free men.

The convict lease system was a natural product of two centuries of chattel slavery. The Emancipation Proclamation stripped the slave owners of the South of their human property but did not change their opinions on the status of blacks in a society dominated by whites. Only six years earlier, in 1857, the Supreme Court of the United States, in the Dred Scott case, had declared that "the right of property in a slave is dinstinctly and expressly affirmed in the Constitution" and that the framers of that document considered blacks as "a subordinate and inferior class of beings."[1] This view had justified the enslavement of blacks and it survived the abolition of slavery. In an address to the National Prison Congress of 1889, an Alabama prison physician asserted

> That there is a vast difference between all the races no one doubts. That there is still a greater difference between the Caucasian and the Negro, occupying, as they do, the two extremes of the human family, I think is true. That, as a race, the Negro is physically and mentally inferior I assert as a fact beyond dispute. Whether this is a result of previous conditions or the discriminating handiwork of the Creator makes no difference."[2]

The ingrained belief in the inferiority of blacks and their reluctance to labor led to the creation of a penal system of forced labor in the South where inhumanity was ignored by the master class because the vast majority—eighty-five to ninety-five per cent—of the convict population was black. Furthermore, the Thirteenth Amendment explicitly authorized "slavery" or "involuntary servitude" as punishment for crime, leaving legislatures dominated by the master class free to reintroduce a species of slavery for Negro criminals and lower-class whites. They were to be forced to do work which would more than compensate the state for their keep. The sole aim of the convict lease system was financial profit to the lessees who exploited the labor of the prisoners to the fullest, and to the government which sold the convicts to the lessees. To this system of slave labor the idea of reformation as an aim of penal "treatment" was completely alien. Speaking to the National Prison Congress of 1890, a physician from Tennessee said,

> We have difficulties at the South, which you at the North have not. . . . We have a large alien population, an inferior race. Just what we are to do with them as prisoners is a great question as yet unsettled. The Negro's moral sense is lower than that of the white man. . . . The Negro regards it as no disgrace to be sent to the penitentiary. He never cares to conceal the fact that he has been there. How we are going to reform that race we do not know.[3]

Sermons and the lash evidently were not the answer.

The history of the South's convict lease system remains to be written. Only its salient ingredients will be described here, showing its derivation from the chattel slavery of antebellum days though lacking its ameliorative features. The most blatant examples were furnished by the states of the Deep South, but by its very nature the system exhibited similar characteristics wherever it existed, whether for petty misdemeanants or violators of county and municipal ordinances or for state prisoners committed for more serious crimes. Our concern will be chiefly with the state convicts.

Mississippi

Mississippi's penitentiary, which had been partly destroyed by Sherman's army, was sufficiently repaired in 1866 to permit the leasing of it to J. W. Young and Company for a period of fourteen years; but within a few months the prison was so overcrowded and the convict population increasing at so rapid a rate that the lessee was authorized to employ prisoners lacking mechanical skills and serving relatively short sentences "at any work, public or private, upon railroads, levees, dirt roads, or other works."[4] In 1868, this arrangement was canceled by the military commander of the Fourth District and the lease given to a rich planter, Edmund Richardson, who, instead of paying for the use of the convicts, received $18,000 annually from the state, which also assumed the costs of transporting the prisoners to and from Richardson's plantations. "There is little wonder that he came to be known as the greatest cotton planter in the world, with a crop that in one year reached the amazing total of 11,500 bales."[5] Profits persuaded the legislature, in 1872, to establish a system of prison farms operated by the state and ready for occupancy in 1876. In the meantime, the lessee would not be allowed to work the prisoners outside the penitentiary except on public roads, a limitation which was removed in 1876, when a new lease was granted, the farm idea having been scuttled.* The new lessee was J. S. Hamilton and Associates, who subleased the prisoners to "planters, speculators, and railroad and levee contractors. . . . Out over the state, in great rolling cages or temporary stockades, on remote plantations or deep in the swamps of the Delta, the convicts were completely at the mercy of the sub-lessees and their guards."[6] From time to time, the press carried reports of the flagrant abuses to which the convicts were subjected in the camps, but it was difficult to stir the conscience of a white public that knew that no tax dollars were spent on prisons and that the camps were almost entirely populated by Negroes. "Of the few white men, who went to prison at all, a remarkably large percentage . . . [had] sentences of more than ten years"

---

*The lease system promised to be more profitable because the legislature had just passed a law "which declared the theft . . . of any kind of cattle or swine, regardless of value, to be grand larceny, subjecting the thief to a term up to five years in the state penitentiary. This was the famous 'pig law,' which was largely responsible for an increase in the population of the state prison from 284 in 1874 to 1,072 at the end of 1877. It was this law that made the convict lease system a big business enterprise" (Wharton, op. cit., 237).

which had to be served in the penitentiary. In the camps, the few white men were used mostly in clerical jobs or as straw bosses.[7]

Critics of the lease system finally aroused the legislature in 1884. Prodded by a press report that "eighteen convicts, being returned to prison [i.e., to the penitentiary] as disabled, proved to be in such a terrible condition from punishment and frost-bite that they had to be smuggled through Vicksburg in a covered wagon,"[8] a legislative committee made an inspection of the camps. Its blistering report, partly reproduced in the Raymond *Gazette* of March 8, 1884, stated that the prisoners on

> farms and public works have been subjected to indignities without authority of law and contrary to civilized humanity. Often . . . sub-lessees resort to "pulling" the prisoner until he faints from the lash on his naked back, while the sufferer was held by four strong men holding each a hand or foot stretched out on the frozen ground or over stumps or logs—often over 300 stripes at a time, which more than once, it is thought, resulted in the death of a convict. Men unable to work have been driven to their death and some have died fettered to the chain gang. . . . When working in the swamps or fields, they were refused pure water and were driven to drink out of sloughs or plow furrows in the fields in which they labored. One instance of this being on the N.O.N.E.R.R., where owners were unable to get contractors to work at a given point known as Canay Swamps. They hired from sublessees the labor of convicts at $1.75 per head per day. They were placed in the swamp in water ranging to their knees, and in almost nude state they spaded caney and rooty ground, their bare feet chained together by chains that fretted the flesh. They were compelled to attend to the calls of nature in line as they stood day in and day out, their thirst compelling them to drink the water in which they were compelled to deposit their excrement.[9]

No action was taken on the report, the "lobby of the leasing system" proving to be effective.[10]

The committee had stated that the convicts in the penitentiary were treated kindly. In July, 1887, a grand jury, which inspected the institution, reported that they saw

> twenty-six inmates, all of whom have been lately brought there off the farms and railroads, many of them with consumption and other incurable diseases and all bearing on their persons marks of the most inhuman and brutal treatment. Most of them have their backs cut in great wales, scars and blisters, some with the skin peeling off in pieces as the result of severe beatings. Their feet and hands in some instances show signs of frost-bite, and all of them with the stamp of manhood almost blotted out of their faces. . . . They are lying there dying, some of them on bare boards, so poor and emaciated that their bones almost come through their skin, many complaining for the want of food. . . . We actually saw live vermin crawling over their faces, and the little bedding and clothing they have in tatters and stiff

148

with filth. . . . As a fair sample of this system, on Jan. 6, 1887, 204 convicts were leased to McDonald up to June 6, 1887, and during this six months 20 died and 19 were discharged and escaped and 23 were returned to the walls disabled and sick, many of whom have since died.[11]

Sixteen per cent of the convicts died that year.

Early in 1887, the Gulf and Ship Island Railroad became the sole lessee. Its camps were no better than those of the sublessees. This lease was terminated the following year and, until 1894, the state leased individual convicts to private planters for eight dollars a month for blacks and seven dollars for whites. The death rate of eleven per cent in 1888 dropped to three per cent in 1889. Mounting public protest finally led the constitutional convention of 1890 to abolish the lease system as of 1894. The legislature was authorized "to establish a prison farm" and also to employ convicts "on levees, roads and other public works under state supervision, but not under private contractors."[12] The reason for this action was well-stated by a legislative committee in 1888. "The leasing system under any form is wrong in principle and vicious. . . . The system of leasing convicts to individuals or corporations to be worked by them for profit simply restores a state of servitude worse than slavery; worse in this that it is without any of the safeguards resulting from the ownership of the slave."[13]

Louisiana

In 1868, the Louisiana legislature leased the Baton Rouge penitentiary to a private firm. At the time, the institution held 85 white and 203 black males and 9 black females, mostly agricultural laborers. The lessee promptly sold the lease, at great profit, to a corporation headed by Major Samuel L. James which, until 1901, conducted "the most cynical, profit-oriented and brutal prison regime in Louisiana history."[14] The penitentiary became the repository for the sick, infirm, or crippled convicts. The able-bodied were moved to camps on the plantations at Angola and Lagona owned by James or to camps at levees or railroads. The work on the levees, to which whites were rarely assigned, was especially hard and dangerous to health. In 1886, a local newspaper reported that "men on the works are brutally treated and everybody knows it. They are worked mostly in swamps and plantations, from daylight to dusk, Corporal punishment is inflicted on the slightest provocation. . . . Anyone who has travelled along the lines of railroads that run through the Louisiana swamps . . . in which the levees are built, has seen these poor devils almost to their waists, delving in the black and noxious mud."[15] Two years earlier, the editor of the New Orleans *Daily Picayune,* June 30, 1884, had written that it would be more humane "to impose the death sentence immediately upon anyone sentenced to a term with the lessee in excess of six years, because the average convict lived no longer than that."[16] The death rate was indeed high—twenty per cent in 1896.[17]

Efforts were made in the eighties to terminate the lease, not because of the brutality of the system, but because it was too profitable to the lessee; his profits should, by right, fill the coffers of the state. In 1883, the convention of the Democratic Party, which controlled the legislature, demanded that the state assume the task of working the convicts on the public levees, but the legislature took no action, the political influence of the lessee being too powerful. The legislature, in 1890, did attempt to alleviate the abuses of the system somewhat by requiring the Board of Control* to set up a method of classifying convicts which would obviate the indiscriminate assignment of the prisoner to labor regardless of their physical condition. Borrowing from the antebellum plantation practice of rating slaves as "full hands," "half hands," and "dead hands," convicts were to be sorted into four classes. "First class men are . . . sound in every respect and accustomed to manual labor. These men are sent to the levee camps where the work is the most severe. Second class men are . . . of moderate strength and capabilities and are assigned to the sugar plantations. . . . Third class men are assigned to the cotton plantation [Angola] and fourth class men . . . to the hospital."[18]

Finally it was decided in 1898, that the lease system would be terminated when the contract with the lessees expired in 1901, and that thenceforth it would be illegal to lease convicts to private persons or firms. The convict population, on December 1, 1901, consisted of 1,143 persons, 984 of whom were black.[19] Thus ended a system in which convicts were "a species of slave labor" and which had, in a sense, made Major James "the largest slave holder in post-bellum Louisiana."[20]

Alabama

In 1866, the governor of Alabama leased the penitentiary to a contractor who was charged the sum of five dollars and given a sizable loan. The legislature granted him permission to work the prisoners outside the walls; they were soon found in the Ironton and New Castle mines.[21] Appalling

---

*The Board of Control consisted of five persons appointed by the governor. It was supposed to supervise the lease system but had little influence. By 1894, its members were literally in the pay of the lessees who paid their salaries. (Carleton, *op. cit.,* p. 17a.)

treatment and working conditions there and at railroad construction camps were reflected in the mortality rate of the convicts, which rose to 41 per cent in 1869, an all-time high. Envious of the financial profits enjoyed by the lessee, the legislature, in 1874, decided to offer railroads, iron and coal mining corporations, and planters the opportunity to lease convicts for short terms of from one to five years and pay the state five dollars monthly for "full hands," half that amount for "medium hands," and nothing for "dead hands."[22] Entrepreneurs quickly took advantage of the offer and numerous camps were established at various work sites. Lessees received not only state convicts through the penitentiary but also convicts leased directly from the counties.* Most males worked in the mines, while females, children, and infirm males were "leased to lumbering companies, turpentine industries and agricultural operators, whose work was not reckoned to be as 'dangerous' or 'arduous' as that in the mines."[23] The deplorable conditions in some of these camps led the Mobile *Register* of February 15, 1875, to report that the convicts "laboring with manacled limbs in swamps and sleeping in the unwholesome atmosphere . . . died like cattle in slaughter pens."[24] Yet, state inspectors, either insensitive, corrupt, or relying solely on information supplied by the lessees, claimed in their biennial report of 1880 to the governor "that the convicts had generally been well clothed and fed, and kindly and humanely treated; and that corporal punishment had only been inflicted in extreme cases."[25] The governor appointed John H. Bankhead warden of the penitentiary in 1881, and the latter's report on convict camps the following year painted a different picture.

I found the convicts confined at fourteen different prisons controlled by as many persons or companies, and situated at as many different places. . . . [The prisons] were as filthy, as a rule, as dirt could make them and both prisons and prisoners were infested with vermin. . . . Convicts were extremely and, in some instances, cruelly punished. . . . They were poorly clothed and fed. . . . The sick were neglected, insomuch that no hospital had been provided, they being confined in the cells with the well convicts. . . . The prisons had no adequate water supply, and I

---

*"Immediately after the Civil War, in an effort to relieve the pressure on the penitentiary, the legislature had established a system of hard labor for the county. Only convicts with sentences of two years or more had to be sent to the penitentiary; when the sentence was less . . . the convict was usually leased out by the county in which convicted. . . . In 1886, there were 904 convicts at labor for counties as compared with 659 state convicts. A large percentage of the county convicts were leased to individuals or firms far removed from the county of conviction; consequently, it was practically impossible for the county commissions to supervise their treatment adequately. County officials and contractors kept such poor records, sometimes none at all, that prisoners were known to have been worked for months or even years after the expiration of their sentences" (Allen Johnston Going, *Bourbon Democracy in Alabama, 1870–1890* [University of Alabama, Press, 1951], p. 174).

verily believe there were men, who had not washed their faces in twelve months. . . . I found the men so intimidated that it was next to impossible to get from them anything touching their treatment. . . . To say that there are any reformatory measures used at our prisons, or that any regard is had to kindred subjects, is to state a falsehood. The system is a disgrace to the State, a reproach to the civilization and Christian sentiment of the age, and ought to be speedily abandoned.[26]

It was—in 1928!

The poor health and the high death rate of the convicts had been a constant concern to the benevolent opponents of the lease system. In 1883, Dr. R. M. Cunningham, who had been appointed physician at the penitentiary two years earlier, was transferred to the mines of the Pratt Coal Company. He found the lessee's prison there "unfit for the habitation of animal beings. The convicts were worked at a task for which they were incapacitated and which required from ten to fourteen hours to perform, thus depriving them of all sunlight. There was no discrimination made as to the fitness or unfitness of any convict to work in the mines, when received. . . . They were bathed in cold water, slept in damp clothes, on damp beds, in an overcrowded dark and damp cell, on a scaffold."[27] Pleurisy and pneumonia were the principal diseases in the prison.

These revelations led to reforms. A ten-hour work day was introduced at the mines and the convict's daily task adjusted to his capacity. "First class" men were to mine five tons of coal daily, "second class" men, "third class" men, and "dead hands," four, three, and two tons respectively, later (1888) reduced by a ton for each class. To facilitate the supervision of the lessees by the state, all convicts, including those of the county who had been brought under state control in 1883, "were concentrated at the Pratt Mines and on two Black Belt plantations" in 1887, and the following year the Tennessee Coal, Iron and Railroad Company secured a twenty-year lease of convicts to work at the Pratt Mines.[28] By September 1890, 801 of the state's 1,123 convicts were working in these mines and housed in two new prisons built by the company at the site. The rest—sick, and crippled males or those otherwise unfit for hard labor, and women—were retained in the Wetumpka penitentiary and "sometimes leased to nearby planters for day labor or worked on a share basis on Thomas William's plantation."[29] That year the system yielded a net profit to the state of more than $36,000.[30]

Since the lessee was only interested in the financial profits from the labor of his convict, corporal punishment was the chief instrument used to ensure that they completed their daily tasks under the vigilant eyes of convict "trusties," who constituted the custodial force.

Cruel punishments such as the "shower bath," crucifix, and yoke and buck were forbidden in 1891, but vigorous methods . . . among them the sweat box and lash were allowed to continue. . . . The sweat box is a coffin-like cell with just enough space to accommodate a man standing erect. Generally made of wood or tin, it is completely closed except for a hole two inches in diameter at nose level. When placed under the blistering southern sun, the temperature inside becomes unbearable. In a few hours a man's body swells and occasionally bleeds."

During the fiscal year 1925–26, "the official Punishment Record Ledger shows that 400 prisoners served 4,000 hours in the sweat box in Alabama."[31] As for the lash, all attempts to stop its use failed. It survived the lease systems for decades.

Opposition to the system was mounting. Humanitarians decried its callous flouting of the most elementary human rights. It was, by its very nature, inimical to the reformation of the offender which postbellum penologists regarded as an important purpose of punishment. Although the state treasury's income from the leases continued to rise, fiscal authorities looked with envy on the huge private profits gained by the lessees from their exploitation of convict labor. It was assumed that if the state abolished the system and took complete control over the labor of its convicts, the spoils of the lessees would accrue to the state. That this could occur only if the state adopted the exploitative philosophy and methods of the lessees may not have been repugnant to those who knew that over ninety per cent of the convicts were black.

In 1915, a legislative committee investigated the lease system. Its report of the findings stated that "the convict lease system of Alabama is a relic of barbarism, a species of human slavery, a crime against humanity. . . . A sentence to hard labor should not impliedly include a deprivation of nourishment, an absence of God's sunlight, the breaking of bones, the maiming of limbs, the disfigurement of persons, the loss of life itself. Lessees should not have the authority, after jury and judges have acted, to add punishment, which no court in the first instance would have imposed." It spoke of convict miners going into the mines before sunrise and emerging after sunset, of daily quotas of ten to fourteen tons, of their enforcement by whipping "so brutal that in some instances brought to the committee's attention the skin was literally broken from the back, causing scars that will be carried to the grave," and of ill-prepared and insufficient food. In the turpentine camps, conditions were as bad, perhaps worse. There the convicts "are made frequently to rise at four in the morning, day in and day out, walk five or six miles to work, toil all day long, with insufficient water and food, in the heat of the sun until darkness comes, and then forced to walk into camp for supper."[32]

Finally, in 1923, the legislature forbade "any person to lease or let for hire any state convict to any person, firm or corporation" after March 31, 1927.[33] White convicts were promptly removed from the mines and lumber camps to state-operated farms and prisons. The state took over the prisons at the mines on a rental basis until June 30, 1928, when the 900 black convicts still there were transferred. On leaving the mine, a convict was heard to say, "Boss, I'm no longer in slavery."[34]

Georgia

At the outbreak of the Civil War the Milledgeville penitentiary held about two hundred white convicts; those willing to serve in the Confederate army were released. After the war, the problem of housing convicts became acute, because Sherman's army had gutted the prison. What could be done with the growing number of ex-slaves convicted of serious crimes? Downgrading some felonies to misdemeanors and authorizing courts to commit misdemeanants to county chain-gangs was only a partial solution,[35] and in 1866, state convicts were leased to contractors on public works.[36] When, as a result of the Reconstruction Acts of 1867, a Union military commander took charge of the government, he leased a hundred convicts the following year to a railroad builder for the total sum of twenty-five hundred dollars, and in 1869, five hundred convicts were leased to seven different contractors. Finally, in 1876, the legislature decided that three years later, all the state convicts would be leased for twenty years to three companies headed by prominent politicians and businessmen, the lessees paying the state twenty-five thousand dollars annually. The lessees constructed three prisons in different counties, each prison having several less permanent branch camps at various sites in the state where "the convicts were put to work mining coal and cutting wood, farming on great tracts of land, making bricks and constructing railroads." [37]

Georgia's lease system did not differ from those already described. The welfare of the prisoners was of no concern to the lessees, who, interested only in gaining maximum profit from the prison labor, looked with equanimity on the growing convict population which spelled increased financial gain. Attempts by the legislature to regulate the system failed miserably. The convicts were left to the mercy of their employers. Reports of brutality in the camps rarely brought official response. "Now and then a governor held investigations, as was the case in 1887, when Governor Gordon had fines of $2,500 imposed on two companies for cruelty to their convicts, and in 1896 when Governor Atkinson levied a fine on the Dade County Coal Mining Company."[38]

Two years before the leases were to expire in 1899, the legislature was stirred to action. It decided to establish a state farm to which women, juveniles, the sick, the aged, and the feeble-minded would be sent when the leases ended. It also decided that afterward the able-bodied convicts—about two thousand—would be distributed to the counties to be put on chain-gangs working on road construction if their sentences were for five years or less. Those with longer sentences would be leased for $100 a year per convict. Later, convicts would be auctioned to the highest bidder, with the result that the annual revenue to the state increased by $200,000 to $300,000. Within a few years lessees were paying $225 per convict and were subleasing them for $630.[39]

The growing opposition to the system bore fruit. The penitentiary committee of the legislature had found it to be brutal and graft-ridden. Practically all the wardens of the camps, the guards, and some camp physicians were in the pay of the lessees. Two wardens who also were state inspectors of camps ran brickyards, lumber mills, turpentine farms, and coal mines for the lessees. The legislature of 1907–8 appointed a special investigatory committee to hold hearings on the system. Some of the testimony elicited was "actually unprintable, much of it was absolutely sickening."[40] The committee learned that

an angry and cruel State officer, selfishly interested in punishing, whipped to the very door of the hospital a boy within eight weeks of a consumptive's death. An inhuman State officer decides that he will sweat a Negro convict and gives orders accordingly. The convict is . . . wrapt head, body and feet in blankets and enclosed in a box. He dies; a camp physician certifies that his death is caused by congestion of the lungs. . . . Another Negro claiming to be sick is whipped and put to work till he falls exhausted and two hours later is dead. A white man refuses to work. The warden orders him to strip to receive a whipping. He draws a razor and starts toward the warden, though shackled. The warden admits that he could have kept out of his way by retreating. He shot to kill him, aiming directly between his eyes. A large percentage of whippings at the two mining camps are for 'shortage on tasks' or for "slate in coal." The evidence further shows that the mining boss, or foreman, an employee of the lessee, fixes the task; that Inspector _____ is seventy-three years old, too old . . . for the arduous duties of an inspector. He declares he never expected to go into a mine to see what is required of these convicts; that Assistant Inspector _____ started into the Durham mines and went about one hundred yards, when the water and mud were so bad he abandoned the inspection. . . . The evidence as to the treatment of the convicts at Chattahoochee Brick Company, showed violations of the rules of the Prison Commission as to food, lodging, eating, and sleeping quarters, excessive tasks and discipline.[41]

The committee also discovered that the law limiting the labor of county convicts to road construction was being violated, that county solicitors were getting fees and the counties revenue from illegally leasing convicts to private persons and corporations. It characterized these "wild-cat camps" thus: "As a rule these camps, the conditions existing therein, and the cruel and inhuman treatment of unfortunate convicts, thus illegally sold into worse than slavery, are a disgrace to a civilized people. . . . The sworn officers of the courts and county government profit from the cruel and illegal labor and sweat of criminals."[42]

All these revelations finally led the legislature to decide that after April 1, 1909, no leases would be authorized. After that date, convicts not committed to the state farm would be sent to the chain-gangs of the counties' road-construction camps.

Florida

The antebellum penitentiary movement bypassed Florida. Governor Reid told the territorial legislature in 1840 that by establishing prisons "the cause of humanity might be advanced, by abolishing the barbarous punishments of whipping, branding and pillory,"[43] but his suggestion fell on deaf ears. After the war, the need for a state prison seems to have become evident, because in 1866, the federal government lent the state its arsenal at Chattachoochee for that purpose. Because of the high cost of its mismanagement during the reconstruction years, the state, once it again assumed full control of the prison, converted it into a mental hospital and sought legislative approval for leasing all state convicts to a private lessee.[44] In 1902, that lessee was the Florida Naval Stores Company, which also subleased convicts to some thirty persons or firms having prison camps and receiving full power of discipline over their inmates. The largest of the camps held about four hundred convicts.[45] In 1909, Governor Gilchrist noted that "our prisoners are now leased to a strong company [Florida Pine Co.] owning many hundred thousand acres of timber lands, operating sawmills and turpentine farms. While using most of the prisoners, they sub-lease some of them to be employed in phosphate mines and on turpentine farms other than their own, and in sawmills."[46] The lessee paid the state the sum of $281 annually for each convict and bore the cost of guarding, feeding, and clothing him, and caring for his health. The state's annual gain from these transactions amounted to about $340,000 in 1911.[47]

156

Since the lessee had to accept all convicts, this meant that women, children, the sick, and the infirm were included. This circumstance may have helped toward the establishment of the state prison provided for in the constitution of 1885, and which at last materialized when the state acquired 15,000 acres at Raiford for s State Prison Farm; it was ready for use by 1914. All state convicts were sent there to be sorted into two classes. Able-bodied males were placed in Class One, and most of them were conveyed to the lessees. Some of them, as well as all women and men "not able to take the shovel and throw dirt and that kind of work, but can do farm work."[48] were assigned to Class Two and retained at Raiford.

The leasing of state convicts ended with the year 1917, when a State Convict Road Force was created under the supervision and control of the State Road Department, which in turn was supervised by the Governor and the Commissioner of Agriculture. All Class One convicts were to be assigned to the Force for labor on the highways. County convicts were not affected by this policy change. The state had little or no concern for them, although they constituted about one-third of all convicts serving prison terms in Florida. The counties continued to lease them until an act of June 7, 1923, provided that "no new contracts shall be made whereby county convicts shall be leased to work for any private interest after the passage of this Act and it shall become a law," and that already existing contracts would become null and void at the end of the year. Counties were authorized to use convicts on their own public works—roads, bridges, etc.—or to lease them to other counties for like employment or to the State Road Force.

The statute also prohibited the flogging or whipping of convicts and ordered the Commissioner of Agriculture to make and enforce "suitable and reasonable rules" for the treatment of convicts in prisons, jails, and camps. It fixed the workday at ten hours, including time to go to and from work. It provided for a state inspector in each of the four congressional districts, such inspector to visit each place of confinement at least once a month and among other things, examine convicts for marks of severe disciplining. These reforms were provoked by the nationally publicized case of Martin Tabert, a young North Dakotan who had been so brutally whipped—119 lashes—by a chain-gang captain that he died. The matter would have been hushed up by the authorities had not the North Dakota legislature demanded an investigation. It disclosed

official corruption in sending individuals to prison for trivial reasons and then leasing them out to a private company that placed them in camps where brutal and barbarous treatment sometimes existed. A Leon County sheriff admitted receiving $20 for each prisoner turned over to the Putnam Lumber Co., a convict leaseholder, and the sheriff and the judge were removed for their activities. . . . The captain was convicted of second-degree murder, but the conviction was reversed by the supreme court for legal technicalities, and he apparently escaped punishment by the state.[49]

There had been previous scandals, and the brutal treatment of convicts under the lease system earned the state well-deserved notoriety.

South Carolina

Before the Civil War the law violators of South Carolina were dealt with by the counties. The decision to construct a penitentiary was reached in 1866; it was opened the following year at Columbia. According to one state official, the reason for establishing it was that "after the emancipation of the colored people, whose idea of freedom from bondage was freedom from work and license to pillage, we had to establish means for their control. Hence came the penitentiary."[50] Construction continued for several years, but overcrowding was a continuing problem and the institution was a financial loss. A few prisoners had been leased as early as 1873, but in 1877 the legislature authorized large-scale leasing. One hundred convicts were handed over to the Concord and Augusta Railroad. "By 1878 South Carolina had 221 prisoners working on railroads, in phosphate mines, and on private plantations. In two years' time, 153 prisoners had died—the death rate on the Greenwood and Augusta being 52.52 per cent—82 had escaped, and many of them returned to state custody were so disabled they could not walk. An investigation showed the prisoners to be suffering from malnutrition, vermin, and beatings, and from living in indescribable filth."[51] Such characteristic abuse of the convicts by the lessees was aggravated by the lack of state supervision. Leasing was terminated in 1885.

North Carolina

The constitution of 1868 provided that death, imprisonment with or without hard labor, and fine should be the only punishments for crime. Previously, the code of 1855 had made seventeen crimes capital offenses, had retained branding, mutilation, whipping, the stocks, and the pillory for certain crimes, and had decreed imprisonment, usually for less than a year, for a variety of offenses.[52] The first General Assembly under the new constitution made murder and rape capital crimes, and in April, 1869, it passed "an Act to provide for the erection of a penitentiary," an institution previously lacking in

158

North Carolina because earlier proposals, from 1801 on, had been defeated in the legislature or by popular referendum.[53] In 1870, the construction of the new prison began at Raleigh. "The buildings ... were of heavy pine logs ... [and] were only temporary ... for the purpose of housing those prisoners who helped in the construction of the permanent buildings. ... In 1875, the first brick cell-block, containing 64 cells was completed, but the entire prison was not completed until Dedember, 1884," and as late as 1932, it had a "normal capacity of only 350 prisoners."[54]

The building of the prison could not keep pace with the rapidly rising convict population. In 1875, when 569 blacks and 78 whites were committed to the institution,[55] the legislature decided that "imprisonment with hard labor" should be interpreted to include convict labor on public works, highways," or other labor for public benefit and the farming out thereof," and that "no prisoner whose labor may be farmed out shall be punished for failure of duty as a laborer except by a responsible officer of the state and that prisoners farmed out shall be at all times, as to their government and discipline, under the supervision and control of the penitentiary board or some officer of the state."[56] The leasing of all able-bodied men began at once, the lame, the halt, and the sick being kept in the penitentiary, and by 1877, some 500 state convicts were in railroad camps. In 1880, there were 800 "scattered in camps on six railroad systems and living under such conditions that 100 [actually 123] escaped during the year in spite of the fact that 11 others were shot down in such attempts."[57] Eleven per cent of those convicts died that year, including 21 "who had been returned [to the penitentiary] from the railroads completely broken down and hopelessly diseased."[58] In 1885, twelve railroads had 1,275 convicts in their construction camps and "judges of a large number of counties were given authority to sentence prisoners convicted before them to be delivered directly into the hands of the railroad corporation, to be receipted for by the warden of the penitentiary and accounted for by him."[59]

Leasing would continue for decades, even though the warden gave it another name. In his June, 1909, report, he noted that "for several years we have had a contract for 150 men with Messrs. Wade and Morrison, who were engaged upon work for the Atlantic Coast Line railroad," and that he had just "made two new contracts, 75 men each, and extending until May 1, 1909, one with the Atlantic Improvement Company, at Fayetteville, the other with the Navassa Guano Company of Selma. Since Sept. 1906, the contract price for prison labor has been $1.50 per day per man."[60] The fact that these convicts were clothed, fed, and disciplined by employees of the state, and only their labor placed at the disposal of the lessees, seemed to set this practice apart from the old lease system, but the difference must have been minimal, because in 1923 the state's commissioner of public welfare reported that the legislature was aroused in 1917, "after a terrific fight," to make several improvements in the prison system, including "a modification, not a complete elimination of the convict lease system."[61] A decade would pass before its last vestiges disappeared.

Arkansas

From 1847, to 1893, the penitentiary at Little Rock was in the hands of lessees whose views of their rights were expressed in 1882 in the response of one of them to a letter from an inquiring opponent of the lease system. He wrote that, "I am sole lessee and work all the convicts, and of course the business of the prison is my private business."[62] The state took control of the institution in 1893, but the leasing of convicts continued. Neither the penitentiary nor its prison farm, purchased in 1901, were able to furnish full employment to the growing number of convicts. The law required the institution to be self-supporting. A financially satisfactory solution was found in the leasing of surplus convicts to a contractor who in turn subleased them to farmers, manufacturers, and railroads. Although the state was responsible for the guarding, maintenance, and health care of the convicts in the lessees' camps, it is evident that conditions, especially in the coal mines and railroad camps, were deplorable. Three-fourths of the cases of sickness and death originated in them. These and other facts were revealed by an investigation which Governor George W. Donaghey undertook in 1912. He uncovered events which "could scarcely be accepted as truth gotten from official documents and personal statements among a civilized people." During the year 1912 for instance,

it was reported by the citizens of Malvern that while working near that town for a contractor on the railroad, a young white boy convict was compelled to work in the hot sun while he had a burning fever, that he was refused the necessary attention, and that the next day he died. Concerning this matter, it was published in the *Times-Journal,* a paper at Malvern, that information had been secured from the convicts that they were fed mostly on sour pork and beans, and were herded in cars at night, twenty-four or twenty-five men to the car, where they slept amid filth and vermin, and that the slightest complaint upon the part of any convict brought him a lashing on his back with a leather strap six feet long and four inches wide, and that men sent out from the walls [i.e., the penitentiary], unaccustomed to labor, to work on the railroads were made to do the hardest work in the hot sun from the start; and that, if they lagged or showed inability to do the work they were thrown to the ground and lashed with a strap to the extent of ten lashes and sometimes as many as fifteen, according to the humor of the warden.

It was reported from Ward station that, while working on the railroad for a contractor, a white boy convict, sentenced for a minor offense, was shot down and, after being delivered to the station to be transported to the hospital, while lying on the platform of the depot in the burning hot sun, his blood trickling down the planks of the platform, many people passed by and saw him. When he cried to passers-by to give him some relief, the warden refused to permit anyone to go near him. He was transported to the hospital, and next day died.[63]

The leasing of convicts ended in 1913.

Tennessee

The old penitentiary at Nashville became so overcrowded after the war that convicts were leased to various private employers, and in 1884, the entire convict population, then about a thousand strong, was leased to the Tennessee Coal and Iron Company for $101,000 a year. Five years later, a physician of the state board of health reported that in addition to the convicts held in the penitentiary, there were elsewhere in the state

the barracks, in which are confined, under the repression of the shot gun, the slaves whom the state has sold to the coal-mining company of the Cumberland plateau. Of their treatment the state knows nothing; the company cares nothing, except the amount of money that can be made out of them, and of that they seem to have rather a good opinion, as they show an evident preference for that sort of slave labor over the paid work of free men. Among the slaves so sold by the state to the company can frequently be found children under fifteen, training for no possible future but that of a felon's life.[64]

In 1893, the legislature decided to erect a second prison at Petros where several thousand acres of coal land belonged to the state. Wooden barracks were constructed to house the coal company's convicts.

Coal mining was the state's largest industry, but of the many mining companies in the state, only one had a convict lease and could underbid and undersell its competitors. Free miners had for years agitated against the system; they had seen convicts used as strikebreakers and their own wages depressed. The recurrent labor conflicts and the accompanying violence and disorders finally caused the state to end the leasing of convicts in 1895.[65]

Texas, Kentucky, and Virginia also used the convict lease system at one time, but the above illustrations suffice to fill in the picture. Designed to save

161

taxpayers the expense of supporting prisons and to make convict labor a source of revenue, it became a windfall for politically powerful lessees who profited from it and therefore resisted its abolition. It was a pernicious system which did nothing to reform offenders and subjected them, temporarily or for life, to a form of chattel slavery even worse than that from which blacks had been freed. It began, grew, and flourished only because almost all who suffered under it were ex-slaves whom the master class still thought of as belonging to an inferior race. This also accounts for the indifference toward the often shocking neglect and brutality of the lease camps, the cause of such abnormally high death and morbidity rates that official investigators in several states concluded that a convict who survived five to seven years in the camps, or two years in some of the lumber camps, could consider himself fortunate.

XII: CHAIN GANGS AND PRISON FARMS

With the demise of the lease system, one might assume that when states and counties took full control of convicts, its worst features—the lash, the sweat box, the stocks, the shackles, the ball-and-chain, and the intolerable working and living conditions imposed by bosses whose sole concern was maximum financial profit—would also vanish. To test this assumption it is necessary to look briefly at what followed: mainly the chain gang and the prison farm or plantation, the one constructing roads and the other raising and processing agricultural products.

The Chain Gang

In the late nineteenth century roads were largely primitive. The limited use of county-jail prisoners or state convicts on road-building was advocated and actually carried out in many states outside the South, but for most of the southern states which had used gangs of leased and chained convicts to build levees and railroads, the construction and maintenance of state highways and county roads by convict labor seemed an excellent way of meeting the rising needs of a new era—the automobile age—and avoid the building of costly prisons. The result was the adoption by most states of a penal institution which generally became known as the chain gang.

Originally, the chain gang was apparently a punishment reserved for ex-slaves or their descendants who committed crimes. This is shown in Alabama by the fact that when the lease system was abolished in 1923 and the State Highway Department was specifically authorized to work convicts on the public roads, it established road camps and hired *black* convicts from the board administering the state's penal system. At the end of 1941, there were twenty-five such camps in which 1,717 blacks were confined. Whites did not appear in them until several years later. Of the twenty-one camps, which in 1948 held about a thousand convicts, the three housing whites were said to be of recent origin. Two of them were listed as "honor camps," but that designation seemed to have been chosen merely "to differentiate them from the camps for Negro prisoners," because they were actually "not operated on the honor basis." [1]

163

Before we take a look at what life in the chain gang meant to its inmates, a brief sketch of this institution in two representative states, the Carolinas, will suffice to illustrate its rise and progress.

Only free blacks were subjected to penal slavery in North Carolina before the Civil War. In 1787, a free Negro or mulatto who was unable to pay a fine for "entertaining any slave on the Sabbath or at night . . . should be sold at auction . . . for the shortest time any one would pay the fine and costs."[2] A proviso added in 1831 specified that if no one paid the fine, the free colored person could be sold to any one who would pay the most for five years of his servitude. The chain gang was instituted in 1866, when the legislature authorized inferior and superior courts "to sentence the offender to work in chain gangs on the public roads of the county or on any railroad or other work of internal improvement in the state" for a term of a year or less. Overseers appointed by the county courts supervised the road workers. In 1870, an act provided that those sentenced to hard labor for less than two years were to be used to build roads, and overseers were authorized "to confine said convicts together with chain, or if need be with ball and chain."[3] In 1887 and 1889, statutes ordered that males punishable by imprisonment at hard labor in the county jail or for ten years or less in the state prison could instead by sentenced to work on the public roads of the county.* They would be under the control of the county authorities who would "have power to enact all needful rules and regulations for the successful working of the convicts on the public roads or in canaling the main drains and swamps or on other public work of the county."[4] Those certified by the county physician as seriously disabled physically would be sentenced to the county jail or the penitentiary.

After 1886, a number of counties established chain gangs which were sent out from the county workhouses which housed the convicts and where men sentenced to the roads for nonpayment of fines mingled with "felons—often degraded convicts—under sentences for loathsome or desperate crimes." [5] According to a report of the State Board of Charities, the management of these "little penitentiaries" was extremely lax in some counties and harsh in others due to the ignorance or inexperience of untrained officers. In the county with the largest chain gang, about a hundred convicts, a system prevailed of "loading with ball and chain the convict on the roads or the

---

*In 1915, two counties were authorized to send convicts to the roads for as long as twenty years, and in 1923, one county saw the upper limit reduced to five years. (Steiner and Brown, *op. cit.,* pp. 49–50.)

quarry, in addition to the armed guard, to prevent elopement. This is torture—instead of punishment." [6]

In his biennial report for 1907–08, the superintendent of the state prison wrote:

Under special acts of the legislature about forty counties in North Carolina have organized what are known as chain gangs [with a total of more than twelve hundred convicts] and use them in the construction and improvement of their public roads and highways. The State has granted to the counties absolutely and unconditionally the full management and control of these prisoners and has endeavored to surrender its responsibility for them, not even reserving a supervisory or inspectionary authority. Without the least concert with one another, each county is in supreme control of its own gang, prescribes its own rules of discipline, of clothing, of guarding, of quartering and of working. Consequently, in addition to what is known as the State Prison, North Carolina has forty wholly independent state prisons, under forty separate and distinct managements, with forty different and distinct rules and regulations, and over which there is absolutely no State supervision and inspection. The hospital facilities, at least, of all these many prisons are inadequate and defective, for in none of the counties is there a place, except the jail or workhouse quarters, where the sick or the enfeebled or the demented can be cared for and cured. I have been informed, but cannot substantiate the statement, that the average life of a road convict is less than five years. . . . The law evidently intends the punishment to fit the crime and that persons convicted of felony and given long terms shall be sent to the State's prison, while those convicted of less serious offenses, especially misdemeanors, shall be given shorter terms and lighter work upon the roads. And yet, under existing conditions, it is strangely true that harsher and more vigorous punishment is inflicted upon the petty offender than upon him who commits the more serious crime. . . . I believe [the present chain-gang policy of the State] . . . to be in every respect as defective and as full of possibilities for wrongdoing, cruelty and inhumanity as was the old convict-lease system.[7]

In 1931, when North Carolina had fifty-one county chain gangs, the legislature transferred the management of the state prison to the State Highway and Public Works Commission and gave that body full control of all prisoners sentenced to terms of sixty days or less, later changed to thirty days or less. This marked the end of the county chain gang. "Scandal after scandal, whisperings of sadistic cruelty, medieval tortures, brutal bosses—these have made the county prison camp in North Carolina notorious. Some of the county camps have been well managed . . . but certain incidents have pointed to cruelty and gross neglect." [8]

In addition to the central prison at Raleigh, which served as a receiving prison for all male prisoners, the Highway Commission in 1950 operated a prison for women for all women misdemeanants and felons, a youth center, opened in 1949, and three large prison farms with a total of eleven thousand acres housing about fifteen per cent of the total prisoner population, as well as eighty-five road camps throughout the state. Thirty-four of these camps were for whites, forty-nine for blacks, one for Indians, and one unsegregated. Twenty-nine of the camps housed misdemeanants, forty-one felons, fifteen both, and four first offenders.[9]

When the lease system was abandoned by South Carolina in 1885, the counties were again given almost complete control over the disposition of convicts. Those convicted of select serious crimes had to be committed to the penitentiary, but the counties could assign other felons to labor on public works. The penitentiary, therefore, became "to a great extent a dumping ground [with a] . . . population to an unusual degree made up of sick, injured, aged, and incorrigibles,"[10] able-bodied males being sent to the county chain gangs. In 1926, all but two of the forty-six counties had such gangs, with a total population of 298 white and 1,017 black inmates.[11] Five years later the number of chain gang counties had declined to thirty-four. The others hired out their convicts to them, as did the municipalities "authorized to place convicts on the county chain gangs" if they had none of their own.[12] A research agency reported in 1968 that

the chain gang has flourished ever since [1885]. . . . It has been entirely under the direction of the county supervisors, without supervision from any state-wide authority and without any notion of treatment or reeducation. The camps are not inspected by the boards of health, although this is required by law. Convicts sentenced to the camps are not medically examined, and the law expressly permits the housing together of tubercular and non-tubercular convicts. . . . We do not know how many chain gang convicts are repeaters. No reports are made to the State; but the number of convicts working for the county is estimated at more than 2000.[13]

A survey of the development of the chain gang in other states of the South would show variations, but the basic character of the institution was the same everywhere. Like the lease system, it was designed to exploit the labor of the prisoners to produce maximum profits at minimum cost. The means previously used by lessees to achieve this end were also adopted—shackles and armed guards to prevent escapes, and the lash and instruments of torture to discipline the laggard and the unruly.

The chaining of the men at work or in the road camps was considered to be a self-evident necessity. The chains, a substitute for the locks and bars of a maximum-security prison, were in use everywhere. In North Carolina, for instance, either an iron or steel band was clamped on the left ankle, or both ankles, in which case they were connected by a twenty-inch chain. In either instance, a three-foot long chain was attached to the ankle iron or the connecting chain and hooked on the prisoner's belt. Some prisoners were hobbled by "a sharp pointed iron . . . resembling an ordinary pick with the 'eye' riveted around the ankle. Its two prongs, each ten inches in length and bent slightly upwards, extended out from the ankle both in front and behind."[14] This hampered a man's mobility day and night.

The practice of chaining varied a great deal as the years passed. In the 1930s, seven of the thirty-seven North Carolina counties having chain gangs dispensed with irons; some of the others chained most of the men, and still others only a few. Generally, "trusties"—i.e., picked men entrusted with chores around the camps—were not chained, nor were prisoners in "honor camps." The chains would not disappear until after World War II.

Chains were worn constantly. Only a blacksmith could remove them. At night in the more or less permanent, crowded bunkhouses, the belt chain mentioned earlier was attached to a metal rod or long chain which ran the length of the lodging at the foot of the beds. The same was done in the large tents which, because they could so easily be moved from one work site to another, were not uncommon. But the worst of the mobile camps, used extensively in the Carolinas, Georgia, and Florida by the smaller rural counties, was the cage on wheels. In his message to the Florida legislature in 1911, Governor Gilchrist, who hoped to see all state convicts placed on the projected state prison farm at Raiford, indignantly described a visit to a Georgia convict road camp where "the men sleep in a movable car placed on four wheels, with bars, constructed very much [like] . . . a car . . . in which animals are conveyed [by] . . . the circuses showing throughout the State, with this exception: in the circus cars there are usually only one or two animals. In the convict cars, there are sometimes ten or twelve convicts. They are shackled and connected with a chain at night." [15] In the 1930s, the typical North Carolina cage was about the size of a small moving van, eighteen feet long and seven or eight feet wide and high. Roof, floor, and ends were of solid steel and the sides "a close network of flat steel bars." Tarpaulins could be rolled down outside in wet or cold weather, leaving the interior dark. Entrance to the cage was through a rear steel door padlocked on the outside. Inside and lengthwise were six three-decker bunks divided by an aisle about two feet wide. The cage was heated by a small stove in the aisle at the front; a kerosene lantern swinging from the ceiling gave light. Each bunk had a mattress, usually without sheet and blankets. "A night bucket and a pail of drinking water completed the equipment. When the cage is filled to capacity, there is no place for the men except in their bunks, which are too low for a sitting posture." [16] The prisoners often had to stay in these cages from Saturday noon to Monday morning and on holidays or when bad weather halted work.

The housing of the Whitfield County chain gang in Georgia, said to be typical of most of the 150 chain gangs maintained in that state in 1933, was described as follows:

Parked along the road among the scrub pine stands a row of great wagons, square like those in which a circus keeps its pacing animals. A lattice of steel bars forms the sides. Within each cage-on-wheels, 12 men are confined. Six bunks are along each side, three deep, end to end. In these, after long hours of back-breaking work on the roads, often chained to each other, men sleep in the same sweat-begrimed clothes in which they have worked all day. A heavy canvas curtain, which may be unrolled to cover the barred sides of the cage, is their only protection against weather. In each cage is a narrow cutoff, above a metal tub suspended just beneath the cage. That is the only sanitary arrangement. . . . These cages . . . meet all the requirements of the State Prison Commission for living quarters "when not in permanent quarters." The rules provide for substantial buildings for "permanent quarters" but this county has never had any.[17]

Pick and shovel were the chief tools of the chain gang, which worked a ten-to-twelve-hour day, depending on the season. The labor was performed under the supervision of the camp warden or captain chosen for his knowledge of road building, and under the guns of poorly paid guards. An official report noted that in North Carolina

the most frequent wage is around fifty dollars a month. Such a wage, coupled with the class of work that a guard on a typical chain gang must do, does not often attract the type of man who is fit to have charge of other men. The guard is usually without even an elementary education, often practically illiterate. He is ignorant, of course, of any method of controlling men except by force.[18]

The chain gang was a purely custodial institution. Since its only purpose was to keep prisoners at hard labor, punishment awaited any man who tried to escape and survived or who failed to perform his assigned task. The nature of the punishment depended on the attitude of the camp captain and on the limits fixed by law or regulation, both of which were widely ignored. Flogging by strap or lash was still legal in the South before World War II, except in Florida, Georgia, and North Carolina, and was the most common of the more severe punishments, but other excruciating legal means were also used, such as the stocks in Georgia and the sweat box in Florida.

In the Whitfield County camp in Georgia,

beneath a scraggly pine stands a curious wood contraption with a row of holes in its face. This is an improved model of stocks, not like the simple model in the history books. These stocks are authorized by the State Prison Commission as one form of punishment called on its books "restricted movement." The convict sits on the sharpened edge of a board, hands and feet stretched out before him and locked in holes between two other boards. An hour, the rules say, is the limit of this punishment, which is inflicted by the camp warden on any prisoners who do not work hard enough on the roads or who break discipline in camp.[19]

When flogging was abolished in Florida in 1923, another form of disciplinary punishment was invented—solitary confinement—but not as this is ordinarily understood. Rules and regulations issued by the Commissioner of Agriculture stated that "for refusing to work, or refusing to do his work in a proper and workmanlike manner, a convict shall be confined in solitary confinement for such time as may be necessary [and] . . . placed on a restricted diet . . . in extreme cases reduced to bread and water." The punishment should last "until he shall faithfully promise to abide by the rules of the prison and to do his work in the best manner of which he is capable, but "in no case shall a convict be required to remain in solitary confinement and on restricted rations long enough . . . as to endanger his life or permanently impair his health." The instrument for this punishment was to be a cell with solid walls and "3 feet wide, 6 feet 6 inches long and 7 feet from the floor to the grating over the top" and "so constructed that it can be divided across in two equal parts, and a convict may be confined in one half of the space in the day time, but shall have the full space in the night time." This cell became known as the sweat box. Its effect on those confined in it caused Dr. W. H. Cox, the state prison physician, to report in 1931 that "if within my power to do so, I would change the mode of punishment. . . . I doubt the constitutionality of the authority to devitalize a man and call it punishment or chastisement." [20]

This observation was dramatized the following year when a New Jersey teenager, Arthur Maillefert, died in the sweatbox at the Sunbeam camp in Duval county. He was ill and unable to work on the road. The camp captain and his "whipping boss" said he was shamming. After beating him mercilessly, they placed him in the sweat box, locked his feet in clamps, and placed a chain attached to an overhead beam around his neck. He was found strangled to death in the morning. A local justice of the peace pronounced it suicide, but an official investigation led to the indictment of the responsible officers on a charge of murder. They were convicted of manslaughter. The investigation revealed that brutal treatment of prisoners was commonplace in the camp, as it was in many other Florida camps in spite of laws and regulations.[21]

The evils of the chain gang system went beyond the terrible conditions and abuses just related. It would be unreasonable to assume that all chain gangs were managed by brutal, unfeeling men. Alabama's road camps were given high marks by northern investigators, for instance, but the very purpose of the system, run by whites in charge of gangs of blacks or of "poor white trash" and "damn Yankees," made it, in the words of an early superintendent of North Carolina's state prison, "in every respect as full of possibilities for wrong-doing, cruelty and inhumanity as was the old convict-lease system." This was not a prophecy, it was a fact.

The reports of southern official agencies or investigators of the chain gangs abound with observations on their filthy, unsanitary conditions, the vermin-ridden bunks, the lack of medical care, the inhumane discipline, the indiscriminate mingling in the racially segregated camps of young and old, first offenders and old hands, felons and misdemeanants; and the callous attitudes of the officials, which reflected the popular sentiment that the punishment of criminals be vindictive and retributive.[22] In that stifling atmosphere prison reformers fought an uphill battle which in some states was not partially won until the mid-fifties, and in others is still being waged even though the old primitive chain gang is now history.

The Plantation Prisons

When leasing ended, some states, especially in the deep South, established huge prison plantations and farms to house and employ convicts not used on the roads. Conspicuous examples are furnished by Alabama, Arkansas, Florida, Louisiana, Mississippi, and Texas,[23] but while these institutions generally proved to be highly profitable financially, the treatment of their inmates did not rise much above the level of the lessee camps and chain gangs.

In Louisiana, for instance, when the monopoly on leased convict labor held by the firm headed by Major James for three decades was broken in 1901, the state promptly bought James's Angola plantation with its prisons and continued the raising of cotton and, later, sugar cane. Additional land was acquired; by 1929, Angola had 18,000 acres, and a smaller plantation at Monticello 3,500 acres. The old Baton Rouge penitentiary served as a receiving and classification depot only, the classification consisting simply of determining the kind of labor to which the convict should be assigned. In a system which regarded the convict as a mere money-making machine there was no room for notions of rehabilitation, especially since 84 per cent of the convicts were black, for whom "agricultural work and Sunday preaching" were deemed adequate rehabilitative agents.[24] This prescription was evidently no cure-all, for in 1908, 99 per cent of the "first class" convicts sent to the back-breaking labor in the levee camps were black, and the percentage of blacks among the "second class" convicts reserved for the sugar plantation was almost the same. Nearly all white convicts were rated "third class" and assigned to the cotton fields of Angola, where the ratio of blacks to whites was 1.4 to 1.[25] Since, according to Professor Mark T. Carleton, historian of the Louisiana state penal system, "black convicts ... were treated very much like black slaves had been treated on any large 'well-run' antebellum plantation," [26] it is clear that white convicts now shared that treatment, including the corporal punishments no longer sanctioned by the criminal law but approved by administrative law. Compared with the era of James, the state is said to have become more paternalistic and less brutal in its treatment of convicts, but the pace of progress was snaillike.

In 1917, in order to save money, the paid guard force was replaced by armed "trusty" convicts, an iniquitous system then also in use in Arkansas, Florida, and Mississippi; there were still 239 such convict-guards at Angola in 1969. Flogging was one method of enforcing obedience to rules and diligence. In 1933, there were 1,547 known floggings, with a total of "23,889 recorded blows of the double lash." From 1928 to 1940, there were 10,000 recorded floggings, some of 50 lashes each. How many were unrecorded, no one knows, for although Governor James ordered a stop to this punishment in 1941, the order was simply ignored. Three years later, an investigating committee reported to the Governor "that sanitary conditions were 'decidedly inadequate', gambling was Angola's only 'organized' recreation, flogging on a scale just 'short of rank torture' was practiced, 'vice conditions' were 'almost universal' and separation of convicts according to nature of offense and length of sentence was 'practically nonexistent'." [27]

In 1951, thirty-seven white convicts in a camp for "uncooperative" prisoners cut their heel tendons in order

to attract public attention to the conditions under which they lived and worked ... being quartered in filthy and overcrowded barracks known as "jungle camps," where hundreds of men sleeping in double and triple-decked beds were jammed into space barely adequate for a hundred men; work in the fields from dawn to dusk with insufficient food and inadequate medical attention, flogging and other brutal punishments for failure to keep up with one's task as well as for disciplinary infractions; the use of armed prisoners as guards; the generally low quality of paid personnel; the almost complete absence of rehabilitation programs and of professionally or technically trained personnel; inequities in pardons and paroles, with preferential granting of releases to prisoners with political influence and/or hard cash; and other evils, large and small. Official investigations revealed that these conditions were real, not imaginary. In 1952 the Angola penitentiary was publicized as "America's Worst prison" . . . although it was not without competition for that dubious distinction.[28]

Reforms were instituted. A highly competent federal prison administrator was appointed head of the prisons, a modern penitentiary capable of housing 2,160 prisoners—240 in cells and 1,920 in 32 sixty-man dormitories—was built, personnel was placed under civil service, flogging, sweat boxes, "and other archaic forms of punishment were abolished," and many other commendable changes made, but a disastrous reduction in the appropriation for the prisons in 1962 started the institution on a down-grade course again.[29] In 1971, Carleton wrote that "today, despite gradual alterations and nominal progress, these institutions remain much as they were at the turn of the century and are thus penologically, socially and economically two generations out of date." [30]

Angola's reputation was unsavory, but the Arkansas penitentiary would have won the prize in any competition for the "dubious distinction" of being "America's worst prison." This is evident from facts uncovered in 1966 by an official investigation of its administration. As early as 1901, Arkansas had established a prison farm to which convicts not leased or needed at the Little Rock penitentiary could be sent to hard labor. After the abolition of the lease system in 1913, a second prison farm was acquired in 1916. When the old penitentiary was closed in 1933, the older Cummins Farm and newer Tucker Farm constituted the penitentiary. They were large farms, Cummins with 16,200 and Tucker with 4,500 acres, on which livestock and rice, cotton, soy beans, cucumbers, strawberries, wheat, oats, field corn, and sorghum were raised. Except for a few blacks on "death row," Tucker had only white male prisoners, while Cummins housed black males and females and some white male "incorrigibles." Of a total of about sixteen hundred prisoners, about three hundred were kept at Tucker, most of them very young. The institutions were managed by a superintendent responsible to a five-member board of superannuated politicians appointed by the governor. An assistant superintendent was in charge of Tucker which, in August, 1966, became the scene of an official inquiry by the Criminal Investigation Division (CID) of the State Police, following complaints that liquor was being smuggled into the institution. The investigation revealed shocking conditions of corruption and maltreatment, all meticulously described in a report submitted to the governor.[31]

172

The main building consisted of a long, wide corridor known as "The Yard" which gave access to offices, an auditorium, a mess hall, three dormitory wings or "barracks," and a block of fourteen cells for prisoners in isolation or awaiting execution. Each dormitory, fifty by one hundred feet in size, had a hundred beds. One barrack was reserved for the "rank men," or farm laborers, another for "do-pops," prisoners holding privileged jobs, and the third for the "trusties," who made up the guard force; this third dormitory was never locked at night.

The mattresses [of the barracks] were filthy and rotten . . . cotton was spilling out of the majority . . . from worn and torn spots . . . sheets were dirty and appeared to have been used for two or three weeks without change. Over half of the beds did not have any pillows. . . . The showers were pouring water from leaks. The commodes were stopped up or would not flush. The urinals were stopped up and in general disrepair. The entire barracks smelled from filth. The floors were dirty and littered. Shake-downs of the barracks uncovered sixty-one knives, five pairs of fighting knuckles, two palm weights for fighting, five blackjacks and clubs, and one hatchet, as well as "whiskey bottles, keys to open all doors, gambling equipment . . . illegal drugs and narcotics," etc.

The mess hall with the kitchen in the center of it was dirty.

Flies were very thick and there was no screen on the door leading to the wash rack and vegetable room. The food and meat were piled on the cook tables completely exposed to the flies. . . . Tin cans with the tops cut out were used as cups. The pitchers and trays were badly bent and damaged. All cooking utensils were in a state of disrepair or damaged beyond repair.[32]

The prisoners ran the institution. Every department—kitchen, commissary, hospital, security, etc.—was headed by a trusty. Armed trusties, preferably chosen from among those serving long sentences for homicide or armed robbery, manned the guard towers on the periphery and the gates and escorted all work gangs. The assistant superintendent, known as "The Man," a bookkeeper, and three "wardens" (in reality mere custodians) were the only "free-world" people in the institution. Next to "The Man," the most important person inside was the chief trusty, or "Yard Man."

When the "long line" of the "rank men," who constituted about a third of the inmate population, filed out at daybreak for work in the fields until dark, they were escorted by a foreman, or "rider," and two "high-powers" on horseback armed with carbines. Two "shotguns" on foot accompanied the line at a distance of fifty to seventy-five yards. Two more "shotguns" and a "sub rider," or straw boss, brought up the rear. Farther behind, two "high powers" backed up the force in case of trouble.[33] The CID investigator saw the laborers brought back from the fields for their evening meal. They seemed to him to be from forty to sixty pounds under weight.

> Their clothing [whites]* were filthy. . . . Several inmates were wearing trousers, torn up the inseam and outseam to the hips. Their shoes were in terrible disrepair and seemed to be several sizes too large . . . worn out, had no strings and had holes along the soles and across the tops. The inmates stated that they had no shoes and either were required to wear the rubber boots or go barefooted . . . they had never been issued underwear, and socks were issued only twice a year [two pairs at a time][34]

The evening meal of the "rank men" consisted, according to one source, of rice, soy beans, corn bread, and ice water.[35] The food seen by the CID investigator was "a very thin, watered-down serving of rice. One large tablespoon per inmate. . . . Meat was served . . . once a month on visiting Sunday . . . in small portions. . . . Milk and eggs were drawn from Cummins prison but were used only for cooking and for trusties. . . . Inmates received one egg per year on Christmas morning and were never given milk to drink." [36] The trusties fared better. "Many of them had steak for breakfast and pork chops and hamburgers." [37] Trusties took their meals apart from the "rank men."

The prison was riddled with graft. "The Man," who was soon to retire, urged the CID investigator to seek his job. It offered many attractions: a fourteen-room mansion, maintenance, a new car each year, an expense account, and a salary of eight thousand dollars which was "the smallest part of the job [because] . . . a lot of gifts would be offered from business people in the farm-supply trade, people in the clothing business, and other 'interested persons' [and] . . . that it was only 'smart' to accept the gifts." As for the rules made by the prison board, they could be ignored with impunity. Both the prisoners and the "wardens" should be taught who was boss. "If a prisoner got out of line he should be 'hit with anything you can get your hands on', because that's the only thing they respect." The wardens should be watched because one was "a drunken whore chaser," another "a good man but a thief and too open with it," and the third new and ignorant.[38] He said that he knew that "gambling, selling jobs, drinking, and so forth," was rampant, but this "was 'as old as the penitentiary', and while it might be slowed down, it will continue regardless of what is done to stop it. . . . A person must learn to turn his back on some things, such as wives and girl

---

*The traditional striped clothing was discontinued in 1929. Only "rank men" wore white clothing. Trusties wore khaki, and "do-pops" one white and one khaki garment.

friends visiting inmates and going off places together," and that "while this is a violation of regulation, it seemed to keep the inmates in a better frame of mind." [39]

The investigation confirmed the prevalence of all these practices. The "Day Yard Man" frankly explained that he was "The Man's" representative "in job-selling and loaning money to the other inmates" at a hundred per cent interest.[40] As much as a thousand dollars had been paid by parents to get, their inmate sons transferred from the hard labor in the fields to jobs in the laundry, for instance. "Almost everything could be had at Tucker farm, if you could get the money"—better food, whiskey brought in by a warden or a trusty, or "pills." [41]

The prisoners were brutally treated. The chief sufferers were the "rank men." Working under the gun for ten or twelve hours and even longer, with only a noon break for a lunch of bread and "weevils, beans, and collards in a kind of soup mixture" spooned out into tin cans or canteen cups from buckets on a mule-drawn wagon,[42] they were constantly in fear of being beaten for failure to complete their tasks, often because of inexperience, weakness, or illness. Then the riders, like the slave drivers of old, belabored them with cudgels, knotted ropes, or canes, or reported them to "The Man" for harsher discipline. Arkansas was the only state to still allow the whipping of prisoners. Regulations required that a prisoner be given a hearing before being whipped and limited the number of blows to ten, but neither of these rules were observed in practice. The instrument used was a leather strap, five feet long, five inches wide, and three eighths of an inch thick, attached to an eighteen-inch long wooden handle.[43] Many inmates reported that they had been tortured, wire pliers being used to pinch fingers, toes, noses, ears, or genitals, and needles inserted under the fingernails. The most dreaded instrument was the "Tucker telephone." Consisting of "an electrical generator taken from a ring-type telephone, placed in sequence with two dry cell batteries," it was "attached to an undressed inmate . . . by means of one electrode to a big toe and the second electrode to the penis, at which time a crank was turned sending an electrical charge into the body of the inmate; . . . several charges were introduced . . . designed to stop just short of the inmate 'passing out.'"* The investigator discovered this instrument in the assistant superintendent's residence and confiscated it.[44]

The findings of the investigation brought results. The state police were

---

*A federal trial of the assistant superintendent on charges of subjecting prisoners to cruel and unusual punishment by the use of the "Tucker Telephone" resulted in a hung jury. (*The New York Times,* October 23, 1969.)

temporarily placed in charge of the institution after the civilian staff was fired. The legislature created a penitentiary study commission to review the penal system and recommend reforms.[45] An experienced and progressive prison administrator was brought in from outside the state to modernize the institutions. His vigorous efforts gave promise of considerable success, but his unorthodox methods antagonized the Establishment and led to his early dismissal.* Some improvements were made, including the official abolition of corporal punishments, but old and ingrained attitudes and habits of management, difficult to eradicate, persisted.

We have only sampled the institutions—chain gangs and prison farms—which state and local governments developed to replace the convict lease system. The assumption that a change from private to public administration of punishment would radically improve the manner and means of dealing with convicts did not prove accurate, because the deeply rooted public view of punishment as retribution had not changed, nor were the governments any less eager than the lessees had been to have the labor of the convicts yield maximum financial profit. Systems which looked upon the convict as a public slave did not offer much room for programs of rehabilitation.

---

*Mr. Tom Murton was superintendent during thirteen months. His book, already cited, is a vivid portrayal of his experiences in office.

Postscript

The survey just completed was begun for the purpose of examining the validity of Radbruch's contention that the punishments for crimes embodied in the criminal law were originally punishments reserved for slaves. Therefore, a final commentary seems proper.

In societies where chattel slavery was regarded as a normal social institution, slaves were articles of property, which like other property could be bought, sold, transferred, inherited, traded, and even discarded. They were their masters' animate tools, useful for the production of wealth by manual labor. As human beings, they were components of a caste possessing none of the rights enjoyed by free men and occupying a status below the bottom rung of the social ladder. Their status was thought to be the natural consequence of their mental and moral inferiority. Being "born for slavery," their exploitation was defended and justified as being their ordained fate, and their labor was the hallmark of their status; it tainted their occupations as "slave labor" unfit or unbecoming to free men.

The intrinsic nature of chattel slavery caused the development of a penal system appropriate for slaves, a system in which the master, as prosecutor, judge, and enforcer, administered justice within his domestic establishment, undisturbed by public authorities. The offending slave could be tortured to extort a confession and reveal his accomplices. Since he owned nothing, he was usually beaten or whipped. In both ancient and modern slaveholding societies, the whip was the instrument used to enforce obedience, but other means were also employed, such as stocks, fetters, and confinement. For gross offenses the slave might be killed by his master. Like other livestock, he could be branded, especially if he was prone to run away.

The prototypes of this domestic penal system are found in ancient societies, which devised a different system for dealing with their offending citizens. In Greece and Rome, citizens could not be subjected to judicial torture for violating the law, nor could they be flogged. They were fined, exiled, their property perhaps confiscated, punishments inapplicable to slaves. As Demosthenes noted, slaves were punished in their bodies, citizens in their property.

The transformation of this system into one which made the domestic punishments for slaves applicable to nearly all free men who broke the law was completed during the Roman Empire and hastened by the granting of

Roman citizenship to practically all freeborn males of Roman or barbarian origin within its borders. Abandoning the old republican principles of the equality of citizens before the law, the upper classes—the *honestiores*— retained for criminals of their own status the traditional punishments of exile, deportation, fines, and confiscation of property, beheading, and freedom from torture. For the lower classes, the *humiliores*, who composed the vast majority of the population, they introduced judicial torture and the old slave punishments of hanging, crucifixion, and burning at the stake, as well as sentences to death in the arena mangled by beasts or killed by gladiators. They were subjected to a punishment which was to become favored for criminals from the lower classes, namely penal slavery in imperial mines and factories and on public works. Manual labor, despised by the upper classes, thus became a new kind of corporal punishment for crime.

A similar evolution, partly indigenous and partly influenced by Roman traditions, would produce in the Germanic nations of the Middle Ages a penal system which oppressed the lower classes and favored the dominant upper classes, who then as later shaped the law and administered justice. By the end of the twelfth century, the capital and corporal punishments, which in the past offending slaves alone had suffered, had been enshrined in law and would become fixtures in the criminal laws of all Western nations. Some of them survive to the present day, evidencing the slavish origin of penal systems and the persistence of attitudes and practices engendered by it, and confirming Radbruch's contention.

Notes

PREFACE

1. Georg Rusche and Otto Kirchheimer, *Punishment and Social Structure.* With a Foreword by Thorsten Sellin (New York: Columbia University Press, 1939), p. 5.
2. *Ibid.* pp. 6–7.
3. "Der Ursprung des Strafrechts aus dem Stande der Unfreien," reprinted in Gustav Radbruch, *Elegantiae juris criminalis* (Basel: Verlag für Recht und Gesellschaft, 1950).
4. *Ibid,* pp. 11–12.

CHAPTER I

1. A. H. M. Jones, *Athenian Democracy* (Oxford: Blackwell, 1964), p. 79.
2. Victor Ehrenberg, *The Greek State* (2d ed.; London: Methuen, 1969), p. 31.
3. William. L. Westermann, *The Slave Systems of Greek and Roman Antiquity* (Philadelphia: American Philosophical Society, 1955), p. 9; *see also* his "Athenaeus and the Slaves of Athens," *Athenian Studies* (Cambridge: Harvard University Press, 1940), pp. 451–70.
4. Gustave Glotz, *Ancient Greece at Work* (New York: Barnes & Noble, 1965), p. 90.
5. Ehrenberg, *op. cit.,* p. 31.
6. *Plato's Statesman,* trans. J. S. Kemp, edited with an Introduction by Martin Oswald (New York: Liberal Arts Press, 1957), 262d.
7. *The Politics of Aristotle,* translated with an introduction, notes and appendices by Ernest Barker (New York: Oxford University Press, 1962), 1327b.
8. *Ibid.,* 1253b, 1254a, 1254b.
9. *Ibid.,* 1252a, 1255a, 1254b, 1260a, 1254b.
10. *Ibid.,* 1252b.
11. *Ibid.,* 1255a.
12. *Ibid.,* 1255b.
13. Quoted by William Chase Greene, *Moira, Fate, Good and Evil in Greek Thought* (New York: Harper & Row, 1963), pp. 238–39.
14. Glotz, *op. cit.,* p. 219.
15. *Plutarch's Lives,* translated from the original Greek with notes, historical and critical, and a life of Plutarch by John Langhorne and William Langhorne (4 vols.; Philadelphia, 1825), I, 171.
16. *Demosthenes' Orations,* introduction by John Warrington (Everyman's Library No. 546; London: Dent, 1967), p. 243. According to Aristotle (*op. cit.,* 1276a), menials were of two kinds, "slaves who do menial duties for individuals, and mechanics and laborers, who do them for the community."
17. In Donald Kagan (ed.), *Sources in Greek Political Thought from Homer to Polybius* (New York: Free Press, 1965), p. 99.
18. Plato, *The Laws,* translated with an Introduction by Trevor J. Saunders (Baltimore: Penguin Books, 1970), 847, 919.
19. Aristotle, *op. cit.,* 1337b, 1328b–29a.
20. Plato, *op. cit.,* 776.
21. Ehrenberg, *loc. cit.*

22. Thucydides, *History of the Peloponnesian War,* trans. Richard Crawley (London: J. M. Dent & Sons, 1910), p. 298.
23. Plutarch, *op. cit.,* I, 126–27. Such exercises must have been rare, according to H. Michell, *Sparta,* (Cambridge: Cambridge University Press, 1964), p. 84.
24. H. D. F. Kitto, *The Greeks* (London: Pelican Books, 1951), p. 128.
25. Glotz, *op. cit.,* p. 212.
26. Alfred Zimmern, *The Greek Commonwealth, Politics and Economics in Fifth-Century Athens* (5th rev. ed.; London: Oxford University Press, 1931), chap. 15.
27. Plato, *op. cit.,* 776.
28. See Glenn R. Morrow, *Plato's Law of Slavery in its Religion to Greek Law* (Urbana: University of Illinois Press, 1939), pp. 33–34.
29. Zimmern, *op. cit.,* p. 400; Edouard Ardaillon, *Les mines du l'aurion dans l'antiquité,* (Paris, 1897).
30. Kagan, *op. cit.,* p. 100.
31. Plato, *op. cit.,* 870.
32. Kagan, *op. cit.,* p. 145.
33. Plato, *Gorgias,* 525.
34. Kagan, *op. cit.,* p. 141.
35. *Ibid.,* p. 40.
36. Thucydides, *op. cit.,* pp. 199–201.
37. Morrow, *op. cit.,* p. 67.
38. Berthold Freudenthal, in *Zum ältesten Strafrecht der Kulturvölker. Fragen . . . gestellt von Theodor Mommsen* (Leipzig: Duncker & Humblot, 1905), p. 14.
39. Piero Fiorelli, *La tortura giudiziaria nel diritto comune* (2 vols.; Milano: Giuffré, 1953), I, 13.
40. Aristophanes, *Plays,* trans. Patric Dickinson (2 vols.; London: Oxford University Press, 1970), II, 250–6.
41. Irving Barkan, "Imprisonment as a Penalty in Ancient Athens," *Classical Philology* 31: (1936), pp. 338–41; Robert J. Bonner and Gertrude Smith, *The Administration of Justice from Homer to Aristotle,* (Chicago: University Press, 1938), pp. 275–76.
42. Plato, *The Laws,* Saunders' Introduction, p. 31, 908.
43. *Ibid.,* 908–9.
44. *Ibid.,* 919–20.
45. *Ibid.,* 880.
46. Glotz, *op. cit.,* p. 193.
47. Freudenthal, *op. cit.,* p. 16.
48. *Diodorus of Sicily,* with an English translation by C. H. Oldfather (10 vols.; Cambridge: Harvard University Press, 1935), II, book 3, 12–14; Glotz, *op. cit., pp. 353, 356–57.*
49. Herodotus, *History of the Greek and Persian War,* (New York: Washington Square Press, 1963), II, 124.
50. Jean Imbert, *La peine de mort. Histoire-Actualité,* (Paris: Armand Colin, 1967), p. 16; Jacques Champollion, *The World of the Egyptians,* (Geneva: Minerva, 1971), p. 14.
51. *Plutarch's Moralia: Twenty Essays,* trans. Philemon Holland (London: J. M. Dent, n.d.), p. 171.

CHAPTER II

1. William L. Westermann, *The Slave Systems of Greek and Roman Antiquity* (Philadelphia: American Philosophical Society, 1955), p. 69; R. H. Barrow, *Slavery in the Roman Empire* (New York: Barnes & Noble, 1968), p. 21.
2. Léon Halkin, *Les esclaves publics chez les Romains* (Bruxelles, 1897); Barrow, *op. cit.,* chap. 5.

3. Moses Hadas (ed.), *Basic Works of Cicero* (New York: Modern Library, 1951), p. 19

4. W. W. Buckland, *The Roman Law of Slavery xii, 735 pp.* (Cambridge: University Press, 1970), p. 36.

5. *Diodorus of Sicily* (12 vols.; London: Heinemann, 1933–67), V. 38.1

6. H. H. Scullard, *From the Gracchi to Nero* (New York: Barnes & Noble, 1963), pp. 95–96.

7. *The Satyricon* (Ann Arbor: University of Michigan Press, 1962), p. 130.

8. *Ibid.*, p. 50.

9. Tacitus, *Annals*, XV, 44.

10. Ugo Brasiello, *La repressione penale in diritto romano* (Naples, 1937), pp. 369–70.

11. Buckland, *op. cit.*, p. 36.

12. *Ibid.*, p. 37.

13. Tenney Frank, *Rome and Italy of the Republic* (Paterson, N.J.: Pageant Books, 1959), p. 384.

14. Tacitus, *op. cit.*, XIII, 27.

15. Westermann, *op. cit.*, pp. 141–42.

16. A. H. M. Jones, "Slavery in the Ancient World," *The Economic History Review*, 2d ser. 9: (1956), p. 198; also reproduced in Finley, *op. cit.*

17. The history of the Roman law of capital punishment is authoritatively treated in Ernst Levy, *Die römische Kapitalstrafe* (Heidelberg, 1931; Sitzungsbericht der Heidelberger Akademie der Wissenschaften, Philos. histor. Klasse, 1930–31, No. 5).

18. A.H.M. Jones, *The Criminal Courts of the Roman Republic and Principate* (Totowa, N.J.: Rowman and Littlefield, 1972), pp. 17, 74.

19. Brasiello, *op. cit.*, pp. 55–56.

20. Piero Fiorelli, *La tortura giudiziaria nel diritto comune* (2 vols.; Milano: Giuffré, 1953), I, 22–25.

21. *Ibid.*, pp. 25–43.

22. The best secondary sources for the history of the development of the discriminatory penal system of the Empire that I have found besides Brasiello's work (already cited) are G. Cardascia's "L'apparition dans le droit des classes d' 'honestiores' et d' 'humiliores'," *Rev. histor. de droit francais et étranger*, 1950, pp. 305–37, 461–84; and Peter Garnsey's *Social Status and Legal Privilege in the Roman Empire* (Oxford: Clarendon Press, 1970). They have all relied heavily on Justinian's *Digest*, which has also been available to me in Pothier's edition of 1818 in its Italian translation, published in Venice in 1841–42.

23. Buckland, *op. cit.*, pp. 277–78, 403–6; Brasiello, *op. cit.*, chap. 15.

24. Ludwig Friedländer, *Roman Life and Manners under the Early Empire* (4 vols.; New York: Barnes & Noble, 1956), II, 40–90.

25. Alban D. Wimper, *Lucretius and Scientific Thought* (Montreal: Harvest House, 1963), p. 48.

26. *Digest* 48.19.40, marginal commentary by Pothier; see note 22.

CHAPTER III

1. Sir Frederick Pollock and Frederic William Maitland, *The History of English Law Before the Time of Edward I* (2d ed., 2 vols.; Cambridge: 1968), I, 49. After the appearance of the first edition in 1895, Pollock wrote his American friend Justice Oliver Wendell Holmes that his only contribution to this monumental work was most of the Introduction, the chapter on Anglo-Saxon law, and the bulk of the chapter on Contract. *See* C. H. S. Fifoot, *Frederic William Maitland: A Life* (Cambridge, Mass., 1971), pp. 139–40.

2. L. von Bar, *Geschichte des deutschen Strafrechts und Straftheorien* (Berlin, 1882), English translation in Carl Ludwig von Bar *et al.*, *A History of Continental Criminal Law* (Boston, 1916), pp. 74–75.

3. "Der Ursprung des Strafrechts aus dem Stande der Unfreien," in Gustav Radbruch, *Elegantiae Juris Criminalis* (2d ed.; Basel, 1950), pp. 1–12. Another version in Gustav Radbruch and Heinrich Gwinner, *Geschichte des Verbrechens* (Stuttgart, 1951), chaps. 1 and 2. The same view was later expounded by Eberhardt Schmidt in his *Einführung in die Geschichte der deutschen Strafrechtspflege* (Göttingen, 1947), without mention of Radbruch, an oversight corrected in the second edition (1951, p. 26). Arthur Wenger, in his *Strafrecht: Allgemeiner Teil* (Göttingen, 1951), p. 42, praises Radbruch and Schmidt for having "sharpened our view of slave punishments as the root of corporal punishments."
4. E. A. Thompson, "Slavery in Early Germany," reprinted in M. I. Finley (ed.), *Slavery in Classical Antiquity* (Cambridge, 1960), pp. 191–203.
5. *op. cit.,* 9. 8.
6. "Under this king the Goths began to have the ordinances of the laws in writing, for before this they were bound only by customs and habit." Isidore of Seville's *History of the Goths, Vandals, and Suevi* (Leiden, 1970), p. 17.
7. *See* Katherine Fischer Drew, "The Barbarian Kings as Legislators and Judges," in Robert S. Hoyt (ed.), *Life and Thought in the Early Middle Ages* (Minneapolis, 1967), pp. 7–29. A brief but richly documented history of German medieval penal law is found in Robert von Hippel, *Deutsches Strafrecht* (2 vols.; Berlin, 1925, 1930), I, 100–158.
8. Katherine Fischer (trans.), *The Burgundian Code* (Philadelphia, 1949). This code was compiled by King Gundobad about 500 A.D.
9. For a history of this custom, *see* George Neilson, *Trial by Combat* (Glasgow, 1890).
10. Georg Meyer, "Die Gerichtsbarkeit über Unfreie und Hintersassen nach ältestem Recht," *Zeitschrift der Savigny-Stiftung für Rechtsgeschichte* (German Abt.), Vol. 2 (1881), p. 92.
11. "The Visigothic compilation [Breviary of Alaric] became the standard source of Roman law throughout Western Europe during the first half of the Middle Ages," Paul Vinogradoff, *Roman Law in Medieval Europe* (Cambridge, 1968), p. 16.
12. Piero Fiorelli, *La tortura giudiziaria nel diritto comune* (2 vols.; Milano, 1953), I, 56, 68 n. 4, 69; A. Esmein, *A History of Continental Criminal Procedure* (Boston, 1913), pp. 107–14.
13. Joseph Balon, *Traité de droit salique* (4 vols.; Namur, 1965).
14. Von Hippel, *op. cit.,* p. 122; Fiorelli, *op. cit.,* p. 65, n. 52, observed that among 614 known French and German court records before 1000 A.D. and 1065 Italian records before 1150 A.D. criminal cases were almost nonexistent.
15. Fiorelli, *op. cit.,* p. 53, no. 9–11.
16. Paul Leseur, "Des conséquences du délit de l'esclave," *Nouv. Revue histor. de droit français et étranger* (1888), p. 660.
17. Rudolf His, *Geschichte des deutschen Strafrechts bis zur Karolina* (Berlin, 1928), p. 84. I have relied heavily on this work and von Hippel's for data relating to the Frankish period.
18. The influence of Frankish law may be seen in William the Conqueror's abolition of the death penalty and the substitution of castration and exoculation. *See* Pollock and Maitland, *op. cit.,* II, 461. A gruesome illustration is given in William Renwick Riddell's "A Glimpse of Law in the Early Thirteenth Century," *Journal of Criminal Law and Criminology* 21 (February, 1930), pp. 568–71.
19. Leseur, *op. cit.,* p. 716.
20. *Ibid.,* p. 589.
21. His, *op. cit.,* p. 49.
22. John B. Wolf, *The Emergence of European Civilization* (New York, 1962), p. 40. Interesting observations are also found in Friedrich Heer *The Medieval World* (New York, 1968), chap. 2, "Aristocracy and Peasantry."
23. Louis Halphen, "La justice en France au XIᵉ siècle," in *À travers l'histoire du Moyen Age* (Paris, 1950), pp. 176–202.
24. Pollock and Maitland, *op. cit.,* II, 557. Comparable data for Lincolnshire in 1202 are cited in Ralph Arnold, *A Social History of England 55 B.C. to A.D. 1215* (New York, 1967), p. 328; for

Northumberland in 1279 by G. G. Coulton, *Medieval Panorama* (Cambridge, 1938), pp. 337–38.

25. Von Hippel, *op. cit.*, p. 158.
26. No mention of punishments applicable only to unfree persons is found in the numerous source documents from the thirteenth and later centuries reproduced in Hans Planitz's *Handhaft und Blutrache und andere Formen des mittelalterischen Rechtsganges in anschaulichen Darstellungen* (Leipzig, n.d.).
27. Pollock and Maitland, *op. cit.*, II, 460, 462.

CHAPTER IV

1. Gregorio Lasala Navarro, *Galeotes y presidiarios al servicio de la Marina de la Guerra en España* (Madrid, 1961), pp. 4–5.
2. Descriptions and some historical data about these punishments can be found in B. Saint-Edme, *Dictionnaire de la pénalité* (5 vols.; Paris, 1824–28); Charles Desmaze, *Les pénalites anciennes* (Paris, 1866); William Andrews, *Bygone Punishments* (London: Allen, 1931); Helmut Schumann, *Der Scharfrichter* (Kempten-Allgäu: Verlag der Heimatpflege, 1964); Robert Anchel, *Crimes et chatiments au XVIIIe siècle* (Paris: Perrin, 1933). For Colonial America, see Alice Morse Earle, *Curious Punishments of Bygone Days* (New York: Macmillan, 1896). Nearly all contain illustrations. Hans Fehr, *Das Recht im Bild,* (Zürich: Rentsch, 1923), is richly illustrated.
3. F. C. B. Avé-Lallemant, *Das Deutsche Gaunertum* (2 vols.; Munich, n.d.); Frank Aydelotte, *Elizabethan Rogues and Vagabonds* (Oxford: Clarendon Press, 1913); J. J. Jusserand, *English Wayfaring Life in the Middle Ages* (New York: Barnes & Noble, 1961 [orig. publ. 1889]; A. V. Judges, *The Elizabethan Underworld* (New York: Dutton, 1930); Frantz Funck-Brentano, *Les Brigands* (Paris: Hachette, 1904); Louis Rivière, *Mendiants et vagabonds* (Paris: Lecoffre, 1902); C. J. Ribton-Turner, *History of Vagrants and Vagabonds* (London, 1887).
4. Hellmuth von Weber, "Calvinismus und Strafrecht," In Paul Bockelmann and Wilhelm Gallas (eds.), *Festschrift für Eberhard Schmidt* (Göttingen, 1961), pp. 39–53.
5. Ugo Brasiello, *La repressione penale in diritto romano* (Naples: Jovene, 1937), p. 367.
6. Adolf Berger, *Encyclopedic Dictionary of Roman Law* (Philadelphia, 1953), p. 610 (*Transaction,* American Philosophical Society, n.s. 43, pt. 2).
7. *Constitutio criminalis Theresiana, oder der . . . Majestät Maria Theresiä . . . peinliche Gerichtsordnung* (Vienna, 1769), p. 12.
8. Suetonius, *Twelve Caesars, "Life of Augustus,"* par. 25.
9. Martin P. Nilsson, Imperial Rome (New York: Schocken Books, 1962), p. 207.
10. Léon Halkin, *Les esclaves publics chez les Romains* (Brussels, 1897), p. 46.
11. J. M. Kenworthy, "Navy," *Encyclopedia of the Social Sciences* (15 vols.; New York: Macmillan, 1930–35) XI, 314.
12. Alexander Adam, *Roman Antiques . . .,* (New York, 1819), p. 389.
13. B. Saint-Edme, *op. cit.* IV, 140. "There is not a single Roman law which indicates that galley slavery was a punishment during the Empire."
14. Fernando Cadalso, *Instituciones penitenciarias y similares en España,* (Madrid: Góngora, 1922), p. 95.
15. Navarro, *op. cit.,* p. 10.
16. P. Masson, "Les galères de France (1481–1781)," *Annales de la Faculté des Lettres d'Aix,* 20 (1937) p. 80.
17. For brief descriptions of galley slavery, see George Ives, *A History of Penal Methods* (London: Stanley Paul & Co., 1914), pp. 101–6, and Georg Rusche and Otto Kirchheimer, *Punishment and Social Structure* (New York: Columbia University Press, 1939), pp. 52–58. The works of Masson and Navarro, already cited, are scholarly histories of the institution in

France and Spain. A more popular account is found in Michel Bourdet-Pléville, *Des galériens, des forçats, des bagnards* (Paris: Plon, 1957), pp. 5–48. Of special interest is the autobiography of Jean Marteilhe, a young Huguenot, who was a galley slave at Marseilles from 1700 to 1713. It was published in 1757 in Rotterdam under the title *Memoires d'un Protestant condamné aux galères de France pour cause de religion.* An English translation by Oliver Goldsmith, using the pseudonym James Willington, was published in London the following year. An American translation was published in 1867 in New York under the title *The Huguenot Galley Slave.* An abbreviated French version was issued in Paris in 1909 under the title *La vie aux galères,* edited by Albert Savine. We are indebted to Professor Paul W. Bamford for the finest studies of galley slavery made by an American historian. (*See* his *Fighting Ships and Prisons—The Mediterranean Galleys of France in the Age of Louis XIV* [Minneapolis: University of Minnesota Press, 1973]; "The Procurement of Oarsmen for French Galleys, 1660–1748," *American Historical Review,* 65 (October, 1959) pp. 31–48; "Slaves for the Galleys of France, 1665 to 1700," in John Parker [ed.], *Merchants and Scholars* [Minneapolis, 1965], pp. 175–91.

18. Masson, *op. cit.,* p. 81.
19. Masson, *op. cit.,* p. 88.
20. *Ibid.,* pp. 109, 190.
21. Bamford, *op. cit.,* pp. 182–83.
22. Masson, *op. cit.,* p. 274.
23. Carl Ludwig von Bar *et al., A History of Continental Criminal Law* (Boston: Little, Brown & Co., 1916), p. 272.
24. Desmaze, *op. cit.,* p. 137n.; Saint-Edme, *op. cit.,* IV, 86.
25. Bamford, *op. cit.,* p. 192.
26. Marteilhe, *op. cit.,* pp. 183–84.
27. Masson, *op. cit.,* pp. 276–77.
28. Felix Gaiffe, *L'envers du grand siècle* (Paris: Michel, 1924), p. 173.
29. Masson, *op. cit.,* p. 74.
30. Bamford, *op. cit.,* p. 226.
31. *Ibid.,* pp. 245–48. Shelby T. McCloy, *Government Assistance in Eighteenth Century France* (Durham, N.C.: Duke University Press, 1946), p. 137.
32. Masson, *op. cit.,* p. 306 ff.; Bamford, *op. cit.,* p. 255 ff.; for a description of a very brief experiment of sending convicts to Louisiana, *see* James D. Hardy, Jr., "The Transportation of Convicts to Colonial Louisiana," *Louisiana History* 7:(1966), pp. 207–21.
33. Bamford, *op. cit.,* p. 235.
34. Navarro, *op. cit.,* pp. 4–5.
35. Cadalso, *op. cit.,* pp. 95–96; Navarro, *op. cit.,* p. 13.
36. Navarro, *op. cit.,* p. 31.
37. Cadalso, *op. cit.,* p. 104; Navarro, *op. cit.,* p. 91.
38. Navarro, *op. cit.,* chap. 14.
39. Alberto Tenenti, *Piracy and the Decline of Venice 1580–1615* (Berkeley: University of California Press, 1967), chap. 6.
40. Louis Th. Maes, *Vijf eeuwen stedelijk strafrecht* (The Hague: Nijhoff, 1947), p. 450. A. Hallema, "Toepassing van galeistraf in de Nederlanden gedurende de 15de en 16de eeuw," *Tijds. v. Strafrecht* 60 (1951), pp. 125–50.
41. Judges, *op. cit.,* p. 1x–1xi.
42. Karl Hafner and Emil Zürcher, *Das Schweizerische Strafrecht* (Bern: Stämpfli, 1925), pp. 5–6; Eduard Osenbrüggen, *Das Alamannische Strafrecht im deutschen Mittelalter* (Schaffhausen, 1860), p. 97; Gotthold Appenzeller, *Strafvollzug und Gefängniswesen im Kanton Solothurn vom 15. Jahrhundert bis zur Gegenwart* (extract from *Jahrbuch für solothurnische Geschichte,* XXX, 1957, 35–40, 94–97).
43. Osenbrüggen, *loc. cit.*

CHAPTER V

1. *Constitutio Criminalis Theresiana oder der ... Majestät Maria Theresiä ... peinliche Gerichtsordnung* (Vienna, 1769).
2. *Sveriges Rikes Lag ... 1734.* The first edition printed in antique, 1780, is reproduced in facsimile in Volume III of *Minnesskrift ägnad 1734 års lag av jurister i Sverige och Finland* (Stockholm, 1934). The sixth of the nine codes in these general statutes is entitled *Missgiernings Balk (Criminal Code)* and the seventh, *Straff Balk (Punishment Code).*
3. *Constitutio ...*, p. 10.
4. M. Koppél, *Die Vorgeschichte des Zuchthauses zu Waldheim* (Leipzig: Wiegandt, 1934), p. 10.
5. L. von Bar, *Geschichte des deutschen Strafrechts und der Straftheorien* (Berlin, 1882), p. 250.
6. Eberhard Schmidt, *Einführung in die Geschichte der deutschen Stafrechtspflege* (Göttingen: Vandenhoek und Ruprecht, 1947), p. 162.
7. Reproduced in Albert Ebeling, *Beiträge zur Geschichte der Freiheitsstrafe* (Breslau-Neukirch, 1935), pp. 67–72.
8. John Howard, *An Account of the Principal Lazarettos in Europe* (Warrington, 1789), p. 72.
9. Ebeling, *op. cit.*, p. 70.
10. Howard, *op. cit.*, p. 102.
11. *Ibid.*, pp. 133–34.
12. R. von Hippel, *Deutsches Strafrecht* (2 vols.; Berlin: Springer, 1925, 1930), I, 318–19.
13. L.-M. Moreau-Christophe, *De l'état actuel des prisons de France* (Paris, 1837), p. 266.
14. Gotthold Appenzeller, *Strafvollzug und Gefängniswesen im Kanton Solothurn vom 15. Jahrhundert bis zur Gegenwart* (Solothurn: Brosmann, 1957), pp. 118–19.
15. Wüllner, "Zur geschichtlichen Entwicklung der Aussenarbeiten im Strafvollzug," *Monatsschrift für Kriminalpsychologie und Strafrechtsreform* 30 (1939), p. 120, n. 24.
16. Unless otherwise indicated, the following summary is based on Fr. Struckenberg, *Faengselsvaesenet i Danmark 1550–1741* (Copenhagen, 1893), pp. 17–48, 166.
17. Knud Waaben, "Misgerning og straf," in Axel Steensberg (ed.), *Dagligliv i Danmark 1720–1790* (Copenhagen, 1971), p. 282.
18. Sigfrid Wieselgren, *Sveriges fängelser och fångvård* (Stockholm, 1895), p. 99.
19. *Ibid.*, pp. 146, 153.
20. *Missgiernings Balk,* chap. 7, par. 1, p. 8; par. 2, p. 40; pars. 3–4, p. 45; par. 1, p. 46; par. 2, p. 47; par. 1, p. 57.
21. Fernando Cadalso, *Instituciones penitenciarias y similares en España* (Madrid: Góngora, 1922), p. 308.
22. *Ibid.*, p. 431.
23. Louis Rivière, *Mendiants et vagabonds* (Paris: Lecoffre, 1902), p. 5.
24. N. Herman Kriegsmann, *Einführung in die Gefängniskunde* (Heidelberg: Winter, 1912), p. 3; Hippel, *op. cit.*, p. 224, n. 9. In many places, the term "stock" simply meant prison. For a discussion of all the many terms used to designate a prison, see A. Hallema, *Geschiedenis van het gevangeniswezen* (The Hague: Staatsdrukkerij, 1958), pp. 18–25.
25. Ebeling, *op. cit.*, pp. 7–11.
26. Appenzeller, *op. cit.*, pp. 66–68.
27. Karl Hafner and Emil Zürcher, *Schweizerische Gefängniskunde* (Bern: Stämpfli, 1925), p. 10.
28. Howard, *op. cit.*, pp. 125–26.
29. Cadalso, *op. cit.*, p. 372.
30. Eugenio Cuello Calón, *La moderna penologia* (Barcelona: Bosch, 1958), I, 367.
31. Cadalso, *op. cit.*, pp. 373–74.

32. *Dei dilitti e delle pene* (no author, publisher, or place given; Printed in Livorno by the press of Marco Coltellini).

33. Quotations from the tract in my translation are from chapters XV and XVI, pp. 381–462, of the edition published in Cesare Cantu, *Beccaria e il diritto penale* (Florence, Barbera, 1862). A recent translation by Henry Paolucci was published by Bobbs-Merrill, Indianapolis, in 1963. The most extensive bibliography of Beccaria's writings, commentaries thereon, and translations is that of Giacinto Manupella, *Cesare Beccaria. Panorama bibliografico* (Coimbra, 1963; Extr. from *Boletim da Faculdade de Direito da Universidade de Coimbra*, vol. 39).

34. Friedrich Hartl, *Das wiener Kriminalgericht. Strafrechtspflege vom Zeitalter der Aufklärung bis zur österreichischen Revolution.* (Vienna: Böhlau, 1973), pp. 408.

35. *Ibid.,* p. 128

36. John Howard, *op. cit.,* p. 72.

37. Schmidt, *op. cit.,* (2d ed.; 1951), pp. 183–84.

38. *Ibid.,* p. 246.

39. Hartl, *op. cit.,* p. 425. He added that "it must be remembered that in contemporary prisons [Zuchthäuser] few prisoners survived sentences of two or three years."

40. Schmidt, *op. cit.,* p. 246.

41. Hartl, *op. cit.,* pp. 23–24.

42. von Bar, *op. cit.,* pp. 159–60.

43. Hartl, *op. cit.,* p. 408, n. 7.

44. Howard, *op. cit.,* p. 66.

45. H. Kaut, "Leibes- und Freiheitsstrafen," in *Strafrechtssammlung des Nö. Landesmuseum im Schloss Greillenstein.* (Vienna, Museum, n.d.), p. 52.

46. Hartl, *op. cit.,* p. 25.

47. Cited by Cantú, *op. cit.,* p. 253.

48. Schmidt, *op. cit.,* pp. 247–48, quoting chap. 1, par. 14, of the Code.

CHAPTER VI

1. 22 Henry VIII, A.D. 1531 (Spelling modernized).

2. Frank Aydelotte, *Elizabethan Rogues and Vagabonds* (Oxford: Clarendon Press, 1913), p. 63.

3. A. V. Judges, *The Elizabethan Underworld* (New York: Dutton, 1930).

4. 14 Elizabeth, A.D. 1572.

5. E. M. Leonard, *The Early History of English Poor Relief* (New York: Barnes and Noble, 1965), p. 33 (reprint of 1900 ed.).

6. The history of the British houses of correction remains to be written. A smattering of information about them may be gleaned from Edward Geoffrey O'Donoghue, *Bridewell Hospital: Palace, Prison, Schools* (London: Lane, 1923); John Ashton, *The Fleet: Its River, Prison, Marriages* (London: Unwin, 1888); Franz Doleisch von Dolsberg, *Die Entstehung der Freiheitsstrafe* (Breslau: Kurtze, 1928); Austin van der Slice, "Elizabethan Houses of Correction," *Journal of Criminal Law and Criminology,* 27, pp. 45–67; (May–June, 1936); John Howard, *The State of the Prisons in England and Wales* (Warrington, 1777, and later editions), *passim.*

7. *Archaeologia: or Miscellaneous Tracts Relating to Antiquity* Published by the Society of Antiquaries of London, Vol. 21, 1827. Endorsed by Lord Burghley, the Prime Minister. The original can be found in the British Museum's Lansdowne Manuscript Collection 5, Art. 30.

8. Victor von Klarwill, *Queen Elizabeth and Some Foreigners* (New York: Brentano, 1928), p. 318.

9. Ashton, *op. cit.,* p. 211.

10. Doleisch von Dolsberg, *op. cit.,* pp. 121–23.

11. W. Page (ed.), *The Victoria History of Somerset* (2 vols.; London: Constable, 1911), II, 312.

12. 39 Elizabeth, A.D. 1598.

13. Sidney and Beatrice Webb, *English Prisons Under Local Government* (London: Longmans, Green and Co., 1922), pp. 14–17.

14. A. Hallema, "Het oudste ontwerp van Dirck Volkertszoon Coornhert," *Tijds. v. Nederl. Taal-en Letterkunde* 45 (1926), pp. 1–14.

15. H. A. Enno van Gelder, *Memorien en adviezen van Cornelis Pieterz. Hooft* (Utrecht: Kemingk, 1925), II, 81–82.

16. Jacobus Koning, *Geschiedkundige aanteekeningen betrekkelijk de lijfstraffelijke regtsoefening te Amsterdam* (Amsterdam, 1828), p. 34.

17. Robert von Hippel believed that the idea of using imprisonment as a means of reforming the prisoner was applied for the first time in the Amsterdam houses. See his "Beiträge zur Geschichte der Freiheitsstrafe," *Zeitschrift für die gesamte Strafrechtswissenschaft* 18, pp. 419–94, 608–66, 1898. The institutions are fully described by Thorsten Sellin, *Pioneering in Penology* (Philadelphia: University of Pennsylvania Press, 1944 [extensive bibliography, pp. 111–20]. The richest source is A. Hallema, *Geschiedenis van het gevangenizwesen* (The Hague: Staatsdrukkerij, 1958).

18. Hallema, *op. cit.*, p. 120.

19. Sellin, *op. cit.*, p. 42.

20. Hallema, *op. cit.*, p. 121.

21. Sellin, *op. cit.*, pp. 69–72.

22. Hallema, *op. cit.*, p. 117. The exploitative nature of the houses of correction is graphically described by Georg Rusche and Otto Kirchheimer, *Punishment and Social Structure* (New York: Columbia University Press, 1939), pp. 41–52, 63–71.

23. Sellin, *op. cit.*, chap. X.

24. Albert Ebeling, *Beiträge zur Geschichte der Freiheitsstrafe* (Breslau-Neukirch: Kurtze, 1935), pp. 17–58.

25. *Ibid.*, pp. 58–63.

26. *Ibid.*, p. 39.

27. Karl Hafner and Emil Zürcher, *Schweizerische Gefängniskunde* (Bern: Stämpfli, 1925), p. 11.

28. Hellmuth von Weber, "Die Entwicklung des Zuchthauswesens in Deutschland im 17. und 18. Jahrhundert," *Festschrift Adolf Zycha* (Weimar, 1941), p. 458.

29. Eberhard Schmidt, *Einführung in die Geschichte der deutschen Strafrechtspflege* (2nd ed.; Göttingen: Vandenhoeck and Ruprecht, 1951), pp. 183–84.

CHAPTER VII

1. Armand Corre and Paul Aubry, *Documents de criminologie rétrospective* (Paris: Maloine, 1902), pp. 129, 205, 260, 520.

2. P. Masson, "Les galéres de France (1481–1781)," *Annales de la Faculté des Lettres d'Aix* 20: 7–479, 1937, pp. 294–97. Paul W. Bamford, *Fighting Ships and Prisons* (Minneapolis: University of Michigan Press, 1973), pp. 236–40.

3. L.-M. Moreau-Christophe, *De l'état actuel des prisons en France* (Paris, 1837), p. 266.

4. *Ibid.*, p. 265. This formula remained in the French *Code pénal* (I, 1, sec. 15) until 1960. Jacques Léauté, *Les prisons* (Paris: Presses Univ. de France, 1968), p. 22.

5. B. Saint-Edme, *Dictionnaire de la pénalité* (5 vols.; Paris, 1828), "Flétrissure."

6. Leon Faucher, *De la réforme des prisons* (Paris, 1838), pp. 218–19. M. Bourdet-Pléville, *Des galeriens, des forçats, des bagnards* (Paris: Plon, 1957), pp. 57–59.

7. Bamford, *op. cit.*, p. 292.

8. *Ibid.*, pp. 293–95.

9. John Howard, *An Account of the Principal Lazarettos in Europe* (Warrington, 1789), pp. 54–55.

10. *On the Prisons of Philadelphia*. By an European. (Philadelphia: Moreau St. Mery, 1796). Also issued in French (*Des prisons de Philadelphie*. Par un Européen.) the same year and reprinted in Paris. The author was the emigré, Duc de la Rochefoucauld-Liancourt. *See* Thorsten Sellin, "Tocqueville and Beaumont and Prison Reform in France," Introduction, pp. xv–xi, to Gustave de Beaumont and Alexis de Tocqueville, *On the Penitentiary System in the United States and its Application in France* (Carbondale: Southern Illinois University Press), 1964.

11. In addition to the already cited works of Moreau-Christophe, Faucher, and Bourdet-Pléville, the following furnish useful descriptions of the bagnes: [P.] Sers, *Intérieur des bagnes* (Paris, 1848); Le Pelletier de la Sarthe, "Histoire générale des bagnes," in his *Voyage en Bretagne* (Paris, 1853); and Marcel Le Clère, *La vie quotidienne dans les bagnes* (Paris: Hachette), 1973.

12. Sers, *op. cit.*, pp. 36–38.

13. *Ibid.*, p. 38.

14. Faucher, *op. cit.*, p. 222.

15. *Compte général de l'administration de la justice criminelle en France pendant l'année 1880 et rapport relatif aux années 1826 à 1880* . . . (Paris: Impr. Nationale, 1882), table 6.

16. *Ibid.*, p. lxxxv.

17. Descriptions of the Spanish bagnes are found in Gregorio Lasala Navarro, *Galeotes y presidiarios al servicio de la marina de querra en España* (Madrid: Ed. Naval, 1961): Fernando Cadalso, *Instituciones penitenciarias y similares en España* (Madrid: Góngora, 1922), and his *L'Espagne et la réforme pénitentiairre* (Madrid: Orrier, 1925); Eugenio Cuello Calón, *La moderna penologia* (Barcelona: Bosch), 1958.

18. Cuello Calón, *op. cit.*, pp. 363–64, n.

19. Navarro, *op. cit.*, p. 107.

20. Reprinted in Navarro, *op. cit.*, pp. 138–54.

21. *Ibid.*, p. 115.

22. John Howard, *The State of the Prisons in England and Wales . . . and an Account of Some Foreign Prisons and Hospitals* (Warrington, 1784), pp. 151–52.

23. *Ibid.*, pp. 109–10.

24. The history of this institution is found in Thorsten Sellin, "The House of Correction for Boys in the Hospice of St. Michael in Rome," *Journal of Criminal Law and Criminology* 20 (February, 1930), pp. 533–53.

25. Howard, *op. cit.*, pp. 115–16.

26. *Report of the Committee of the Society for the Improvement of Prison Discipline . . . 1820* (London, pp. 137–38).

27. *Actes du Congrès Pénitentiarire International de Rome . . . 1885,* II, part 1, 134–35.

28. Ugo Conti, *La pena e il sistema penale del codice italiano* (Milano: Soc. ed. Libraria, 1910), pp. 151–63, *passim*.

CHAPTER VIII

1. Sidney and Beatrice Webb, *English Prisons Under Local Government* (London: Longmans, Green and Co., 1922), p. 44 n.

2. A. G. L. Shaw, *Convicts and the Colonies* (London: Faber and Faber, 1966), p. 24.

3. *Ibid.*

4. John Howard, *The State of the Prisons . . .* (1st ed.; 1777), pp. 482–84. The movement to reduce the number of crimes defined as capital by the law and to substitute other punishments

has been exhaustively studied by Leon Radzinowicz in the first volume of his *A History of English Criminal Law and its Administration from 1750* (London: Macmillan, 1948).

5. In addition to the works of the Webbs, Shaw, and Howard, the description of the bagnes is based largely on the following works: W. Branch-Johnson, *The English Hulks* (London: Christopher Johnson, 1957); Lionel W. Fox, *The English Prison and Borstal Systems* (London: Routledge & Kegan Paul, 1952); Abbot Emerson Smith, *Colonists in Bondage* (Chapel Hill: University of North Carolina Press, 1947); D. L. Howard, *The English Prisons* (London: Methuen & Co., 1960); George Ives, *A History of Penal Methods* (London: Stanley Paul, 1914); Edmund F. Du Cane, *The Punishment and Prevention of Crime* (London: Macmillan, 1885); Luke Owen Pike, *A History of Crime in England* (2 vols.; London, 1876); Henry Mayhew and John Binny, *The Criminal Prisons of London and Scenes of Prison Life* (London, 1862).

6. Branch-Johnson, *op. cit.*, p. 3.

7. Quoted by D. L. Howard, *op. cit.*, p. 15.

8. 19 Geo. III, c. 74, sec. 33.

9. Du Cane, *op. cit.*, p. 118.

10. 24 Geo. III c. 56 [Patrick Colquhoun] A Magistrate, *A Treatise on the Police of London* . . . (Philadelphia, 1798), p. 235.

11. Shaw, *op. cit.*, pp. 363–68.

12. Joseph Adshead, *Prisons and Prisoners* (London, 1845), p. 224.

13. Basil Thomson, *The Story of Dartmoor Prison* (London: Heinemann, 1907).

14. Mayhew and Binny, *op. cit.*, p. 154 n.

15. Branch-Johnson, *op. cit.*, p. 4.

16. Louis Becke (ed.), *Old Convict Days* (London: T. Fisher Unwin, 1899), pp. 27–28.

17. Quoted by Branch-Johnson, *op. cit.*, p. 5.

18. John Howard, *Lazarettos* . . ., p. 217.

19. Becke, *op. cit.*, p. 28.

20. Mayhew and Binny, *op. cit.*, pp. 199–200 n.

21. *Ibid.* Conditions and practices in the hulk *Leviathan* at Portsmouth in 1842 are described in J. F. Mortlock, *Experiences of a Convict* (Sydney: Sydney University Press, 1965), pp. 51–56.

22. Howard, *Lazarettos*, p. 217.

23. Mayhew and Binny, *op. cit.*, p. 199.

24. *Ibid.*, pp. 201–2.

25. Branch-Johnson, *op. cit.*, pp. 172–73.

26. *The Works of the Rev. Sydney Smith* (3 vols. in one; New York: Appleton, 1878), pp. 162, 164.

27. John Vincent Barry, *Alexander Maconochie of Norfolk Island* (Melbourne: Oxford University Press, 1958).

28. Du Cane, *op. cit.*, chap. 6.

29. Fox, *op. cit.*, p. 44.

30. Webb, *op. cit.*, p. 187.

31. Fox, *op. cit.*, p. 427.

32. *Report of the Committee of the Society for the Improvement of Prison Discipline* . . . *1820* (London, pp. 19–20).

33. Ives, *op. cit.*, p. 189.

34. Crawford, *op. cit.*, pp. 168–74 (table).

35. See Chapter 6, fn. p. 73.

36. Ives, *loc. cit.*

37. Computed from data in the table referred to in note 34, *supra.*

38. R. F. Quinton, *Crime and Criminals, 1876–1910* (London: Longmans, Green and Co., 1910), p. 58.

39 Mayhew and Binny, *op. cit.*, pp. 305–7. Thomas Archer, *The Pauper, the Thief, and the Convict* (London: Groombridge & Sons, 1865), pp. 161–63.

40. Sir John Cox Hippisley, *Prison Labour, Etc.* (London, 1823), p. 31.

41. Crawford, *op. cit.*, p. 107.
42. Webb, *op. cit.*, p. 98.
43. Hippisley, *op. cit.*, p. 121. Plate illustrating crank operated by several prisoners on p. 190.
44. Mayhew and Binny, *op. cit.*, p. 308.
45. Webb, *op. cit.*, p. 146 n.
46. *Ibid.*, pp. 169–76. Graphically reported in Charles Reade's novel *It is Never Too Late to Mend* (1856).
47. Mayhew and Binny, *op. cit.*, pp. 308–10.
48. *Ibid.*, pp. 310–13; Webb, *op. cit.*, p. 207.Galley 138
49. Fox, *op. cit.*, p. 51. *A propos des bruits sur les prétendues oppressions des détenus dans les prisons russes,* (St.-Petersburg: Impr. "Russo-Française," 1910).

CHAPTER IX

1. Nicholas Karamzin, "Memoir on Ancient and Modern Russia," in Thomas Riha (ed.), *Readings in Russian Civilization* (3 vols.; Chicago: University of Chicago Press, 1964); II, 289.
2. George Vernadsky, "Medieval Russian Laws," in Riha, *op. cit.*, I, 44.
3. Jerome Blum, "Lord and Peasant in Russia," in *ibid.*, p. 171.
4. Vernadsky, *op. cit.*, pp. 37–38.
5. Blum, *op. cit.*, p. 165.
6. *Ibid.*, p. 169.
7. Jesse D. Clarkson, *A History of Russia* (New York: Random House, 1961), p. 235.
8. *Ibid.*, p. 248.
9. Geroid Tanquaray Robinson, *Rural Russia under the Old Regime* (New York: Macmillan, 1917), p. 63.
10. George Vernadsky, "The Mongol Impact on Russia," in Riha, *op. cit.*, 189.
11. Anatole G. Mazour, *The First Russian Revolution, 1825* (Stanford: Stanford University Press, 1937), p. 5.
12. Solomon, *op. cit.*, p. 510 n.
13. Riha, *op. cit.*, II, 258–59.
14. Mazour, *op. cit.*, pp. 212–13; Avrahm Yarmolinsky, *Road to Revolution* (London: Casswell, 1957), p. 52.
15. M. Borovitinoff, "Le rôle de la peine de mort en Russie," *Actes du Congrès pénitentiaire international de Washington, Octobre 1910,* V, 70.
16. In addition to the most informative report by Alexander Solomon cited earlier, useful data for a study of Russian penal practices before the First World War are found in the more or less extensive reports made periodically to the International Penitentiary Commission and published in the Proceedings of its quinquennial congresses: (a) Report by Galkine-Wraskoy, *Actes du Congrès pénitentiaire international de Saint-Pétersbourg, 1890,* IV, 471–672. (b) N.S. Tagantzew on transportation, *Bulletin de la Commite, pénitantiaire international,* April, 1895; pp. 43–54. (c) A. Solomon, *Actes du Congrès pénitentiarire international de Bruxelles,* 1900, I, 74–82. (d) A. de Stremooukhoff, "Exposé sommaire des progrès réalisés en Russie ... depuis ... 1900," *Actes du Congrès pénitentiaire international de Budapest, 1905,* IV, 473–514. (e) E. de Khrouleff, "Notice sur le développement ... en Russie de 1905 à 1910," *Actes du Congrès pénitentiaire international de Washington, 1910,* V, 343–410. These reports are forthright statements of policies and actions taken by the government. Most of their authors were heads of the prison administration in the Ministry of the Interior. For a graphic description of what penal slavery was like in practice, *see* George W. Kennan's remarkable investigative report *Siberia and the Exile System* (2 vols.; New York: Century Co., 1891), and Peter Kropotkin's *In Russian and French Prisons* (New York: Schocken Books, 1971; originally published in 1887).
17. Solomon, *Rapport,* p. 503.

18. Solomon, *op. cit.* in note 16c, *supra,* p. 80.
19. *Ibid.,* pp. 80–81.
20. John Howard, *op. cit.,* pp. 87, 90–91.
21. Kropotkin, *op. cit.,* p. 126. Map 54 in Martin Gilbert, *op. cit.,* shows some of the places to which convicts were assigned.
22. Solomon, *Rapport,* pp. 548–49.
23. Kennan, *op. cit.,* I, 87, 89, 90–91.
24. *Ibid.,* pp. 97–99.
25. *Ibid.,* II, 138.
26. *Ibid.,* p. 207 n.
27. Khrouleff, *op. cit.,* p. 384.
28. Kennan, *op. cit.,* II, 162.
29. *Ibid.,* p. 280.
30. *Ibid.,* p. 307.
31. Solomon, *Rapport,* p. 539.
32. *Ibid.,* p. 547.
33. Galkine-Wraskoy, *op. cit.,* pp. 496–97.
34. Kropotkin, *op. cit.,* p. 47.
35. Kennan, *op. cit.,* II, 549 n.
36. Khrouleff, *op. cit.,* p. 315. In 1911–12, several thousand convicts labored on constructing the Amur railroad in far-eastern Siberia. *Travaux des détenus sur la grand artère du Chemin de fer de l'Amour,* (St. Petersburg: Impr. "Russo-Française," 1913).
37. Jules Patouillet (trans.), *Les Codes de la Russie soviétique. IV. Code pénal de la RSFSR avec les modifications jusqu'au ler octobre 1933* (Paris: Librairie géneral de droit et de jurisprudence, 1935).
38. A translation of the 1924 code is found in Luis Jiménez de Asúa *et al. La vida penal en Rusia* (Madrid: Ed. Reus, 1931), pp. 233–314.
39. The following are a small sample of many laudatory reports: The works of de Asúa, Calcott, and Reswick already cited, and Elias Tobenkin, *Stalin's Ladder* (New York: Minton Balch & Co., 1933), part 3; Lenka von Koerber, *Sowjetrussland kämpft gegen das Verbrechen* (Berlin: Rowohlt, 1933); D. A. Pritt, "Bolshevo: a Russian Labour Colony for Criminals," *Howard Journal,* III, (1933), No. 4; 78–82; John L. Gillin, "Russia's Criminal Court and Penal System," *Journal of Criminal Law and Criminology* 24, (May–June, 1933); pp. 290–312; Nathan Berman, "Juvenile Delinquency under the Soviets," *Journal of Criminal Law and Criminology* 30 (May–June, 1939), pp. 68–76.
40. David J. Dallin, *The Real Soviet Russia,* (rev. ed.; New Haven: Yale University Press, 1947), p. 237.
41. Conquest, *op. cit.,* p. 81; Paul Barton, *L'Institution concentrationnaire en Russie, 1930–1957* (Paris: Plon, 1959), pp. 53–54.
42. Dallin, *op. cit.,* p. 231.
43. Conquest, *op. cit.,* p. 78; United Nations, International Labour Office, *Report of the Ad Hoc Committee on Forced Labour* (Geneva, 1953), p. 496.
44. B. Yakovlev, *Concentration Camps in the USSR* (Munich; Institute for the Study of the History of Culture of the USSR, 1955 [in Russian]). Diagram of the table of organization of the GULAG, pp. 51–52, and map of eight camp zones, p. 71. Location of camp zones and units are also found in maps 109–11 in Gilbert, *op. cit.*
45. Dallin, *op. cit.,* p. 241.
46. Bernhard Roeder, *Katorga, Aspect of Modern Slavery* (London: Heinemann, 1958), p. 16.
47. Barton, *op. cit.,* pp. 161–62.
48. *Ibid.,* p. 320.
49. Conquest, *op. cit.,* p. 82.

CHAPTER X

1. Alice Morse Earle, *Curious Punishment of Bygone Days* (New York: Duffield, 1907).
2. Abbot Emerson Smith, *Colonists in Bondage* (Chapel Hill: University of North Carolina Press, 1947).
3. Raphael Semmes, *Crime and Punishment in Early Maryland* (Baltimore: John Hopkins Press, 1938), chap. 5.
4. Winthrop D. Jordan, *White over Black* (Baltimore: Penquin Books, 1969), p. 75.
5. *Ninth Census of the United States,* I, table 1.
6. Quoted in Arthur P. Scott, *Criminal Law in Colonial Virginia* (Chicago: University of Chicago Press, 1930), p. 199.
7. *Ibid.,* p. 200.
8. *Ibid.,* pp. 202–3.
9. John Roles, *Inside Views of Slavery on Southern Plantations* (New York, 1864), chap. 7. Roles had for ten years been an overseer on several large plantations.
10. Stampp, *op. cit.,* p. 225.
11. *Ibid.,* pp. 206–9. Clement Eaton, *The Growth of Southern Civilization, 1790–1860* (New York: Harper & Row, 1961), pp. 77–78.
12. Scott, *op. cit.,* p. 300.
13. *Ibid.,* p. 301.
14. *Fourth Annual Report of the . . . Prison Discipline Society, Boston, 1829,* pp. 280–81.
15. Stampp, *op. cit.,* p. 211.
16. Thorsten Sellin, "Philadelphia Prisons of the Eighteenth Century," *Transactions of the American Philosophical Society,* n.s., XLIII, part 1 (March, 1953), 327.
17. *On the Prisons of Philadelphia.* By an European (Philadelphia: Moreau St. Mery, 1796). The author was Duc de La Rochfoucauld-Liancourt, a refugee French noble. Robert J. Turnbull, *A Visit to the Philadelphia Prison* (Philadelphia, 1797).
18. Thomas Jefferson, *Notes on the State of Virginia* (Chapel Hill: University of North Carolina Press, 1955), pp. 144–45. On the practice of gibbeting in the American colonies, *see* Thorsten Sellin, "The Philadelphia Gibbet Iron," *Journal of Criminal Law, Criminology, and Police Science* 46 (May–June, 1955), pp. 11–25.
19. Quoted in William Crawford, *Report on the Penitentiaries of the United States* (Montclair, N.J.: Patterson Smith, 1969) reprint of 1835 ed., p. 114.
20. Stampp, *op. cit.,* pp. 215–17; Jordan, *op. cit.,* pp. 125–27, 406–14; E. Franklin Frazier, *The Negro in the United States* (New York: Macmillan, 1949), chap. 4.
21. O. F. Lewis, *The Development of American Prisons and Prison Customs, 1776–1845* (New York: Prison Association, 1922), chaps. 17 and 20.
22. *Ibid.,* pp. 265–66. Blake McKelvey, *American Prisons* (Chicago: University of Chicago Press, 1936), pp. 22–23.
23. Lewis, *op. cit.,* p. 268.
24. Malcolm C. Moos, *State Penal Administration in Alabama* (Bureau of Public Administration, University of Alabama, 1942), p. 2.
25. Quoted in Paul B. Foreman and Julien R. Tatum, "The Short History of Mississippi's State Penal Systems," *Mississippi Law Journal,* 10 (April, 1938), p. 256.
26. Lewis, *op. cit.,* p. 257.
27. Crawford, *op. cit.,* p. 117.
28. Lewis, *op. cit.,* p. 259.
29. George Thompson, *Prison Life and Reflections* (Hartford: A. Work, 1855). They had tried to aid slaves to escape.

30. *Ibid.*, p. 121.
31. *Ibid.*, p. 120.
32. *The Complete Works of Edward Livingston on Criminal Jurisprudence* (2 vols.; New York: National Prison Association, 1873), II, 537–606.
33. McKelvey, *op. cit.*, p. 33.
34. Moos, *op. cit.*, p. 5.
35. Quoted in Claude G. Bowers, *Jefferson and Hamilton* (Boston: Houghton Mifflin Co., 1966), p. 101.
36. Thompson, *op. cit.*, pp. 131–132, 354.
37. Foreman and Tatum, *op. cit.*, p. 257.
38. Moos, *op. cit.*, p. 6.
39. Crawford, *op. cit.*, p. 99.
40. Ulrich B. Phillips, *American Negro Slavery* (Baton Rouge: Louisiana State University Press, 1966); (originally published in 1918), pp. 456–57.

CHAPTER XI

1. Oscar Handlin (ed.), *Readings in American History* (New York: Knopf, 1957), p. 348.
2. R. M. Cunningham, "The Convict System of Alabama in its Relation to Health and Disease," *Proceedings of the National Prison Association* (1889), p. 138.
3. P. D. Sims, *ibid.*, pp. 120–21.
4. Paul B. Foreman and Julien R. Tatum, "The Short History of Mississippi's State Penal Systems," *Mississippi Law Journal*, 10 (April, 1938), p. 260.
5. Vernon Lane Wharton, *The Negro in Mississippi, 1865–1890* (New York: Harper & Row, 1965), p. 238.
6. *Ibid.*, p. 239.
7. *Ibid.*, pp. 239–40.
8. *Ibid.*, p. 240.
9. Quoted in Foreman and Tatum, *op. cit.*, p. 263n.
10. Wharton, *op. cit.*, p. 241.
11. Quoted in *ibid.*, p. 241.
12. *Ibid.*, p. 242.
13. Foreman and Tatum, *op. cit.*, p. 264.
14. Mark T. Carleton, *Politics and Punishment: The History of the Louisiana State Penal System* (Baton Rouge: Louisiana State University Press, 1971), p. 20.
15. *Ibid.*, p. 36.
16. *Ibid.*, p. 37.
17. Robert H. Marr, "The Institutions of Louisiana," *Proceedings of the National Prison Association*, 1902 p. 268.
18. Carleton, *op. cit.*, p. 100.
19. Marr, *op. cit.*, p. 272.
20. Carleton, *op. cit.*, p. 45.
21. Malcolm C. Moos, *State Penal Administration in Alabama* (Bureau of Public Administration, University of Alabama, 1942), p. 11.
22. Fletcher Melvin Green, "Some Aspects of the Convict Lease System in the Southern States," in J. Isaac Copeland (ed.), *Democracy in the Old South and Other Essays*, (Nashville: Vanderbilt University Press, 1969), p. 279.
23. Moos, *op. cit.*, p. 14.
24. Green, *op. cit.*, p. 283.
25. Quoted in George W. Cable, "The Convict Lease System in the Southern States," *The Silent South* (Montclair, N.J.: Patterson Smith, 1969; reprint of 1889 ed.), pp. 167–68.

26. *Ibid.*, p. 168.
27. Cunningham, *op. cit.*, pp. 110–11.
28. Green, *op. cit.*, p. 279.
29. Going, *op. cit.*, pp. 178–79.
30. *Ibid.*, p. 181.
31. Moos, *op. cit.*, p. 18.
32. Quoted by Hastings H. Hart in *Proceedings of the American Prison Association,* 1919. pp. 202–3.
33. Moos, *op. cit.*, p. 20.
34. *New York Times,* July 1, 1928.
35. A. J. McKelway, "Abolition of the Convict Lease System of Georgia," *Proceedings of the American Prison Association,* 1908, p. 219.
36. E. Merton Coulter, *A Short History of Georgia* (Chapel Hill: University of North Carolina Press, 1933), p. 393.
37. *Ibid.*, p. 394; Cable, *op. cit.*, p. 154; E. C. Wines, *The State of Prisons and Child-Saving Institutions in the Civilized World* (Cambridge: University Press, 1880), p. 191.
38. Coulter, *op. cit,* p. 395.
39. *Ibid.*
40. McKelway, *op. cit.*, p. 223.
41. *Ibid.*, pp. 223–24.
42. *Ibid.*, p. 224.
43. W. K. Doyle, A. M. Laird, and J. S. Wise, *The Government and Administration of Florida* (New York: Crowell, 1954), p. 181.
44. *Ibid.*
45. S. H. Blitch, "Conditions of Penitentiary Affairs in Florida," *Proceedings of the National Prison Association,* 1904, pp. 285–86.
46. Albert W. Gilchrist, "Prison Reform in the South," *Proceedings of the American Prison Association,* 1909, p. 126.
47. A. W. Gilchrist, "The Jails and Prisons of Florida," Proceedings of the American Prison Association, 1911; pp. 261–62.
48. J. S. Blitch, in *Proceedings of the American Prison Association,* 1921, p. 43.
49. Doyle *et al., op. cit.*, p. 182.
50. Norton W. Brooker, in *Proceedings of the National Prison Congress,* 1888, p. 70.
51. John Samuel Ezell, *The South Since 1865,* New York: (Macmillan, 1963), p. 367.
52. Jesse F. Steiner and Roy M. Brown, *The North Carolina Chain Gang* (Chapel Hill: University of North Carolina Press, 1927), pp. 11–13.
53. Roy M. Brown, "Prison Reform in North Carolina," *University of North Carolina Newsletter,* XXXIX, no. 6 (April 15, 1953).
54. *Biennial Reports of the North Carolina Charitable, Penal and Correctional Institutions,* for the two years ending June 30, 1932. (Raleigh: North Carolina), pp. 449–50, 473.
55. Steiner and Brown, *op. cit.*, p. 15.
56. *Ibid.*, p. 22; Green, *op. cit.*, p. 281.
57. Blake McKelvey, *American Prisons* (Chicago: University of Chicago Press, 1936), p. 178.
58. Cable, *op. cit.*, p. 143, citing report of the prison physician.
59. F. H. Wines, in *Proceedings of the National Prison Congress,* 1900, p. 88.
60. McKelway, *op. cit.*, p. 79.
61. Kate Burr Johnson, "North Carolina's Prison System," *Proceedings of the American Prison Association,* 1923, p. 235.
62. Cable, *op. cit.*, p. 125.
63. George W. Donaghey, "Why I Couldn't Pardon the Contract System," *The Annals of the American Academy of Political and Social Science* 46; (March, 1913), pp. 22–23.
64. D. F. Wright, "Prison Reform from a Sanitary Point of View," *Proceedings of the National*

Prison Congress, 1889; p. 241. "In 1874, Tennessee leased 123 convicts under eighteen years of age; 15 of them were under 16. 3 were twelve and one only ten years of age" (Green, *op. cit.*, p. 282).

65. McKelvey, *op. cit.*, p. 187; Green, *op. cit.*, p. 284.

CHAPTER XII

1. *Report of the Osborne Association, Inc. on the Alabama Prison System: Summary of Findings* (New York: The Association, 1949), p. 15.
2. Jesse F. Steiner and Roy M. Brown, *The North Carolina Chain Gang* (Chapel Hill: University of North Carolina Press, 1927), p. 19.
3. *Ibid.*, p. 28.
4. *Ibid.*, pp. 30–31.
5. *Biennial Report, North Carolina State Board of Charities, 1893–1895*, p. 16, quoted in *ibid.*, p. 35.
6. *Ibid.*, p. 123.
7. Quoted in A. J. McKelway, "Three Prison Systems of the Southern States of America," in C. R. Henderson (ed.), *Penal and Reformatory Institutions* (New York: Charities Publishing Committee, 1910), pp. 78–79.
8. W. T. Bost, Commissioner of Public Welfare, North Carolina, in *U.S. Daily*, June 8, 1931.
9. Robert S. Rankin, *The Government and Administration of North Carolina* (New York: Crowell, 1955), p. 176.
10. Paul W. Garrett and Austin H. MacCormick (eds.), *Handbook of American Prisons and Reformatories, 1929* (New York: National Society of Penal Information, Inc., 1929), p. 877.
11. *Seventh Annual Report of the State Board of Public Welfare of South Carolina, 1926*, p. 84.
12. Columbus Andrews, *Administrative County Government in South Carolina* (Chapel Hill: University of North Carolina Press, 1933), p. 169.
13. W. Hardy Wickwar, *Criminal Policy in South Carolina* (Columbia, S.C.: Bureau of Governmental Research and Service, University of South Carolina, 1968), p. 41.
14. Steiner and Brown, *op. cit.*, p. 95.
15. Quoted in E. Stagg Whitin, *Penal Servitude* (New York: National Committee on Prison Labor, 1912), pp. 134–35.
16. Steiner and Brown, *op. cit.*, pp. 55–56.
17. *The Philadelphia Record*, February 6, 1933.
18. *Biennial Report, North Carolina State Board of Charities and Public Welfare, 1920–1922*, p. 83.
19. *The Philadelphia Record, loc. cit.*
20. *Twenty-First Biennial Report of the Prison Division of the Department of Agriculture, State of Florida, 1920–1930*, pp. 24–25, 13.
21. Jack Sloan, "Prison Camp Hells," *Real Detective* 26:24–29, 83–86; Walter Wilson, "Chain Gangs and Profits," *Harpers Magazine*, April, 1933, p. 533.
22. Frank Tannenbaum, "Southern Prisons," *Darker Phases of the South* (New York: Putnam's, 1924), chap. 3.
23. Garrett and MacCormick, *op. cit.;* Fred E. Haynes, *The American Prison System* (New York: McGraw-Hill, 1939), chap. 8; John L. Gillin, *Taming the Criminal,* chap. 9; McKelvey, *op. cit.*
24. Mark T. Carleton, *Politics and Punishment,* (Baton Rouge: Louisiana State University Press, 1971), pp. 87–88.
25. *Ibid.*, p. 101.
26. *Ibid.*, p. 108.
27. *Ibid.*, pp. 189, 131, 112, 141.

28. *Report of a Study of the Louisiana State Penitentiary made by Austin H. MacCormick, Executive Director of the Osborne Association, Inc., in July, 1964, at the Request of Governor John J. McKeithen* (New York: The Osborne Association, 1964; mimeo), p. 2.

29. *Ibid., passim.*

30. Carleton, *op. cit.,* p. 197.

31. *Case-Report, Criminal Investigation Division, Arkansas State Police,* File No. 916-166-66 (Little Rock, 1966; mimeo). The report, marked very confidential, was suppressed by Governor Faubus but released by his successor, Governor Winthrop Rockefeller.

32. *Ibid.,* pp. 8, 10, 31, 6.

33. Tom Murton and Joe Hyams, *Accomplices to the Crime,* (New York: Grove Press, 1969), p. 24.

34. *Case Report, op. cit.,* pp. 7–8.

35. Murton and Hyams, *op. cit.,* p. 36.

36. *Case Report, op. cit.,* p. 7.

37. Murton and Hyams, *op. cit.,* p. 33.

38. *Case Report, op. cit.,* pp. 12–13.

39. *Ibid.,* p. 29.

40. *Ibid.,* p. 17.

41. *Ibid.,* p. 11.

42. Murton and Hyams, *op. cit.,* p. 36.

43. *Ibid.,* p. 5.

44. *Case Report, op. cit.,* p. 14.

45. *Report of the Arkansas Penitentiary Study Commission, Jan. 1, 1968,* 144 pp. Little Rock, 1968.

Index

Stalin, Joseph, 131
Stockhouses, 57–61, 63
Sweat box, 169–170
Sweden
    public works, penal slavery
      on, 61–62
    punitive imprisonment, 56
Switzerland
    galleys, 54–55
    houses of correction, 81
    public works, penal slavery on,
      60, 64

Tacitus, 30–32, 34
Tennessee, convict lease system in,
    161
Theognis, quoted, 13
Theresiana, 56, 57, 66, 81
Thucydides, 1, 9, 18
Tiberius, 21, 22, 27
Treadmill, use of, 106–109
Tuchthuis, 76–79

"Tucker Telephone," 175*n.*
Turner, Nat, 137

Ulfila, Bishop, 33
Ulpian, 56

Virginia, antebellum slave population
    in, 134
Visigothic law, 36, 38, 43
Vladimir II, 114
Vouglans, Muyart de, 56

Wedel, Leopold von, 73
Westermann, William, 2
Wolfgang, Marvin E., vi

Yaroslav the Wise, 113

Zimmern, Alfred, 10
Zuchthaus, 80–82